Teaching with
Shakespeare

Teaching with Shakespeare

Critics in the Classroom

Edited by
Bruce McIver and Ruth Stevenson

DELAWARE

Newark: University of Delaware Press
London and Toronto: Associated University Presses

Associated University Presses
440 Forsgate Drive
Cranbury, NJ 08512

Associated University Presses
25 Sicilian Avenue
London WC1A 2QH, England

Associated University Presses
P.O. Box 338, Port Credit
Mississauga, Ontario
Canada L5G 4L8

The paper used in this publication meets the requirements
of the American National Standard for Permanence of Paper.

Library of Congress Cataloging-in-Publication Data

Teaching with Shakespeare : critics in the classroom / edited by Bruce
McIver and Ruth Stevenson.
    p. cm.
    Lectures delivered throughout the academic year 1990–1991 at Union
College, under the sponsorship of the English Dept.
    Includes bibliographical references.
    ISBN 0-87413-491-9 (alk. paper)
    1. Shakespeare, William, 1564–1616—Study and teaching.
2. Literature—History and criticism—Theory, etc. I. McIver,
Bruce, 1943– . II. Stevenson, Ruth, 1939– . III. Union College
(Schenectady, N.Y.). English Dept.
PR2987.T38   1994
82.3'3—dc20   92-59966
                                                 CIP

For Isabel McIver,
Bill Hendricks,
and Harry Marten

Contents

List of Figures

Acknowledgments

The editors thank not only the English Department of Union College, whose Thomas Lamont Fund provided major support for the Shakespeare Lecture Series presented here, but especially the individual critics—R. A. Foakes, Leah Marcus, Patricia Parker, Annabel Patterson, Helen Vendler, and John Wilders—whose presentations themselves and cooperation throughout the entire project made this book possible.

Because Patricia Parker has published the lecture and workshop she presented at Union elsewhere, she has prepared for this volume an alternative lecture and workshop. Annabel Patterson has read all of the workshops and written the "Palinode" that concludes the book. We thank them both.

The editors also thank the following institutions: the Harvard Theatre Collection for providing, with permission, the photograph of Sarah Bernhardt appearing on the book cover; the Houghton Mifflin Company for permission to quote extensively throughout the lectures and workshops (as well as to use textual reproductions) from *The Riverside Shakespeare*, ed. G. Blakemore Evans, Boston, 1974; International Business Machines Corporation for permission to use their advertisement in *American Way Magazine* (15 December 1992); Parker Pen for permission to use their advertisement in *The New Yorker* (25 November 1991); A. P. Watt Ltd. for permission to reprint text and photographs from *"Henry V": A Screen Adaptation* by Kenneth Branagh, London: Chatto & Windus, 1989; and Yale University Press for permission to quote from *Shakespeare's Sonnets,* ed. Stephen Booth, New Haven and London, 1977.

Introduction

BRUCE MCIVER and RUTH STEVENSON

The English Department of Union College invited the six Shakespearean critics whose presentations compose this book to visit the campus individually throughout the academic year 1990–91 as participants in the Lamont Shakespeare Series. We asked them to explain to our students the bases and nature of their critical procedures and to put these procedures into practice by teaching Shakespearean texts of their own choice in follow-up workshops. We did not request our guests to represent particular schools of criticism, but all of them addressed basic issues vigorously debated by such schools. While the presentations were diverse, they held in common a concern for directly correlating criticism with teaching. In particular they took care to encourage the students to establish receptive relationships with Shakespeare's work through developing some awareness of its multiple and intricate demands and some knowledge of influential reactions of past and present critics to those demands.

Helen Vendler began her lecture by describing her own experience as a student. She explained the distinct critical procedures and ways of thinking about literature, especially poetry, that she had learned at home, at college, and in graduate school, and that she had assimilated into her own manner of responding to poems. She led the students to think about their responses and to work at establishing closeness between themselves and Shakespeare's poems in order to discover not only their logical precision but especially their undercurrent of emotion that increasingly urges the student to respond. Professor Vendler never used the language of critical strategy, of interpretative assertion or aggression; rather, she encouraged students to discover how poems themselves dictate the appropriate critical procedures and how to become close to them through reimagining their compositional processes, as she did:

> I found my way into poems by imagining that it was my own hand that had written them, that had chosen this form, and this word rather than that

13

word. It was a habit with me to write out in longhand any poem I was going to think about for some time; and it became a habit to learn the poem by heart, too. Then it was "my" poem, and I could feel its inner exfoliation from a kernel of imaginative and formal intention.

Following the process of exfoliation requires, she explained, discovering the important though not always obvious questions that each poem poses, questions generated within and by the complex interactions of its multiple elements. She demonstrated how to identify some of the key questions posed by Shakespeare's poems as she introduced the students to five sonnets that present quite different problems. For example, in Sonnet 33 ("Full many a glorious morning"), she drew attention to the inconspicuous but insistent inversion of traditional sonnet structure which leads us to ask "why the octave of this sonnet is so luxuriously expressive and the human 'application' in the quatrain so bare" and to see and to feel exactly why this sonnet was written "the wrong-way round." On the other hand, in Sonnet 60 ("Like as the waves") she pointed out the sequence of life models developed quatrain by quatrain that makes us wonder why they occur in just the way they do and that thus encourages us slowly through a process of expectation, surprise, and gradual adjustment, to discover how unrearrangeable, how inexorable those quatrains are. In identifying questions that become progressively precise and provocative, Professor Vendler demonstrated how familiarity with poetic conventions and techniques enables readers to develop gradual awareness and enjoyment of the demanding aesthetic systems of Shakespeare's poems. But reference to poetic technique itself was only a point of departure in her teaching. Even as she introduced the students to specific, technical ways of learning to respond to specific poems, she led her audience to increasingly intellectual and emotional immediacy with these strange and complex poems that lie "just at the brink of our horizon of perception."

In her workshop she arranged at the front of the class a panel of five student experts (on Latin, Shapes, Psychology, Gender, and plain Kibitzing) and by asking them questions began to trace an intricate series of more and more exact discoveries about Sonnet 129's quick, complex movement to different states of perception about "the expense of spirit." Through her direction of the students to particular questions posed by this poem, through her precise attention to numerous student responses, and through the evocative power of her own lyric phrasing, she developed a reading that not only answered those questions detail by detail but also awakened the students to notions of aesthetic value and to glimpses of the gathering, empathetic power of a receptive imagination.

Shakespeare's prominence undoubtedly derives from the extraordinary aesthetic power of his poems and plays, but authorities have used the artistic reputation of "the Bard" to develop non-aesthetic programs. In fact, as R. A. Foakes points out, students might well be on guard for special interests which covertly influence standard interpretations of Shakespeare's work. In "Cutting the Bard Down to Size," Professor Foakes took into particular account the way previous audiences of Shakespeare's work may definitely but indirectly have influenced the responses of today's students. He traced a history of the gradual but crucial shift from the Elizabethan-Jacobean theatergoers who actually attended Shakespeare's plays during his lifetime to twentieth-century highbrow spectators, especially educators, who, unlike the "nut-cracking Elizabethans," have used Shakespeare's work for the implicitly political purpose of encouraging belief in the plays' "unity," "truth," and "stable, finite meaning." Foakes did not try to expose the various motivations that might direct this purpose, but he did explain one kind of influence pertinent to his American student audience. He pointed out that in the United States, during the major periods of mass immigration, teaching Shakespeare as a bard-idol who created profound, determinate, absolute meanings in all of his work was politically useful in assimilating —and, Foakes implied, indirectly subjugating—diverse groups of immigrants while discouraging differences. In opposition, poststructuralist approaches have arisen from a "crisis in confidence" in authority and have challenged "traditionalist" views through five major poststructuralist lines of attack which Foakes described in some detail: deconstruction, American new historicism (and British cultural materialism), feminism, performance criticism, and new textualism. While he warned about the extremes to which poststructural practice can lead and offered two vivid examples of such extremism by professional critics, in his own analysis of *Hamlet* he skillfully exposed the limitations of determinate, unified, and ultimately, if indirectly, political interpretations of the play. In the spirit of poststructuralism, he directly encouraged the students to question traditional authority and to trust their discoveries of plural meanings.

In his workshop, "Making a Start on *King Lear*," Professor Foakes set the stage for such questioning and discovery by introducing basic questions about history, genre, and language ("the imaginative resonances of the text"), by establishing parameters for critical freedom in interpretation, and by tracing something of the critical history of *Lear*. He then involved the class in a process where questioning, discovery, and confidence emerged. He recruited student volunteers to become actors representing characters in the first scene of *Lear,* while he himself took the role of the king. The students and Professor Foakes did not read the text but improvised it out of their own experience of the play, and gradually there developed a flurry of dramatic accusations and vivid debates while Foakes/Lear provoked and guided the students to a clearer understanding of the powerful forces involved in that scene and in the play as a whole.

If students in Professor Foakes's class welcomed the heated debate of his role-playing workshop as a highly stimulating, though still a normal extension of classroom discussion, students in Leah Marcus's lecture and workshop found Shakespeare's texts not only open to debate and multiple interpretation but also subject to "disestablishing." Professor Marcus explained in detail recent critical practices which programmatically challenge schools of criticism which have privileged traditional institutions at the expense of diverse and unstable elements in the plays, and she introduced the students to current debates about the "established" materiality of the printed texts themselves. Perhaps the most striking aspect of disestablishing emerged as she traced the radical redefinition of Shakespeare himself, "not as a man but as a cultural construct remade in different ways by different human agents with competing critical and social agendas." However, having led the students to theoretical poststructuralist ideas about Shakespeare himself, Shakespearean textuality, and Shakespearean interpretation, she led them back to practical kinds of criticism by explaining how the approaches of three of the most conspicuous objects of recent theoretical attack—A. C. Bradley, E. M. W. Tillyard, and New Criticism—enable students to deal closely and intelligently with specific texts in ways that recent critical practice may not.

In her workshop, Marcus returned to the question of "establishing" Shakespearean text and offered different versions of lines from *Hamlet* and *Lear* for the students to interpret from as many angles as possible. As she conversed with the students about their readings of these lines, she demonstrated to them the problems of interpretation created when we deal with plays which exist in radically different textual versions and which may be presented to readers in radically different formats. In particular, the students gained unexpected insights when they tackled the problem of explaining "To be or not to be," whose 1603 "Bad" Quarto version seems extremely strange in comparison to the "polished, lovely, accepted [later] version" of *The Riverside Shakespeare.* At the close of the workshop, Marcus's students came to an intriguing discovery that the Shakespeare of Hamlet's soliloquy presents a less certain view of the afterlife in the later version than in the earlier, while the Shakespeare of the concluding lines of the two *King Lear*s (First Quarto [1608] and First Folio [1623]) seems to move in precisely the opposite direction.

John Wilders led the students to Shakespeare's texts directly through the stage door. In his lecture, "Dramatic Structure and Dramatic Effect," he concentrated on actual stage activity to explain his method of teaching Shakespeare, which varies sharply from those of his own teachers as well as from those of other critics working today. Like Helen Vendler, John Wilders told his audience something about his own experience as a student; unlike her, he exposed the ways it had constrained and chafed him because its emphasis was literary rather than dramatic. In his view, traditional (or even poststructuralist) emphases may work for novels or poems but not for plays, where the structure of dramatic performance is much more akin to the abstract patterns of music. He urged students to become parts of Shakespearean texts by actually assuming roles in plays; not to do so, or at least not to attend productions frequently, "is like studying Mozart and never actually hearing a note of his music." He encouraged students to seek dramatic precision that depends not on verbal logic or psychological feeling but on perception of discrete units of hearing, silence, rhythm, pace, and apartness, rather than combinations of words. Thus, he encouraged the students to pay attention to parts of Shakespeare's plays that lie beyond or under language and that form abstract patterns with a life of their own.

In his workshop, "Teaching *A Midsummer Night's Dream*," he involved the students as actors and audience physically, as several of them performed the first scene of the play. He explained how its musical flow of repeated words, patterns, and segments of dialogue is set against the different, brick-like, often tiny units of dramatic composition which he distinguished in precise detail. He made clear to them how the first scene is divided into five clear structural segments that introduce all major elements of the drama, and he encouraged actors and audience alike to try to sense "what had been in the dramatist's mind" as he composed the structural interaction of these different parts.

Both the lecture Patricia Parker presented at Union as well as the one printed in this volume concentrated on verbal rather than performance energy. In her essay printed here, "Interpreting through Wordplay: *The Merry Wives of Windsor*," she has carefully identified and traced several series of associations and transformations of "translation" in the play which spread from concentration in specific words in one part of a scene outward to increasingly expanded as well as increasingly well defined networks of aesthetic and cultural meaning. Professor Parker focused her attention on scene 1 of act 4 in *Merry Wives* in which the Welsh parson gives a lesson in translation to the boy Will Page, and she demonstrated how the episode is not self-contained and dismissible, as influential critics have suggested, but is implicated in a broad discursive network that extends to multiple meanings of "translation." Starting from the episode's "double translation," with its aim of eradicating difference in the reciprocal translations between Latin and English, she demonstrated the impossibility of eliminating such difference and the concomitant inevitability of having the meanings that escape create flows of association. "Translation" of language has become, in her tracking, related to conveyance of property and to conveyance in every sense, that is, to theft, deception, duplicity, to pages and porters, to construing and construction, to "cozen Germans" who appear out of nowhere, and to an intricate series of other "translations" that finally implicate women as secondary and accessory, genitive and generative, conveyed and cozening—in effect, as figures, from the time of Eve onward, of derivation and decline. Parker's following the process of translation not only has deconstructed the stable meaning of specific diction but also has traced the cultural history that finally links women with decline, with irrepressible utterance, and with the varied, "translated" textual versions of Shakespeare's voice itself.

In "Teaching and Wordplay: The Wall of *A Midsummer Night's Dream*," Professor Parker involved her own students in a counterpoint of voices as they worked out the implications of wordplay originating in one textual crux, that is, in the difference between the Quarto and Folio versions of the wall in "Pyramus and Thisbe." Following the implications of such textual difference provides a crucial basis for making an editorial decision about whether to use the Quarto or Folio. The Quarto reads, "Now is the *moon used* between the two neighbors," in contrast to the Folio's "Now is the *moral down* between the two neighbors." From this textual discrepancy and with student scrutiny directed to the Folio version, Parker led the group from associations with "more," "moral," and "mural" to a demonstration of the numerous verbal links that extend through intertextual references to words in French, Latin, and Greek and to such works as Canticles, Revelation, *The Metamorphoses, Ovid moralisé,* and the *OED*. Perhaps some of her students are still following forces of verbal transformation and association that she and they unleashed and that reflect the high energy and unexpected networks that the Folio's words produce.

Whereas R. A. Foakes, Leah Marcus, and Patricia Parker all dealt to some degree with the influence of indirect cultural interests on and within

Shakespeare's texts, Annabel Patterson, in her lecture on *Henry V*, introduced our students directly to an issue-oriented cultural criticism that clearly exposes how Shakespearean text can be and has been altered for ideological purposes. Professor Patterson introduced her audience to some of the new methodology of analyzing historical and cultural contexts and proceeded to involve the students in a process of historical detective work that combined her close reading of the primary texts of the play (the 1600 Quarto and the 1623 Folio) with careful examination of the interpretive uses of these texts by successive generations of influential historians, critics, editors, and directors. Her focus was the way nonliterary interests have influenced the interpretation of Shakespeare's handling of Henry V's victory in the Battle of Agincourt. She pointed out the crux of this handling—Henry's controversial order to kill the French prisoners—and proceeded carefully to compare successive interpretations with the original texts. In particular she examined the precise chronology between the command itself and the episode interpreters have traditionally but inappropriately used to justify it: the French slaughter of the English camp boys. In her careful examination of the cinematic versions of the play by Olivier and Branagh, she demonstrated how interpretations of these episodes have had political rather than aesthetic motivation. She showed the students that despite Branagh's claims for significant differences between his and Olivier's overtly propagandistic production, Branagh's film, through its handling of the two episodes, both promotes nationalistic celebration quite like Olivier's and glorifies war.

After Professor Patterson reviewed all of the practical teaching applications of the contributors to this book, she wrote an essay in which she reconsiders her own critical procedures in the light of those of her colleagues in the Shakespeare Series. Her essay serves as a fitting conclusion to this volume. Despite her lecture's marked success as "a test case" of issue-oriented criticism, Patterson suggests in her "Palinode" that, while such an approach can "expand the boundaries of literature and literary inquiry" to show how Shakespeare can be used to promote partisan political views, it may exact too high a price. Instead of discovering the power of Shakespeare that emerges from the texts themselves, even the best students, she suggests, can be tempted to construct "prefabricated edifices" in substitution for the intricate process of precise, close reading.

What is lost in the extraliterary construction of such prefabricated edifices, of course, is the enjoyment of working within the literary and dramatic construction of Shakespeare's poems and plays themselves. Our critics clearly described continuities and revisions in critical history and generously demonstrated interpretive procedures of their own; but above all they brought the students into vital touch with parts of Shakespeare's text. They did so by methods that were diverse yet complemented each other in unexpected ways. Helen Vendler, for example, led students to Shakespeare's sonnets as interrelated aesthetic voices to whose questions they might respond with precise intellectual and emotional perception, while John Wilders drew attention to the unfamiliar, quasi-abstract, dramatic patterns positioned within the stage-text of Shakespearean drama. Patricia Parker enticed students to pursue the unruly verbal energies of *Merry Wives* in order to perceive a variety of underlying cultural suppositions, including those about the inferiority of women, while Annabel Patterson showed how a close reading of early versions of *Henry V* could allow students to perceive and expose historical and current manipulations of Shakespeare's text for deliberate political purpose. R. A. Foakes and Leah Marcus further traced cultural-political formations of "Shakespeare," but in their workshops they brought the students back to specific lines and words and to heated debates about the passions and puzzles within the texts themselves. In short, the critics displayed a remarkable diversity while creating among themselves and in concert with the students a design of constructive, lasting pleasure.

Teaching with Shakespeare

Poems Posing Questions

HELEN VENDLER

To talk about one's own critical procedures is to go back to first principles, and often to first teachers. Each of my poetry teachers, I think, gave me one or more of the procedures that I still use. The first, Sister Marie Barry, who taught me in an undergraduate seminar in modern poetry, urged us to trust our own judgment: "Would you print it, Miss Hennessy?" she would ask about a poem by Auden. "Would I?" It meant I had to think about what I admired in the poem, that the first procedure was to write about what you admired. Many people are content to write about what is culturally present in any given period, and minor works are as interesting to them as major works; even wholly failed works—perhaps especially failed works—offer insights into cultural obsessions, as Harlequin romances or Disneyland tell us something about our own culture. But I find failed works like music played off-key; they hurt the ear. Works we find great, though, are often exhausting to think about, and make for strenuous reading; Keats spoke of having to "burn through" *King Lear* when he sat down, almost unwillingly, to reread it.

Nonetheless, we are drawn back again and again to works we admire. My second poetry teacher, Morton Berman, taught me the power of empathy; as he told the story of an author's struggle, he was so deeply engaged with it that one thought in turn that he must be an Evangelical becoming a skeptic (as we read Arnold), or a grieving mourner speculating on evolution (as we read Tennyson), or a Protestant realizing he wanted to be a Catholic (as we read Hopkins). The deep life-engagement of poetry was brought home to me in his class. I was too young then to realize that he was Jewish; and yet he mediated the Victorian Christian anguish to us in all its various forms without a moment's lack of empathy. Later, I remember eating a kosher dinner in the house of a religiously observant Jewish colleague, Morton Bloomfield, and I saw on the wall of the dining room, as I glanced up, a reproduction of Fra Angelico's *Annunciation*. I admired the

23

breadth of empathy in both of these teachers, as they felt their way into life-experiences wholly different from their own.

My third teacher, Reuben Brower, was a classicist by training, and from him I learned that every English text has classical antecedents of which it is fully conscious; the names of Virgil and Ovid, Horace and Catullus were as often on his lips as the names of Pope or Swift. He had a professional interest in translation and in linguistics, and made us conscious of the impossibility of finding equivalent linguistic structures in differing languages. Brower was a critic, rather than a historian of ideas or a biographical writer; he had trained under I. A. Richards at Cambridge, and had learned to ask us the most provocative question after "Would you print it?"—to wit, "What do you see as a critical problem in this text?" We learned what he meant by "a critical problem" as we went along in his seminar; it meant, "What made the writer write this rather than that?"

The livingness of learning in reading poetry was clear to me not only in him but also in my fourth teacher, Douglas Bush, for whom classical mythology was the great mine in which Renaissance poets like Spenser and Milton had found pure gold. Bush had learned *Paradise Lost* by heart, and he never needed to look up a passage in his Milton; I learned from him, as well as from some others, that the best way to possess a poem is to know it by heart.

My fifth teacher, Rosemond Tuve, was a genre critic, and taught us in a seminar called "Romance, Allegory, and Pastoral, with special reference to Spenser." By teaching us the subgenres, and then showing us how *The Faerie Queene* incorporated them all, she showed me how useful it is to think what subgenre a poem belongs to—whether it is a boast, or a recantation, or a homily, or a wedding-poem, or what. She and my sixth teacher, Northrop Frye, taught me the beauty of structure; for Frye, to see overarching architectonic forms was to perceive how the details fit into a whole.

My seventh teacher, John Kelleher, a historian by profession, knew Yeats's poetry by heart, and saw it as intimately related to the Irish history from which it sprang, and of which it became a part. From him I learned that poetry, and especially poetic forms, have ideological meaning; if a Protestant Anglo-Irish poet borrowed a form from the Catholic folk, it was a gesture of homage where homage had often been refused.

Finally, my eighth teacher, I. A. Richards, taught me that a single poem was worth all my time. Richards taught a twelve-week course which considered exactly twelve major poems, ranging from "The Garden" to "Ode on a Grecian Urn." Each poem received two hours of lecture time; but one was left longing for several more hours on that poem. Richards had an

unparalleled sense of poetic import—of how much a given word summoned up, of how many functions a single word could perform in a line or
a stanza. One cause for his depth of understanding was his philosophical
temper; he had done "Moral Sciences" at Cambridge, and remained an
epistemologist and ethicist all his life. Another cause was his prodigious
memory; for him any text had multiple intertextual relations, usually ranging back to Plato.

These teachers all gave me ways of dealing imaginatively, intellectually, and critically with poems. I had learned from my first teachers, my
mother and father, to care for poetry and for the language in which it was
written; my mother knew a great deal of English poetry by heart, and my
father introduced us to poems in Spanish, French, and Italian. At school we
sang the Latin liturgy and Latin hymns, and chanted the Psalms in antipho-
nal chorus. Behind every word in English is a word in Latin or Greek or
French or some other language, and I heard, from early on in my life, the
undersong of etymology in the song of the poem.

I was dissatisfied with the short period of time one spent on an author
in courses, and with the short papers which were all one had time to write.
When it came time to do my dissertation, I had, at last, world enough and
time to read every word Yeats had written, and to write three hundred
pages about him. That wasn't enough, exactly, but it was certainly better
than twelve weeks and twenty pages. However, both my first and second
books were on long works, and when I was beginning my third book, on
George Herbert, I wondered what it would feel like to take a short work and
really write all I wanted to say about it, to show exactly what its poet was
up to. I took a poem of sixteen lines, "Vertue," wrote till I was finished, and
found out that I had typed sixteen pages. Ah, I thought, so that's the ratio:
a page per line. Later, in my fourth book, I wrote fifty pages about a thirty-
three line poem, Keats's "To Autumn," and so I now suspect the ratio
changes with the poem. I was happiest writing about short works, imagining the compositional process that had produced them.

None of my teachers had, I think, come at poems in this way. But I
found my way into poems by imagining that it was my own hand that had
written them, that I had chosen this form, and this word rather than that
word. It was a habit with me to write out in longhand any poem I was going
to think about for some time; and it became a habit to learn the poem by
heart, too. Then it was "my" poem, and I could feel its inner exfoliation
from a kernel of imaginative and formal intention.

I turned, finally, to a project I had had in mind for a long time: to work
on Shakespeare's sonnets. I had learned many of them by heart when I was

fifteen, but I hadn't felt able to deal with them until recently. They are the most ingenious poems of their time, and they are just at the brink of our horizon of perception. The Renaissance begins modern literature, and we feel akin to Hamlet as we do not, I think, to Chaucer's Troilus. And yet, the Renaissance is very far from us, and we are perhaps deluded in thinking it close. To work on Shakespeare's sonnets was to ask myself what questions these remote and yet immediate poems would propose to me.

It is possible to think comparatively about these sonnets: after all, Shakespeare comes at the very end of the sonnet vogue, and was preceded by Dante, Petrarch, Ronsard, du Bellay, Wyatt, Surrey, Sidney, and others. It is interesting to ask (but I don't yet know the answer) how close Shakespeare is to his predecessors. At the same time, the more I looked at his predecessors, the more he seemed to me different from them, notably because he made his own a form not invented by him but realized by him, the form we now call "the Shakespearean sonnet," consisting of four movable parts—three quatrains rhyming alternately and a couplet. The first question that Shakespeare's sonnets put to me is the question of the usefulness of four parts over two. The Italian sonnet has two parts, an eight-line octave and a six-line sestet, which often present a question and an answer, or a problem and its resolution. Many of Shakespeare's sonnets are crypto-Italian sonnets, with a true eight-line beginning. The six remaining lines, which in the Italian model would compose the sestet, often contain a "shortened sestet" of four lines (the third quatrain), followed by something interesting being done in the couplet.

The Italian sonnet often describes a life-situation in the octave, and then metaphorizes it in the sestet; a good example in English of this practice occurs in Keats's "On First Looking into Chapman's Homer":

> Much have I traveled in the realms of gold,
> And many goodly states and kingdoms seen;
> Round many western islands have I been
> Which bards in fealty to Apollo hold.
> Oft of one wide expanse have I been told
> That deep-browed Homer ruled as his demesne;
> Yet did I never breathe its pure serene
> Till I heard Chapman speak out loud and bold;
> Then felt I like some watcher of the skies
> When a new planet swims into his ken;
> Or like stout Cortez when with eagle eyes
> He stared at the Pacific—and all his men

> Looked at each other with a wild surmise—
> Silent, upon a peak in Darien.

Keats writes in the octave about his acquaintance with other poets and his ignorance of Homer until he came across Chapman's translation. The sestet enters into the realm of metaphor, and offers two striking similes, which "correct" the tame earlier metaphor for reading, namely the metaphor of traveling from known isle to known isle. What was it like to read Homer for the first time? "Then felt I like some watcher of the skies . . . / Or like stout Cortez." Homer's demesne turns out to be not another isle, but a whole new ocean.

My first example from Shakespeare, "Full many a glorious morning have I seen," looks structurally like this sort of Italian sonnet, with eight lines of situation (seeing the morning cloud over) followed by four lines of a comparison—"Even so my sun one early morn did shine." [For full texts of sonnets discussed in the lecture and workshop, see pp. 57–59.] We realize as we read this that the comparison is the wrong-way round. Normally, the speaker would say, "My beloved, who is my sun, has hidden from me; what is this like? It is like seeing the sun cloud over." In short, the illustration from nature should follow the life-situation, and clarify it. But Shakespeare's speaker seems to expend all his emotion on the natural phenomenon, as he describes it first with a distinct luxury of adjectival and verbal expressiveness:

> Full many a glorious morning have I seen
> Flatter the mountain tops with sovereign eye,
> Kissing with golden face the meadows green,
> Gilding pale streams with heav'nly alchemy,
> Anon permit the basest clouds to ride
> With ugly rack on his celestial face,
> And from the forlorn world his visage hide,
> Stealing unseen to west with this disgrace.

Nobody has ever felt so bad in print about a cloud-cover before. When we come to the four-line human comparison, it seems, as it turns clouded, barely and sparsely sketched by contrast to the opulence that has preceded it:

> E'en so my sun one early morn did shine
> With all triumphant splendor on my brow;

> But out alack, he was but one hour mine,
> The region cloud hath masked him from me now.

In the couplet, the friend's absence is excused, with apparent generosity and proverbial wisdom:

> Yet him for this my love no whit disdaineth;
> Suns of the world may stain when heav'n's sun
>   staineth.

When we ask why the octave of this sonnet is so luxuriously expressive, and the human "application" in the quatrain so bare, we find the explanation of why this sonnet has been written the wrong-way round. In reading the bare quatrain, we instinctively "fill in" all the verbs and adjectives from the description of the clouded-over sun:

> Even so my sun one early [glorious] morn did shine
> With all-triumphant splendor on my brow,
> [Flattering me with his sovereign eye, kissing me with
>   his golden face, gilding my pallor with his
>   heavenly alchemy,]
> But out, alack, he was but one hour mine,
> The region cloud [the basest cloud, which he permitted
>   to ride with ugly rack on his celestial face] has
>   masked him [as he hides his visage and steals to
>   west unseen with this disgrace] from [forlorn] me
>   now.

No explicit critique of the young man's behavior is voiced in quatrain 3; his disappearance is explained by the active agency of the "region cloud" which masks him. But as we know from the octave, the sun has *permitted* his disgrace by the "basest clouds," themselves moralized; and thus he has been judged as a flatterer, one who gilds and then retracts his gilding. By prefacing the critique of the friend with the critique of the sun, Shakespeare ascribes blame indirectly, even while absolving the friend as performing "only naturally" in the couplet. What remains in the mind from this sonnet is the heartbreaking remembrance of what it was to be kissed and flattered and gilded, even for one hour; and the shaming recollection of the baseness of the clouds that supplanted you as the company of the sun. It is no accident that what rhymes internally in this poem are the words "morn" and "forlorn," and that "grace" becomes hidden in "disgrace." This is what results from asking what, in one instance, Shakespeare made of the Italian octave-sestet structure. It may be time to ask what he made of his own favored structure, which is divided not after eight lines, but after four; and after four again; and after four again. Shakespeare liked his quatrains most for the succinct presentation each could give of a life-model. Though there are many possible choices here, I have taken Sonnet 60: in each of its four parts we have an image of life. How are we to label these images? Why do they occur in the way they do? The first is spoken deliberately and even equably, and shows a steady-state partitive model of life, in which each minute resembles exactly every other minute, in a well-regulated and formal, if mortal, motion:

> Like as the waves make towards the pebbled shore,
> So do our minutes hasten to their end,
> Each changing place with that which goes before,
> In sequent toil all forwards do contend.

Every word of this could be spoken by a philosopher making an abstract point, except one: the odd-word-out is "pebbled," affording us for an instant the sensual feel of the beach. The poet flashes out from under his philosophical cover. And in the next quatrain, the poet-playwright dominates: we see the history of a single soul as the second quatrain, forsaking the partitive steady-state model of the first, describes the unitary tragic arc by which the soul rises to glory and then sinks in ignominious defeat:

> Nativity, once in the main of light,
> Crawls to maturity, wherewith being crowned,
> Crookèd eclipses 'gainst his glory fight,
> And time that gave doth now his gift confound.

The general "theme" is the same: our minutes hasten to their end; nativity crawls to maturity. But halfway through the second quatrain, agency passes away from us, from nativity, and is ascribed (as the tragic arc begins its decline), to the crooked eclipses and to Time. They are now the subjects of the verbs. The small linear drama is enacted in terms of the "cr" words: *crawls, crowned, crooked.* (That drama is finished in the couplet, which seals the end in mentioning Time's *cruel* hand.) The tragic model is summed up in the last line of the quatrain; first time gave (the rising arc) and now Time confounds its gift. A: then B.

If quatrain one shows a recurrent steady-state model, and quatrain two a single tragic model of rise and fall, quatrain three invents yet another model of life, which we might call the death-in-life model. Whereas in quatrain two the crowning came after the crawling, and the crookedness after the crowning, in quatrain three sequence has been abolished, and death is simultaneous with life. In fact, as the quatrain is phrased, death is always pre-positioned to value. In telling the story linearly, we would say, "Once there was youth, and a flourish set on youth; then Time transfixed that flourish." That is how it would be put in the mode of quatrain two; but quatrain three, for three lines, puts the evil action first. And in each line a new evil action occurs, so that the life-and-death process which took two lines in quatrain one, and four lines in quatrain two, now takes place instantaneously in the anticipatory verb pre-position of every line:

> Time doth transfix the flourish set on youth,
> And delves the parallels in beauty's brow,
> Feeds on the rarities of nature's truth.

Value seems at some remove from time in the first two of these savage lines. There is youth; there is the flourish set on youth; it is the flourish that is transfixed. There is beauty; there is the brow of beauty; it is the parallels in the brow of beauty that Time delves. But in the third line, Time has direct access not only to value, but to value in the highest degree. There is truth; there is nature's truth; and there are the rarities of nature's truth, the quintessences of nature's essences. Time devours these rarities as its choicest morsels.

We can see how unrearrangeable these three quatrains are. One could not have the speedup in quatrain three without the stateliness of the tragic arc in quatrain two; one could not sense the tragedy in quatrain two if it were not for the philosophical sangfroid of quatrain one.

What is unexpected is the twelfth line. When we had met Time in line eight, he resembled the Lord: "The Lord giveth and the Lord taketh away; blessèd be the name of the Lord." When we meet him in line twelve, he is the Grim Reaper, and we have apparently returned from simultaneity to linearity: "And nothing stands [now] but for his scythe to mow [soon]." As we see the providential intent in "but for," however, we realize that "stands" is not a temporal present but a philosophic present, and that the line really means, "And nothing exists save what has from all eternity been destined for extinction." The line is not narratively linear, then, but necessitarian. This is to return to the simultaneity of life and death postulated by the third quatrain, but to see the simultaneity not as circumstantial but as evilly providential.

These three models have all been based on life and time; on nativity and minutes and the Grim Reaper. The couplet proposes yet another model, and repeats the verb "stands" so that we realize that its model is placed in opposition to that of quatrain three: "*Nothing stands* but for his scythe to mow. / And yet . . . *my verse shall stand.*" The couplet repeats a version of the tragic arc, rising gradually from "And yet" to "stand, / Praising thy worth," and then sinking under Time's "*cruel hand.*" "*Times* in hope" are in a literal *stand*off with "*Time.*" This model of a perpetual combat between *Time* mowing everything that *stands* and verse that *stands* to *times* in hope is the last of the four models in the sonnet. Shakespeare has used each of his movable parts to good effect in lodging a model in each; and he has made the parts irreversible and nontransposable. This is what he found to do, among other things, with his four-part form. In that sense, each of the sonnets that exploits its four-partedness poses the question, "What models am I suggesting, and why are they in the order in which I present them?"

We might pause, at this point, to recall that Shakespeare's earliest sonnets had none of this complexity of organization. In *Romeo and Juliet*, the charm of the embedded sonnet comes from its being written in dialogue, rather than in any intensity of poetic elaboration:

> *Romeo.* If I profane with my unworthiest hand
> This holy shrine, the gentle sin is this,
> My lips, two blushing pilgrims, ready stand
> To smooth that rough touch with a tender kiss.
>   *Juliet.* Good pilgrim, you do wrong your hand too much,
> Which mannerly devotion shows in this:
> For saints have hands that pilgrims' hands do touch,
> And palm to palm is holy palmers' kiss.
>   *Romeo.* Have not saints lips, and holy palmers too?
>   *Juliet.* Ay, pilgrim, lips that they must use in pray'r.
>   *Romeo.* O, then, dear saint, let lips do what hands do,
> They pray—grant thou, lest faith turn to despair.
>   *Juliet.* Saints do not move, though grant for prayers' sake.
>   *Romeo.* Then move not while my prayer's effect I take.
>   (1.5.93–106)

There are plays on words here but not really a play of thought in the manner of the sonnets in the 1609 volume. Juliet is not really a shrine, nor Romeo a palmer; the metaphors are well-worn ones, and the moves are well-known to both participants.

There is a literary shock in turning from the Petrarchan Shakespeare of *Romeo and Juliet* to the subtle analyst of narcissism that we find in Sonnet 94. The critical problem posed by Sonnet 94 arises from the sudden turn, in quatrain three, away from the human imagery that dominates the octave. Out of nowhere we have something called "the summer's flower," which rapidly summons up images of weeds and lilies. The fit between octave and sestet is difficult to articulate precisely, and the sonnet has provoked much commentary. Here it is:

> They that have pow'r to hurt and will do none,
> That do not do the thing they most do show,
> Who moving others are themselves as stone,
> Unmovèd, cold, and to temptation slow—
> They rightly do inherit heaven's graces
> And husband nature's riches from expense;
> They are the lords and owners of their faces,
> Others but stewards of their excellence.
> The summer's flow'r is to the summer sweet,
> Though to itself it only live and die,
> But if that flow'r with base infection meet,
> The basest weed outbraves his dignity.
> > For sweetest things turn sourest by their deeds;
> > Lilies that fester smell far worse than weeds.

I will not attempt to take up all the questions posed by this sonnet, but I will ask what deflects the speaker from his tortured contemplation of one subset of men and makes him suddenly talk about flowers. The thing that is argued about the flower is that, even though the flower is totally self-regarding ("to itself it only live and die"), it is beloved by its spectators, who ask nothing of it except its beauty. The flower "moving others, [is itself] as stone, unmovèd, cold." Nobody expects more from it. Why, then, do we expect more of a beautiful person? Why can we not admire his beauty and leave it at that? Why, if he is not drawn to us, are we disposed to call him stony-hearted and cold? Why cannot we bring ourselves to admire his character, since he is slow to temptation?

Most commentators have seen the ambivalence in the speaker's remarks about those cold and self-possessed people. In spite of his attempt to praise such people as virtuous and even divine, his resentment of their inhumanity leaks out in his noun "stone" and his adjective "cold." We realize, when we come to the third quatrain, that the poem has not really been about a subset of people at all, but rather about one certain person, who is like "the summer's flow'r." The singular comparison gives the speaker away, as he attempts to excuse the young man; "Since I ask nothing of the flower, why can't I take you simply as an aesthetic object as well, and ask nothing of you in the same way?" The relenting naked adoration in "The summer's flow'r is to the summer sweet," with its folded *summer-summer* reciprocity, reminds us of the speaker's remark elsewhere to the young man:

> For nothing this wide universe I call
> Save thou, my Rose; in it thou art my all.
>
> (Sonnet 109)

The deflecting move away from the world of human beings and ethical choices to the simpler world of flowers and their lovers lasts only two lines. The resentment bursts out in the warning,

> But if that flow'r with base infection meet,
> The basest weed outbraves his dignity.

Summer's flower met summer's adoration; but here it meets base infection and turns its own dignity into sub-baseness, as it becomes baser than the basest weed. "Dignity" is the Latin version of "worth," and we recall that Shakespeare's verse wants to praise worth. "Infection" has as its root *facio*, to do; and this makes us notice the strangeness of the couplet:

> For sweetest things turn sourest by their deeds;
> Lilies that fester smell far worse than weeds.

It is clear that the second line of the couplet refers to our images of flowers and weeds and festering, and that the "far worse" relates to the fact that the flower is of less worth than the basest weed. But what does the first line of the couplet refer to? "Sweetest things" would seem to refer to the summer's flower which is to the summer sweet. But flowers cannot perform deeds, though they can be *infected*. It is only now, I think, that we recognize the multiple appearances of the verb belonging to "deeds"—the verb "do"—in the octave of the sonnet; we also recognize the presence of the word "thing":

> They that have power to hurt and will *do* none,
> That *do* not *do* the *thing* they most *do* show . . .
> They rightly *do* inherit heaven's graces.

We perceive that the first line of the couplet chiefly "belongs to" the octave of deeds, and that the second line of the couplet "belongs to" the quatrain of the flower. Disgrace and expense, the obverse of quatrain two, haunt the couplet. Those inheritors of heaven's graces, those good husbanders of riches, fall by their deeds into base infection and sour all their former sweetness. Lest the warning seem too personal, too greatly driven by rejection, the speaker ends his sonnet with a proverb: "Lilies that fester smell far worse than weeds." If his own warning cannot keep the young man away from base company, let the wisdom of the ages do it. With the final proverb, we realize that the summer's flower has been the lily of the field that toils not, neither does it spin, and that the speaker's relenting toward it in the third quatrain is also prompted by Jesus' parable. The lilies of the field simply are; they do no deeds. They are to be admired as forms of existence, not desired as lovers. But that attempt to have desire give way to pure aesthetic contemplation cannot endure; the poem falls back into desire.

From these examples, it can be seen that each poem poses its own question, phrased in terms of its own imagery, or focus, or stance. The sonnets are sometimes serious, sometimes frivolous, sometimes both together, as in my closing example, Sonnet 105. The main question posed by this poem is what it needs all its repetitions for. The fiction of the poem is that a Christian interlocutor, wishing the poet to worship only the Trinity, accuses the poet of idolatry because of his worship of the beloved. Not at all, replies the poet, maintaining that his beloved—a unitary combination of the Good, the True, and the Beautiful—is as much worthy of worship as the other's one God in three persons:

> Let not my love be called idolatry,
> Nor my belovèd as an idol show,
> Since all alike my songs and praises be
> To *one*, of *one*, still such, and ever so.
> Kind is my love today, tomorrow kind,
> Still constant in a *won*drous excellence;
> Therefore my verse, to constancy confined,
> *One* thing expressing, leaves out difference.

That is the octave; it is, as I have tried to emphasize through the added italics, all about oneness.The next quatrain is all about threeness:

> Fair, kind, and true, is all my argument,
> Fair, kind, and true, varying to other words;

> And in this change is my invention spent—
> Three themes in *one*, which *won*drous scope affords.

It will be seen that the terms of the Platonic triad have been translated into common English, in which, of the Good, the True, and the Beautiful, only the true remains untranslated: *good* becomes *kind*, and *beautiful* becomes *fair*. It will also be noticed that the foremost quality of the beloved, which in the octave was virtue ("Kind is my love today, tomorrow kind") in quatrain three has become beauty ("Fair" twice takes first place).

The couplet displays three-in-oneness:

> Fair, kind, and true, have often lived al*one*,
> Which three, till now, never kept seat in *one*.

The poem rings changes on two culturally available Renaissance trinities: the first is the Christian trinity of three persons in one God, the second the Platonic trinity of the Good, the True, and the Beautiful, which go to make up the One. By arguing that the second is at least as worthy of worship as the first, Shakespeare engages in blasphemy, literally speaking. By organizing his sonnet in three parts—oneness, threeness, and three-in-oneness—Shakespeare acts out the common trinitarian motif. But by placing the unitary word/syllable/phoneme *one/-one/won* exactly twice in each of the four parts of his poem, he slips two-ness into one-and-three-ness, making the emphasis on the reciprocity of the couple underlie his mock-heresy with respect to Christianity and his mock-adherence to Petrarchan Platonism. The sonnet is a good example of the sort of poem that can only be written under specific cultural conditions—here, the Renaissance adherence to both these trinities, and the Renaissance fondness for schemes of words.

If I return to my beginning, it is to say that each poem must raise its own questions, and that to those questions we must bring whatever is necessary: here, a knowledge of trinities; there, a knowledge of the root of *infection;* here, a sense that poems generally put their life-situations first and illustrative phenomena second; there, that a philosophical steady-state model does not resemble the dramatist's tragic arc; here, that concealed wordplay is one of literature's ways of making jokes; there, that the scythe means we are to think of the Grim Reaper. In a sense, in reading poems, nothing that we know comes amiss; and yet, we have to sort out the relevance of what we know by means of the questions the poem proposes in its very structure. Needless to say, none of this is any good without empathy and a sense of the human situation that might engender a poem like "They that have power to hurt"; equally, none of it is any good if one cannot be delighted by a mind that splits up the block-like form of the sonnet into a dialogue between tentative lovers, who are unconscious that they are writing a joint sonnet together. The strenuousness of reading the sonnets arises because we are following a mind at once imaginative and playful, moved and moving without ever forgetting the wayward possibilities of linguistic ingenuity. The poems, even after we have solved one aspect of them, go on posing questions.

Reading for Difference:
The Sonnets

HELEN VENDLER

Workshop

This is a workshop, so you're all supposed to work with me. Why don't I have some volunteers come up with me on the stage? This I know is excruciating, but it would be nice to have some individual people to work with because it's hard to work with a whole group of people. And I thought I'd ask, Is there anybody who knows Latin in this group? Dare you raise your hand? Would you be the grammar expert? People who know Latin know grammar. What, another one? We have two grammar experts? Good. Let's have two grammar experts. Will you come up with me—you two? Now I have to get somebody who is a psychologist or has some interest in psychology or knows something about psychology. I see people being pointed to. Was that a hand? Somebody join this noble volunteer. Who at least thinks about psychological influences? Come on down.

Is somebody interested in structure—like architecture or cell structure or organ structure? Geometry? Anything like that? Anybody interested in shapes? Good. You have to leave in fifty minutes? Okay. We need another psychology volunteer. Anybody interested in love and lust? Anybody interested in gender questions? Is there anybody who would like to volunteer just in general, to put in two cents worth? Is there a kibitzer in the audience? That's always helpful. That's somebody who doesn't have a specific function, just to put in two cents worth.

This is not a good shape. Let's pull the chairs around.

Let me read the poems first, and then we'll have a kind of ground to analyze the poems from. Does everybody have a handout? The first one is Sonnet 116, which is usually thought of as the sonnet about love. The second one is Sonnet 129, which is usually thought of as the sonnet about lust. Have any of you read these before? Some of you—some of you have, some of you haven't. Fine.

Let me read them both so we'll have a sense of what's in the field of interest about love and lust.

> Let me not to the marriage of true minds
> Admit impediments. Love is not love
> Which alters when it alteration finds,
> Or bends with the remover to remove.
> O no, it is an ever-fixèd mark
> That looks on tempests and is never shaken;
> It is the star to every wand'ring bark,
> Whose worth's unknown, although his heighth be taken.
> Love's not Time's fool, though rosy lips and cheeks
> Within his bending sickle's compass come,
> Love alters not with his brief hours and weeks,
> But bears it out e'en to the edge of doom.
>   If this be error and upon me proved,
>   I never writ, nor no man ever loved.

> Th' expense of spirit in a waste of shame
> Is lust in action, and till action lust
> Is perjured, murd'rous, bloody, full of blame,
> Savage, extreme, rude, cruel, not to trust,
> Enjoyed no sooner but despisèd straight,
> Past reason hunted, and no sooner had,
> Past reason hated as a swallowed bait,
> On purpose laid to make the taker mad:
> Mad in pursuit, and in possession so,
> Had, having, and in quest to have, extreme,
> A bliss in proof, and proved, a very woe,
> Before, a joy proposed, behind, a dream.
>   All this the world well knows, yet none knows well
>   To shun the heaven that leads men to this hell.

Vendler: All right. You all have your appointed duties. Who would like to make a remark on grammar, gender questions, shape, the psychology of the speaker in either of the poems? Okay, gender.

Aud.: First of all, gender is not even involved. The speaker could be either a man or a woman.

Vendler: What about the second one?

Aud.: As far as action, there's expressive action, and it usually denotes male sensuality. A male has the passion and in fulfilling passion . . .

Vendler: Is there any indication of the presence of a woman in the second one? Maybe at the end when it talks about bliss. Does anybody want to add anything? Anybody can kibitz at any time. Yes?

Aud.: I don't think the second one is so much about a woman being involved, but sort of a lust of the self. Perhaps it's a masturbatory situation and he knows that what he's doing is wrong but he's compelled to do it.

Vendler: That's another distinction. I'm not saying yes or no. These are just things to float. In an original sort of prewriting session everything is allowed to float. So, at least some distinctions have been drawn between the first and the second. Can you give a further distinction between one and two at the overall level? Yes.

Aud.: Number two is much more violent and has much stronger language—it's harsh and hard. That's an interesting question. I mean, how do you decide when language is violent? Is it only by what the words say, or is it anything else that makes it seem violent?

Vendler: "Murderous" is, of course, a violent word, so on the semantic level,—if you do a semantic scan of the poem, what are the words? It's interesting sometimes just to run through and say the words without saying what they say, leaving out the verbs and just reading things like "expense," "spirit," "waste," "shame," "lust," "action," "lust," "perjured," "murderous," "bloody," just to get a sense of the semantic drift of the whole thing without thinking "What is it saying about these things?" but, "How many violent words per square inch are there if you do a kind of drift over the words?" Now it's certainly the case that there are a lot of violent words per square inch. Do they go through the whole poem? The violent words?

Aud.: No. As was mentioned earlier, there is sort of a bottom where things soften a little bit.

Vendler: Okay. Softens at the bottom so in semantic scanning you hit "bliss," "joy," woe," "dream"—not like "murderous," "bloody," "savage."

Aud.: And not just like the meaning of the word but just the fact that they're listed: "savage," "extreme"—and there's nothing to connect it or break it down.

Vendler: When you're saying "listed," you mean there's a series of similar words that keep "hitting." What kinds of words are these? Where's our grammar expert?

Aud.: Adjectives.

Vendler: Adjectives. Okay. [Laughter.] That's why we need an expert.

It's always a bit tricky. There are trickier moments to come. So we have a list of adjectives. Where do the adjectives start? What's the first adjective?

Aud.: "Perjured."

Vendler: Yes. What has preceded adjectives, grammatically speaking? "Expense," "spirit," "waste," "shame"—what parts of speech are those? Nouns. All right. Another grammar expert. So you have a group of nouns; then you have a group of adjectives. What happens after the adjectives, since we're doing a grammar scan? It's always helpful to do a grammar scan of anything. What happens after "not to trust," which winds up the adjectives? "*Enjoyed* no sooner," "*despised* straight," "past reason *hunted,*" "no sooner *had,*" "past reason *hated*"?

Aud.: Verbs.

Vendler: And what version of those verbs? They are all verbals of what sort?

Aud.: Past participles.

Vendler: Past participles. Yes. What do they attach to? What is "*enjoyed* no sooner, but *despised* straight"?

Aud.: Lust.

Vendler: Lust, yes. So what function are they performing if they modify a noun?

Aud.: Adjectives.

Vendler: Adjectives, yes. They are past participle adjectives, "hunted," "had," "hated," "despised," and so forth. There's a whole set of verbal adjectives there. Let's leave it all at that for the moment, just in terms of the grammar. Yes?

Aud.: I think what Shakespeare's doing is using comparisons to emphasize. It's hard to explain, but in artwork you can have a relief work with a foreground and background, and you can emphasize certain things by this. You can see it visually. I think Shakespeare does it with words. In the comparison of both poems, he creates a relief so to speak—lust and love. You can see it, and he does it by this verbal relief work; I'm not sure exactly what to call it. As in the first poem, love is all these different things and love is set apart from these other things—from tempests, and stars, and things like that. In that way, in the second poem the same thing happens and he emphasizes these ideas with these comparisons.

Vendler: What you bring up is what the formalists invented a new word for, which is "to foreground" *x* or *y,* exactly from that sense of what is foregrounded in a painting or in a sculpture vs. what is in the background. What do you push up front and what do you leave as a sort of background? What aspect of lust? And this goes back to the observation about the softening later. If you're doing the violent aspects for a while, you're foregrounding violence, and then you go into "bliss," "woe," "joy," "dream," where you're not foregrounding the semantic idea of violence. There was someone out here who wanted to say something a minute ago and I missed you.

Aud.: I thought it was interesting to look at the language used to describe in both sonnets, because in the first one love is described in usual conventional language used in love poetry, whereas with lust the play of the words is more like sexual warfare: that's representative of the inner struggle between appetite and reason.

Vendler: Yes. Well, that too would be conventional. We're now into culture. Anyone—I nominate you the culture expert. That would have been a useful thing to have, too. And you bring up the conventionality, really, of both these treatments. If you think about the conventional descriptions of love in the Renaissance, one of them is indeed that it is the star to every wandering bark; Petrarch described the lover as somebody conducting his ship in a terrible storm, where the rain was his tears and the clouds were his sorrows and his will was broken; he had a broken rudder. He could no longer steer the boat, and Shakespeare says there is a way to steer this bark through storms and tempests by the star of love, which is the fixed north star by which you navigate. So that is a Petrarchan convention about love that is used. And certainly the marriage of minds compared to the marriage of bodies in sacramental marriage is a convention. Shakespeare takes the marriage convention and lifts it into the mental realm. In the same way, in the lust sonnet, the internal war between reason and passion sometimes is called by its Greek name of *psychomachia;* the fight between one part of yourself and another part of yourself is a conventional way to represent passion struggling against reason and reason sometimes being overcome by passion. These are commonplaces about love and lust that up to a point he draws from his cultural surroundings and then inquires into. That is to say, the Petrarchan lover who is tossed in the tempest of sighs and tears doesn't have, in Petrarch's sonnet, the star to look at. Shakespeare puts in the star to govern, you might say, the wandering of this ship which can never err because it always has the star. And similarly, we'll go onto the struggle of reason and passion and—did you want to say something about the struggle of reason and passion? Do you see any signs of reason?

Aud.: I guess, maybe.

Vendler: Is there a positive pole mentioned in the lust poem? Maybe our psychologist would like to talk about that? You can imagine—do you know the sonnet by Sir Philip Sidney, "Leave me O love which reaches but to dust / And thou my soul aspire to higher things"—you know, so now you have a pole of higher things vs. the love that leads but to dust. Is there such a positive pole in this lust problem?

Aud.: Joy.

Vendler: All right! That's a positive word, "joy." Is there another positive word?

Aud.: "Dream."

Vendler: Well, dream is a little funny in Shakespeare. Is there another positive word?

Aud.: "Bliss."

Vendler: Bliss, sure. Bliss and joy. Are they connected to reason or are they, too, connected to lust?

Aud.: I say they're still connected to lust.

Vendler: Still connected to lust. Okay, so we now have some positive words connected to lust—"bliss" and "joy"—and we have some negative words connected to lust—"perjured," "bloody," "murderous"—which signals to us that the speaker of the sonnet has, as we say, ambivalent feelings. I mean sometimes he feels good about it—it's a "joy proposed." Sometimes he feels good about it—it's a bliss "in proof"—that is to say, while you're doing it. And sometimes he feels bad about it. When does he feel worst about it?

Aud.: After the consummation when all's said and done. He conquered someone.

Vendler: Okay. So this is a "morning after" poem. He says, "What did I do?" So then we have to explain how do we get from the repentance mode that he starts in when he feels worst about it, to some of the things that he says later.

Aud.: I just—noting that all of the verbs are in the past participle, I think he uses the word "dream" to mean quick, transient things that come and go, you know. Indicative of his feeling that lust is very quick, fleeting pleasure.

Vendler: The aftermath is named as "woe" even in the good moment "bliss . . . woe." The second time, though, it isn't named as bad. It's named as a "dream," which is different from woe and you might want to think more what that means as a rethinking. First, you said it was bliss and then it was woe after. He said many things with the "after" words. The after word was "shame," it was the "expense of spirit" and a "waste of shame" and he said other things with the "after" words. Yes?

Aud.: I was just going to hit on that line, "Before, a joy proposed, behind a dream"—that in the past maybe he was hoping for something better and greater, perhaps love, and perhaps it's a misguided person who thinks sex is love. And if you go back to 116, it's love versus lust or strong versus weak and can you visit temptation like lovers tempted by tempests and stuff. If they're strong and resist it they get the rewards, and the weak person just gets the disappointment—disappointment in his own lack of resistance. It's just the thing "behind" it—dream, the hope that they will find love through this act.

Vendler: You're looking "behind this" in a sort of Freudian sense— you can see a motive behind it. But in this poem there'd be another way of defining "behind" a bliss, and I think that's what you meant.

Aud.: Yes.

Vendler: When does something seem like a dream to you? I mean, when would you say something is a dream?

Aud.: When it's gone.

Vendler: Well, anything can be gone when it's over with, though. I mean, you could have gone shopping and it would be gone and over with. When do you judge an experience to be a dream?

Aud.: When it was unreal to you. Maybe you employ your reason to review it in hindsight and your reason makes it unreal.

Vendler: Yes. There's something about unreality. In hindsight this whole experience that you actually went through all seems as if it was unreal in whatever way you want to think about a dream. It's different from judging it to be woe afterwards when you judge it to have never happened—"I was deluding myself"—the way you say about a dream, "I really thought I was in this situation but now I know it wasn't real."

Aud.: Well, generally, the whole body is involved. It talks about it and relates how it feels and what it is and in the end it says "The world well knows." Everybody has experienced this but then "none knows well / To shun this heaven that leads men to do this hell." Yet nobody can avoid this. It's something that is universal, yet no one "knows well enough to shun the heaven." I see that as women—the heaven—that lead men to "this hell." No man can shun women and avoid this.

Vendler: Okay. Do you think there is a final value judgment on the heaven and the hell?

Aud.: I think it's very ambiguous. I think Shakespeare's very ambiguous here. Because in the second to last line he says "none knows well." It seems that he says "none," and this seems to invalidate what he said before. If the world knows this, and yet nobody knows this, it raises questions of what is "knowing," and maybe you "know" but you can't avoid it. And it's very difficult.

Vendler: The question of whether knowledge is virtue is an old one. Any comments out here?

Aud.: It's denial in a dream. Dreams don't happen and therefore I could never have been taken by that much lust because I'm not like that, so I don't think the heaven is the "woman" herself, but the consummation or the urge or the sex that's already happened there.

Vendler: Okay, more? These are all important things. All of the effort that's put into trying to figure out what the poem intends to say,—is it a remark about orgasm, is it a remark about women, is it a remark about knowledge versus virtue?—one would like some conclusive way of settling these things, and sometimes by further describing of the poem you get a way to judge *x* against *y*. Maybe we should go back for a minute to our grammar expert.

Aud.: Well, I have one more thing to say. I suppose people do beat the last two lines to death, but the last line, the dichotomy that heaven is salvation and hell is damnation, and oftentimes virtue and vice and heaven are spirits and nontemporal, and hell is this indulgence of the flesh, and yet heaven can be the hell, so there's this connection for good or bad. Add whatever value judgment you'd like to it, but it becomes very problematic. I think Shakespeare's suggesting that there's this problem. You try to separate heaven and hell, but in our daily life they're so close together, because we partake of the sensual and the spiritual at the same time. It's difficult to separate them so easily, like in the Scriptures where things are made so crystal clear and separate. You know, in the reality and practicality of daily life it's hard to separate the two.

Vendler: Yes. And would you, for instance, call it a heaven that leads to hell? Of course not. So this is clearly not said in the tones of a preacher, though some people have thought this was something a cleric could get up in the pulpit and say. Yes?

Aud.: I think, going back to what you said earlier, I don't think there is anything ambiguous about the last two lines. I think he's just pointing out the discrepancy between reason and passion and the tendency of the appetite to override the reason.

Vendler: All right. That's very good. Can you say something about the way it's phrased? You say "All this the world well knows" stands in for "reason," and that "none knows well" is the phrase you would put a bracket over and call it "appetite." Anything about the way he says this? Anything about the pattern on the page? Who's the shape expert? You're the shape expert. How could you rephrase the first one, "well knows," so it would match the second?

Aud.: "All know this well"? I don't know.

Vendler: Well, it could exactly match it: "all this the world knows well, yet none knows well." Okay? How come we have it flipped over?

Aud.: Isn't it called a chiasmus?

Vendler: Yes, it's called a chiasmus. It's a figure of speech.

Aud.: It's for emphasis.

Vendler: Well, certainly all figures of speech are for emphasis in one way or another. That's why they are there. Matching is also a figure of speech, though. And matching—meaning the two things are identical—is also for emphasis. Flip-over-chiasmus-crossing—means the two things are unlike. Yes?

Aud.: I think the first part is more passive—it's the knowledge that you have—and the second part is the active part, but you don't know how to translate the first part into action.

Vendler: So the "knows" means something different in each phrase. The first one is you "know" it—everyone sort of has it as an internalized cultural norm, but nobody "knows how to"—it's the difference between *savoir* and *savoir faire*. It's the distinction between knowing and knowing how, and they really are two different verbs: "to know," and "to know how." So this pun or play on the chiasmus is one of the little shape-items of the poem—"well knows" and "knows well"—a little flip over at the end which calls attention to a kind of fulcrum in "knows." What does that "knows" really mean? Any more shape items? We had a shape item when we said the poem began with nouns and went on to adjectives. And then after the adjectives—"savage," "extreme"—it went to the past participles "enjoyed," "despised," "hated"—what does it go onto after that? After those past participles? What about "mad" and "extreme"—what are they? "Mad, mad in pursuit, in possession so." "Had, having and in quest to have extreme." Adjectives again. So, we have another set of adjectives, and then we have "A bliss in proof, and proved, a very woe, / Before a joy proposed, behind a dream." These are?

Aud.: Nouns.

Vendler: Nouns. And they go back to? Where did we have nouns before?

Aud.: At the beginning.

Vendler: At the beginning. So the first set of nouns which you have are "expense," "spirit," "waste," "shame." And then you found another set of matching nouns down below: "bliss," "joy," "woe," "dream." And you can see that they set up what we call cognitive dissonance. I mean, in describing it in way "A," you are letting in one way; in describing it in way "B," you are letting in some other way. Can anyone distinguish among the nouns? I mean, what kind of things do "bliss, woe, joy, dream" refer to versus "expense, spirit, waste, shame"?

Aud.: "Bliss, woe, joy, dream" naturally refer to orgasm while "expense, spirit, waste, shame" probably refer to after the act.

Vendler: Well, the lust is experienced "in action"—"the expense of spirit" in "a waste of shame"—so the rest would be orgasm, too. Lust in action. Question: if you have two descriptions of orgasm, which part of you is one coming from and which part of you is the other one coming from?

Aud.: One seems to be logic and moral virtue while the other is sexual, biological.

Vendler: And which one is which?

Aud.: The "dream, bliss" . . . all the positive ones would be the physical sensations, and the negative ones would be the mind's feeling guilty.

Vendler: Okay, so you have one kind of "aftermath description" and a different kind of "the middle of it" description. In the middle of it, while you're living it, versus "how I think about it now that it is over." So that, the shape is a summing up of the two views of the experience. One is the view you're expressing at the end—"Oh bliss!" "Oh joy!" "Oh woe!" "Oh dream!"; and the other is "expense, spirit, waste, shame." What is the word "shame" played off against, that it rhymes with?

Aud.: "Blame."

Vendler: Okay. What is the difference between "shame" and "blame"?

Aud.: One is interior, and the other is exterior.

Vendler: Yes. One is interior, and the other is exterior.

Aud.: And one follows upon the other in a sense. I guess, you feel a sense of shame if you are responsible.

Vendler: Okay, and where does blame come from?

Aud.: From somebody else.

Vendler: From somebody else. Okay, who are the people blaming you, would you say, if you looked at the lines in which that occurred?

Aud.: I don't see a specific person being blamed. You blame yourself.

Vendler: Blame really isn't shame. Some blame has to be called self-blame because "blame" means something coming from other people. What did you do that was bad? Do you see any sense in this first quatrain that you did bad things to other people?

Aud.: Yes. There's "murder" and "perjure" and "blood" and . . .

Vendler: All the violent stuff. When you perjure yourself what do you do?

Aud.: You lie.

Vendler: Yes. Under oath, theoretically, to somebody else. You say, "I swear on my mother's grave, or something, that I'm not interested in her. I know she's your girlfriend and I'm not interested in her"—and then you've perjured yourself. What about "murderous?"

Aud.: You kill somebody else and you've sinned and the sin is going on throughout the sonnet.

Vendler: And when do you commit these sins? Which phase?

Aud.: Do you mean in action?

Vendler: Well, yes. You have a definition of lust in action, right. And the next definition is?

Aud.: Till action.

Vendler: And what does "till action" mean?

Aud.: Before it happens.

Vendler: Okay, before it happens. And what did you do before it happened, on your way to it?

Aud.: He perjured himself.

Vendler: Okay.

Aud.: Before the act you've had the will to commit the act. You can't be murderous or deceitful unless you've had murderous feelings and I think it's in you. You internalize it within you and externalize it to other people. That's not being studied in the poem, so to say, but . . .

Vendler: Most of these adjectives (and we saw that whole store of adjectives) can mean doing something bad to someone else, and they do— "perjured, murderous, bloody, savage, extreme, not to trust," etc. Is there one that doesn't fit? This is the college board test. Is there one that doesn't have an object to which it is done?

Aud.: Rudeness.

Vendler: Well, rudeness has an object, too. Is there something else?

Aud.: "Extreme"?

Vendler: "Extreme." Sure. "Extreme" is the only form that doesn't say, "I did something blameworthy to someone else." I mean, "not to trust" means you did something awful to someone else so they don't trust you. "Cruel" means you had to have a victim. "Perjured" means you had to perjure yourself to somebody. And so there are all these adjectives that are social—doing something bad to others that causes them to blame you for something, which is entirely different from your sense that you have betrayed

your more noble part in "expending your spirit in a waste of shame."
"Extreme" is odd. Is there something else odd about "extreme"?

Aud.: It isn't negative. It's just sort of a quantifier.

Vendler: Okay, it's an absolute arithmetical theory: there's the mean
and then there's the extreme. So it should stand out for you in a thing like
this because when you're doing a semantic scanning and you're just saying
the words over to yourself, you say "that's strange—'extreme'"—you should
have had another word like "mean," or "cruel" or "oppressive," in which
case you had a victim to oppress. Does "extreme" do something else in the
poem?

Aud.: Even in Shakespeare's time, they had a sense of perfect geometry and symmetry and things that fit, and Shakespeare surely had those in
mind. I think "extreme," actually, in the context of his time, could be a
negative.

Vendler: Yes, exactly. It can be a negative in the sense of the golden
mean. But it's not an adjective of social trespass. It's not negative like the
others that presuppose a victim. It's a victimless—as you say "victimless
crimes"—it's a victimless adjective and so it's not like all the others that
presuppose a victim. The scheme of the poem was nouns, then a set of
adjectives, then a set of past participles, then nouns again. What ends the
poem? Is it more adjectives of social trespass? Is it more "enjoyed" and
"despised"? In grammatical terms, I mean, as we're doing grammar.

Aud.: A lot of verbs: "knows," "knows," "shuns," "dreams."

Vendler: Yes, that's fine. A whole lot of active verbs. What else do we
have at the end?

Aud.: Heaven and hell.

Vendler: We've got nouns. Heaven and hell. We have a new combination, at the end, of some things we've seen earlier. This makes us want to
put together what this says about doing these acts, and the active verbs, and
the nouns of heaven and hell. Heaven and hell are different from "bliss, joy,
woe, dream." They have those cultural overtones that have been mentioned. Let me open it to something else. We've left out an important line
which is the climax of the octave, line 8. The sonnet is an octave with a
sestet, if you want to think of it that way. Or an octave, a quatrain, and a
couplet. And we've left out this odd thing at the last part of line 7 and line
8. What do you say about "a swallowed bait / On purpose laid to make the
taker mad"? Yes?

Aud.: It seems to be a woman as seductress.

Vendler: What makes you say that? And what would you connect it to?

Aud.: Well, there's kind of a dark lady and he "swallowed the bait" and in the last line we have woman being more than she appears to be—sort of this ambiguous image.

Vendler: Who was the first person who swallowed the bait that Eve offered? What image is there now? "Bait."

Aud.: Fishing.

Vendler: Fishing, yes. But actually, in the image "on purpose laid to make the taker mad," a fish isn't made mad by swallowing a piece of bait. But who could be made mad by swallowing a piece of bait? What could you leave to make the swallower mad? People don't do this any more. Can you think of anybody eating something and then going mad afterwards?

Aud.: Are you looking for something herbal?

Vendler: No, not necessarily an herb. But a poisoned something that would drive you literally crazy if you ate it—like a poisoned meat that you might put out for a dog, or that you might want to put out to drive some animal away. There's a sense of bait and swallowing that makes man into a beast. Someone laid out the poison bait on purpose—it's a terrific indictment of the woman. What do you make of that indictment? What did Adam say?

Aud.: Well, I don't recall his exact words. All I recall is that the sequence of events led him to do it anyway, and he and Eve are reconciled.

Vendler: But how does he excuse himself concerning his sin? Do you recall?

Aud.: He knows what he's going to do is wrong and so definitely a sin, but he doesn't want to be lonely and he is almost in the external process of woman pulling man.

Vendler: Does Adam say, "It was my fault and I did it"? No, he says, "She made me do it." And when you say that about anybody else, the woman tends to be an excuse. This is not so much a remark about the woman as a remark about your own wish to get off the hook. I mean, you're looking around for someone to blame and you blame her when you really should be blaming yourself. It's the classic response of projection, denial, or whatever you want to call it. Getting it off yourself and onto somebody else. This results in the discredit of the speaker as soon as he refuses to take responsibility for his own action. "It's all her fault." "She did it on purpose." "She laid the bait." "Well, did she make you swallow it?" "Well, no, but if she hadn't done it, then I wouldn't have swallowed it." So that's another defense reaction, and of course people have many defense reactions when they've done something they disapprove of. Yes?

Aud.: Just another observation. The whole tone of it is that the lustful person is the villain and this sort of switched it around. Earlier we said the recipient of the lustful act was the victim and this puts a twist on the whole thing in that the person who is lusting is the victim and the person who is reacting to the lust is the instigator of the whole thing.

Vendler: Absolutely, it does switch it around. And if you track the responses of this speaker saying these things about himself—waking up to the morning after —gradually the blame begins migrating, as it often does in morning-after poems, so that the migrating blame has now landed on her. And then, does the blame have an end? And then whom does he blame?

Aud.: Everybody.

Vendler: Yes. He blames everybody. Everybody does it and nobody knows it. So this kind of migration of blame is an interesting thing. A lot of Shakespeare's sonnets don't have "a" point of view. In fact, almost none of them has "a" point of view. They have one point of view, and then another point of view, and then another point of view . . . and these tracings of how the human mind works are a remark about lust. Yes?

Aud.: Do the last two lines refer to just men, or would they include women and men responding to other men and women?

Vendler: This is a parody of a homiletic stance, though no cleric would actually say this—"the *heaven* that leads men to this hell." But the poem begins like a homily. You can imagine a cleric standing up and saying the "expense of spirit" and "the waste of shame," "lust in action." And then you start saying odd things like "a bliss in proof" and then you know it's someone else saying these things. It becomes a deceptive poem because it's not in the first person like most of Shakespeare's sonnets. It doesn't say, "I'm waking up on the morning after and I feel horrible." You have to deduce, as it goes on, that it's not a clerical statement but rather a tracking of a set of responses. In George Herbert's poem "Man," he says man does this, man does that, man is terrible, man is disgraceful, and then he says, "My God, I mean myself!" He realizes how foolish a cleric looks saying how bad man is and never saying "I'm one of you too," whereas this poem really says, "We're all in this soup together." Which is different from maintaining a clerical distance. This poem occurs in the Dark Lady sonnets, where she is represented as sexually avaricious—she is the "bay where all men ride." It's not as if she is an innocent virgin and the man is wreaking his lust upon her. This is a case where people are bound to each other by horrible chains of lust. "Therefore . . . / in our faults by lies we flattered be." In this case I do think it means everybody, whereas in another case it might just mean men. You have to examine those cultural questions.

Vendler: We've seen the word "extreme" once. Do we see it again?

Aud.: Line 10.

Vendler: Okay, it turns up as the climax of line 10. And of course when a word turns up again we always have to ask ourselves, "Why?" Because when Shakespeare makes a word turn up again it is golden on the page. In a little short poem when a word turns up again it means, "I want you to notice this word." Shakespeare knew more words than anybody else—he could think of a synonym for "extreme" if he wanted to. But let's notice the fact that it was the only victimless word in the list of adjectives, semantically speaking, if you're doing a semantic scanning; and you've come to it again. And what's interesting about the line in which it comes up—if you were describing that line? Grammatically?

Aud.: The tenses all in one . . .

Vendler: Past, present, and future: "had, having, and in quest to have . . ." Have we defined what's the use of past, present, and future tense before?

Aud.: It seems, in my opinion, to communicate the progress of "expense of spirit" and a "waste of shame." Not long into it and the word "before." And then the line "Enjoyed no sooner, but despised straight."

Vendler: And "in action"—there's a lot of "in action"—and then "after action." And then do you have some more before, during, and after?

Aud.: Then the reference "past reason hunted" and "past reason . . ."

Vendler: "Hated"—what's in the middle? You hunted, and then you have it, had, and then hated. So that sets up another "before, during, and after" pattern: hunted, had, hated. So we've had various patterns of lust: before action, in action, after action, so you're fitting it out along a tense-spread—before, during, and after. And finally it's all summed up in "had"— you had that before—in line 6. "No sooner *had*," "past reason *hated*." And so you've had "had"; and "having" while you're having it; and "in quest to have"—that's lust till action. And then you have the word that sums up all three. It was "extreme" *having* it, it was "extreme" *before* you had it, and it was "extreme" *after* you had it. Had there been one word suiting before and after earlier? I mean, the before and after phrases—"enjoyed no sooner, but despised straight" (you can see he's been inclined to distinguish between the before and after)—"enjoyed" at one time and "despised" after. But then you get to "had, having, and in quest to have, extreme," and you see you get one word that suits all three phases. So it makes moral sense of all the flashbacks that have gone before. You've taken such pains to say "the expense of spirit" and "the waste of shame" is lust in action; his action was all "enjoyed" and "despised," "hunted," and then "hated"; you're making all these contrasts until finally you say, "You know what? There is one word that fits all of these things, 'had, having, and in quest to have,' and this word refers to the speaker." You stop referring to social trespass, the blame, the shame, and you finally say, "Blame, shame, or anything else, what I can say about the *whole* thing is that when I was *wanting* it I was extreme, when I was *doing* it I was extreme, and in hating myself *afterwards,* I was extreme." The hating is just as extreme as the hunting; the having is just as extreme as the hating; the hunting is just as extreme as the having. I mean, it makes you crazy, all the time, before, during and after, as we see, because "mad" is the other word that sums up the three phases: "On purpose laid to make the taker *mad"* afterwards—after he's taken it; *"mad* in pursuit" when he's hunting it; and "in possession *so"*—mad when he's having it. We had already found one adjective that covers all three phases. "I was crazy when I was wanting it, I was crazy when I was doing it, and I was crazy after I had taken the bait." And then why do you have to do it all over again and call it "extreme"? After you've already found a nice adjective, "mad," that will suit all three? What poems often do is substitute more correct descriptions for less correct descriptions; you've found an adjective, "mad," that will suit all three stages—before, during, and after. But then you immediately sum it up differently in a single line: "Had, having, and in quest to have, extreme." You find the real adjective you've been looking for all along. It suits everything, clearly. Why is "extreme" preferable to "mad"? (We assume what comes later is preferable to what came before.) That's a kind of rule of thumb in poems—the rule of thumb of inertia. Poems tend to go along in the same vein until something makes them go in another direction.

Aud.: "Extreme" is more objective. It's not saying it's "terribly extreme" or "wonderfully extreme"—it's just "extreme."

Vendler: It's a judgment. The question is whether it's a value judgment. Are you saying "mad" is a value judgment?

Aud.: "Mad" has bad connotations, while "extreme" could be used either way. He could be "extremely" violent or "extremely" generous.

Vendler: That's the adverbial form: extremely. But the adjective form—"extreme"—does at least have a connotation of going beyond at least sensible behavior.

Aud.: I think it has to do with proportion. You do things to conform to a certain way—having to do with the sensibility of the time, and this brings in proportion, and geometry, and shape. I think it involves—as the first part talks about love—love in the proper proportion. I don't think the love Shakespeare talks about is courtly love, really, but I think that there are rules about loving in all different forms, so that you don't go off the beaten path like the narrator.

Vendler: Is "mad" a defense? Are you responsible if you're crazy?

Aud.: No.

Vendler: Of course not. You're crazy if you swallowed the bait. That's all part of the defense: "She laid this bait and I swallowed it and it made me crazy, so I'm not responsible for what I did." So "mad" is a taking-your-self-off-the-hook adjective, but when you say "extreme," it's a different sort of summing up. If you say "I was crazy," then you're saying you weren't responsible, but if you say "I was extreme," then it's a judgment of the norm imposed by the word "extreme." It suggests that you know you went beyond the bounds. Yes?

Aud.: On a scale, it seems to be getting more and more neutral.

Vendler: Yes. It's getting more neutral in the sense that "extremity" only says, "I went beyond convention." In that sense you're right that it's not such a value judgment as if somebody said "sinful" or somebody said "criminal." "Extreme" does simply imply a norm, but it isn't a social norm so much as an "aesthetic" norm. There's a wonderful poem by Zbigniew Herbert, a contemporary Polish poet, that says finally that what he was objecting to in communism wasn't really something ethical or social; it was all just in such dreadful taste. All that socialist, realist art—who could stand it? His fundamental objection was an aesthetic one. And finally when you see yourself transgressing limits, you think of it as inhuman in some way, or unbecoming. It's almost an aesthetic judgment, "extreme" is. In that way it's more neutral than "sinful" or "criminal." It would apply to either the internal or heavenly code. From that point, you can say that you can remember the way lust was when you were really in it: "It was a joy, it was bliss." In settling on the word "extreme," you're not really judging yourself by social or religious codes so much as by some internal norm; and then you can go back to remember how it really was when you were living it.

Aud.: The word "extreme" combines the two words. "Mad" is a state of extreme thought—a state of mind that's extreme. When you're "mad" you're focused on the internal, whereas with "extreme" you're more focused on numbers or categories or levels of emotion. So one is a subcategory of the other, and, if you're talking about a kind of history that exists in the past, present, and future and violates social norms and conventions and sensibility, then you need a word like "extreme"—an emotion word that describes you psychologically.

Vendler: That's true. "Extreme" is a philosophical analysis of the situation rather than a social analysis ("What I did to all those people") or a moral, legal one ("I perjured myself to them, in order to get where I wanted to go") or a psychological judgment ("I was crazy when I did this"). You get to the most philosophical, comprehensive word, the word "extreme," which judges the situation in a most analytical and removed way.

Aud.: The power of "extreme" is that it's a superlative and a powerful superlative. It's quite supreme—the highest you can get—because it's the furthest out you can get. In other words, you've gone beyond all bounds. He puts it at the climax because it is obviously a climactic word. This is totally out of bounds.

Vendler: Yes. That's why it's the one aesthetically productive word that he can retrieve from the first list. It appears careless in the first list, just one of those many adjectives describing the experience; but then it's the one that is the truest. That's why it's the last description before you go into the chronology. And it is the climactic word. You think "mad" is the climactic word because it comes at the end of the octave and it looks as though everything has been leading up to "On purpose laid to make the taker mad." But Shakespeare is often playing interestingly with the form of the Italian sonnet and he says here, "You thought I had made my climax here at line 8, the way you would have expected from an Italian sonnet, but I am making it at line 10. You thought the high point was at 'mad,' but the real point is 'extreme.'"

That is the knot. That one line—"Had, having, and in quest to have extreme"—is the knot that ties together all previous past, present, and future actions by which you have been describing lust, and it shows all your previous contrasts. It's an interesting description; it's a philosophical description—"extreme." You could have those three other possibilities: "criminal" according to the civic code, "sinful" according to the religious code, and "mad" according to the psychological code. Instead you have "extreme," which really goes back to the ethics of Aristotle, in which the mean of temperance is judged by the two extremes of excess and defect. So that you always have the synonyms of excess and defect. The absence of virtue is either a defect, a lack of something, or the absence of virtue is due to an excess of something; the extremes of excess and defect are two forms of the same thing. So you go in the middle of the poem to a classical definition of ethical sobriety, which of course is then wiped out by the recollection of all this bliss and woe. This time you see that the account of lust is going in chronological order—first it was a "bliss," then it was a "woe" (before, "a joy proposed," behind, "a dream"), whereas "had, having, and in quest to have" runs backwards in time. Then you're back to linear time: first it was a "bliss," then it was a "woe." So the way you think about what something was like is determined by whether you are thinking of it back to front, or from front to back. Front to back it was just lovely. You proposed a joy, you had a bliss. Then you felt sorry, that's front to back too. Back to front, on the other hand, goes "had, having, and in quest to have, extreme," and it shows that you can think of your experience chronologically in the sequence in which it was happening—first it was a joy, then it was a bliss—or you can think about it retrospectively: "had, having, and in quest to have." There is in the poem a tracking of all the ways we have of thinking about an experience, whether along a temporal axis or all together: chronologically, the way it was when it was happening ("joy, bliss, woe") or retrospectively ("had, having, and in quest to have"). The poem tracks many of our ways of memory, and you can see all of these states being tracked as it goes along. Then finally, with the couplet, you have the summation of what had gone before. You have the chronology— how it was when it was happening ("it was a joy, a bliss, a woe") and then you have the aftermath ("I was murderous, shameful, blameful"), all the rest of it. And finally comes the circle at the end of it. "All this the world well knows yet none knows well / To shun the heaven that leads men to this hell." Like a broken record. And finally you see that the thing will keep going around. First, you will live life chronologically: you will propose a relationship to your girlfriend—joy! Then you will have a bliss—love! And then you'll have a woe. So that the heaven that leads to the hell is really present in the couplet that summarizes both ways of seeing it. "The heaven" when you look at it chronologically becomes "this *hell*." When you look back on it—the "this" in "this hell" tells you that which you started with; "The expense of spirit in a waste of shame" is what you feel now. So it's a perfectly circular thing, the couplet that says, "You can think of it this way; you can do it this way, you can think of it afterwards this way. But you're going to keep on doing it no matter what!" So you have three separate parts: the morning after part, the remembering "bliss, joy, woe" part, and then the "it's going to start all over again" part. These are three modes of thinking about your life—the retrospective mode, the chronological mode, the ironizing circular mode in the couplet. Shakespeare shows us three ways of thinking about the "same" experience. He says we're always going to have these three ways and they're never going to match up. What you think afterwards is never going to be what you think as you go along. There's always going to be this trap-like circle, and you're never going to have a perfect match between life as it's lived chronologically and life as it's lived retrospectively. So you're trapped.

Sonnets for "Poems Posing Questions" and "Reading for Difference"

(With permissions from Houghton-Mifflin for lines quoted from *Romeo and Juliet* in *The Riverside Shakespeare*, ed. G. Blakemore Evans, 1974, and from Yale University Press for selections from *Shakespeare's Sonnets,* ed. Stephen Booth, 1977.)

33

Full many a glorious morning have I seen
Flatter the mountain tops with sovereign eye,
Kissing with golden face the meadows green,
Gilding pale streams with heav'nly alchemy,   4
Anon permit the basest clouds to ride
With ugly rack on his celestial face,
And from the forlorn world his visage hide,
Stealing unseen to west with this disgrace.   8
E'en so my sun one early morn did shine
With all triumphant splendor on my brow;
But out alack, he was but one hour mine,
The region cloud hath masked him from me now.   12
    Yet him for this my love no whit disdaineth;
    Suns of the world may stain when heav'n's sun staineth.

60

Like as the waves make towards the pebbled shore,
So do our minutes hasten to their end,
Each changing place with that which goes before,
In sequent toil all forwards do contend.   4
Nativity, once in the main of light,
Crawls to maturity, wherewith being crowned,
Crookèd eclipses 'gainst his glory fight,
And time that gave doth now his gift confound.   8
Time doth transfix the flourish set on youth,
And delves the parallels in beauty's brow,

Feeds on the rarities of nature's truth,
And nothing stands but for his scythe to mow.   12
    And yet to times in hope my verse shall stand,
    Praising thy worth, despite his cruel hand.

Rom. [*to Juliet.*] If I profane with my unworthiest hand
This holy shrine, the gentle sin is this,
My lips two blushing pilgrims, ready stand   95
To smooth that rough touch with a tender kiss.
    Jul. Good pilgrim, you do wrong your hand too much,
Which mannerly devotion shows in this:
For saints have hands that pilgrims' hands do touch,
And palm to palm is holy palmers' kiss.   100
    Rom. Have not saints lips, and holy palmers too?
    Jul. Ay, pilgrim, lips that they must use in pray'r.
    Rom. O then, dear saint, let lips do what hands do,
They pray—grant thou, lest faith turn to despair.
    Jul. Saints do not move, though grant for prayers'
       sake.   105
    Rom. Then move not while my prayer's effect I take.

                         (*Romeo and Juliet*, 1.5.93–106)

94

They that have pow'r to hurt, and will do none,
That do not do the thing they most do show,
Who moving others are themselves as stone,
Unmovèd, cold, and to temptation slow—   4
They rightly do inherit heaven's graces,
And husband nature's riches from expense;
They are the lords and owners of their faces,
Others but stewards of their excellence.   8
The summer's flow'r is to the summer sweet,
Though to itself it only live and die,
But if that flow'r with base infection meet,
The basest weed outbraves his dignity.   12
    For sweetest things turn sourest by their deeds;
    Lilies that fester smell far worse than weeds.

.

105

Let not my love be called idolatry,
Nor my belovèd as an idol show,
Since all alike my songs and praises be

To one, of one, still such, and ever so.   4
Kind is my love today, tomorrow kind,
Still constant in a wondrous excellence;
Therefore my verse, to constancy confined,
One thing expressing, leaves out difference.   8
Fair, kind, and true, is all my argument,
Fair, kind, and true, varying to other words;
And in this change is my invention spent—
Three themes in one, which wondrous scope affords.   12
   Fair, kind, and true, have often lived alone,
   Which three, till now, never kept seat in one.

116

Let me not to the marriage of true minds
Admit impediments. Love is not love
Which alters when it alteration finds,
Or bends with the remover to remove.   4
O no, it is an ever-fixèd mark
That looks on tempests and is never shaken;
It is the star to every wand'ring bark,
Whose worth's unknown, although his heighth be taken. 8
Love's not Time's fool, though rosy lips and cheeks
Within his bending sickle's compass come.
Love alters not with his brief hours and weeks,
But bears it out e'en to the edge of doom.   12
   If this be error and upon me proved,
   I never writ, nor no man ever loved.

129

Th' expense of spirit in a waste of shame
Is lust in action, and till action lust
Is perjured, murd'rous, bloody, full of blame,
Savage, extreme, rude, cruel, not to trust,   4
Enjoyed no sooner but despisèd straight,
Past reason hunted, and no sooner had,
Past reason hated as a swallowed bait,
On purpose laid to make the taker mad: 8
Mad in pursuit, and in possession so,
Had, having, and in quest to have, extreme,
A bliss in proof, and proved, a very woe,
Before, a joy proposed, behind, a dream.   12
   All this the world well knows, yet none knows well
   To shun the heav'n that leads men to this hell.

Cutting the Bard
Down to Size

R. A. FOAKES

When in London in 1989 there were found the remains of the Rose Theatre (built 1587)—the theater where Shakespeare's earliest plays, *Henry VI* and *Titus Andronicus,* for example, were probably staged—a special excitement was generated by the discovery of masses of crushed hazelnut shells in the arena where the "groundlings" stood. Sober archaeologists thought the shells might have been used deliberately to create firm standing for spectators, but the press seized on the image of nut-cracking Elizabethans as representative of the common people, much as they might one day in centuries to come the popcorn-eating audiences at today's cinemas; the shells confirmed an image of Shakespeare dear to traditional conceptions of him as one of us, the Stratford boy who got Anne Hathaway pregnant, went off to London to make his fortune, and wrote for the people—a popular dramatist, accessible to everyone. So long as the theater remained a major popular form of entertainment—as it was at first in the sixteenth and seventeenth centuries, along with executions and bearbaiting, and later in association with shows of all kinds, burlesques, circuses, and acrobatics (that is to say, well into the nineteenth century), Shakespeare continued to be a dramatist for the people. Widespread illiteracy was the norm (compulsory education for children was not introduced in Britain until 1870), and books and newspapers were expensive luxuries for the most part, but there were theaters everywhere, both grand and rudimentary. In America in the early nineteenth century Shakespeare was integrated into popular culture, and his plays were "presented as part of the same milieu inhabited by magicians, dancers, singers, acrobats, minstrels, and comics. He appeared on the same playbills, and was advertised in the same spirit."[1] His most popular play in performance seems to have been *Richard III,* which perhaps was seen as reinforcing a populist American ideology and buttressing American values. As late as 1906, Martha Baker Dunn, a minor novelist, looking back over a long association with Shakespeare's plays, could say:[2]

> Shakespeare's message is the message of a robust manhood and woman-hood: Brace up, pay for what you have, do good if you wish to get good; good or bad, shoulder the burden of your moral responsibility, and never forget that cowardice is the most fatal and futile crime in the calendar of crimes.

No one could accuse Richard III of cowardice, whatever else one might say about him. Thousands of theaters, large and small, operating in Britain and across America performed Shakespeare's plays, or at any rate the best-known ones, in the context of farces, entertainments and afterpieces, and as an integral part of the popular culture of the day. We catch glimpses of this in, for example, Dickens's *Great Expectations* (1861), in which the ambitious "provincial amateur," Mr. Wopsle, faces a running commentary from the audience while attempting to make his mark on the stage in London by playing Hamlet. (Three other actors represented the whole of the Danish nobility.) Mr. Wopsle's Hamlet—played, as was normal at the time, with the audience almost as well-lit as the actors—was treated as available for friendly banter by the audience, and on the question whether " 'twas nobler in the mind to suffer, some roared yes, and some no, and some, inclining to both opinions, said 'toss up for it.'"[3] Dickens, was, of course, presenting a satirical picture of such performances, but this close involvement by the audience must have been common. The image of Shakespeare as popular dramatist is neatly caught in some movies, as for example, in John Ford's great western *My Darling Clementine,* in which Henry Fonda as Wyatt Earp is angered by the villains, the Clantons, when they attempt to prevent a drunken touring actor from reciting, very melodramatically, one of Hamlet's soliloquies.

The later nineteenth century brought radical changes in the theater, most notably the split between vaudeville or music hall stages and the so-called "legitimate" theater, that is to say, between popular and highbrow entertainment. On the "legitimate" stages in the fashionable parts of town, plays were performed on their own, with little or no music, to educated audiences. Then movies replaced theater as basic mass entertainment, and Shakespeare was taken over as a part of bourgeois culture: Shakespeare the popular dramatist gave way to Shakespeare as cultural idol. As early as 1882, one critic saw what was coming when he predicted that Shakespeare was "destined to become the Shakespeare of the college and university, and even more the Shakespeare of private and select culture."[4] The development of select theaters for those who could appreciate serious drama coincided roughly with the establishment of the study of English and American literature as a discipline in its own right in schools and colleges. Taken over by educators, Shakespeare was institutionalized as a great teacher and philosopher whose works could only be understood through special training. Shakespeare took a central position in the literary syllabus, as was shown by the new growth industry in providing scholarly editions and interpretations of his works. The New Variorum edition was promoted by Horace Howard Furness, who established a Shakespeare library in Philadelphia. A Shakespeare archive was built up in Stratford-on-Avon, where the Shakespeare Memorial Theater was erected. Later the Folger Shakespeare Library was established in Washington, next to the Library of Congress. Mr. Wopsle's *Hamlet*, with spectators actively taking part, gave way to that of Forbes Robertson, whose classical rendering of the role seemed to Bernard Shaw in 1897 to present a "dramatic hero whose passions are those which have produced the philosophy, the poetry, the art and the statecraft of the world."[5] This was Shakespeare the Great Bard, who merited the "Book of Homage" produced in 1916 on the tercentenary of his death. Already in the advertisement for the New International Shakespeare in 1903, Shakespeare had been presented as the "supreme teacher" who "shows the way—more clearly than any other author—to the higher intellectual and moral life."[6]

In this way Shakespeare was recreated for educational purposes at the beginning of this century, and so acquired an immense cultural authority. There was a political motive too in this shift. He was seen by the first director of the Folger Shakespeare Library in his dedication speech in 1932 as the "cornerstone of cultural discipline" in welding together the millions of immigrants flocking into the United States:

> On every ship they came . . . not only Germans and Scandinavians, but Italians, Poles, Slavs, Hungarians, Czechs, Greeks, Lithuanians, Rumanians, Armenians—from almost every clime under the sun. They swarmed into the land like the locust in Egypt; and everywhere, in an alarming way, they tended to keep to themselves . . . America seemed destined to become a babel of tongues and cultures. Fortunately . . . there was initiated throughout the country a system of free and compulsory education. . . . On the side of the humanities that schooling concerned itself mainly with the English language and literature . . . [and] in our fixed plan of elementary schooling, [Shakespeare] was made the cornerstone of cul-

tural discipline. . . . Not Homer, nor Dante, nor Goethe, not Chaucer, nor Spenser, not even Milton, but Shakespeare was made the chief object of their study and veneration. . . . This study and veneration was carried into the colleges and universities, and there pursued with still more intensity.[7]

We now take for granted this veneration and cultural authority of Shakespeare, as is shown in the use of his name in advertising pens, computers, hotels, liquor, almost anything (figures 1 and 2). Here we see Shakespeare fetishized as the "quintessential playwright," a measure of supreme excellence or value by which to establish the quality of any commodity, to the point where he is treated with extravagant devotion. It has its comic side in that it allows actors to get away with anything: when Ian McKellen was acting Shakespeare in San Francisco in 1987, he was asked if he ever forgot a soliloquy, and replied, "You can usually say some rubbish or other. It's Shakespeare and nobody will ever know."[8] It has its absurd side too, as when the Rose site in London was in danger of being built on, and a group of actors led by Dame Peggy Ashcroft, and, I think, including Ian McKellen, knelt there in protest, apparently praying, as if they were trying to preserve a religious shrine.

The cultural authority accorded Shakespeare has tended to make him at once very familiar, so that everyone has heard of him and takes his stature for granted (as in the use of his name in advertisements), and at the same time very remote, a figure to be treated with reverence. The educational establishment's adoption of Shakespeare as a central author in the syllabuses of schools and colleges led to his being treated as a fount of wisdom. As the great teacher or philosopher, he had a message to give, and so each play seemed to offer the possibility of a "single determinate meaning." Teachers and critics thought of themselves as seeking the truth about the plays, as though by correcting the errors of their predecessors (for Shakespeare was recognized to be very complex, and his meanings not easy to penetrate), eventually, if not in our time, a proper understanding would be reached. Many students and some critics still would like to sum up a play in terms of a message, a simple statement, to pin it down like a dead butterfly, named and summed up once for all. So in 1982 Harold Jenkins produced his edition of *Hamlet* as part of the Arden Shakespeare, one of the most respected series of our time; he belongs to an older school of critics, and the style of his comments is representative of them. He says, for example, "*Hamlet* is not simply a tragedy of revenge in which the crucial deed has to be deferred until the end: it is a play about a man with a deed to do who for most of the time conspicuously fails to do it."[9] The play,

Fig. 1. Parker Pen's Use of the Image of Shakespeare (Courtesy of Parker Pen USA Limited)

Fig. 2. IBM's Use of Shakespeare's Name (Courtesy of International Business Machines Corporation)

he goes on, "imposes on its hero the duty of revenge. . . . The essential subject . . . suggested by and focused in the old story of a son's revenge, is, then, as I see it, the intermingling of good and evil in all life."[10] Notice the tone of certainty; he knows what the play is about, and what its "essential subject" is, though this turns out to be rather platitudinous; the mingling of good and evil in life is the topic of any number of works from the Bible onwards. The point I am making is that such a critic is certain of his bearings; he has, for instance, no doubt about the Ghost's command, as he calls it, to Hamlet to revenge his father's murder, and pours scorn on those who question it: "In our day a race of critics has arisen who maintain that Hamlet should have disapproved of his father's ghost as much as they do themselves."[11] The disparaging tone shows his confidence that he is right and others wrong: if Shakespeare is the great philosopher, then the good critic should be able to tease out what Shakespeare's meaning and purpose were.

Such criticism has the virtues of clarity and confidence, and the best of it is still read, for in many ways it can help students, though too often exerting pressure on them to accept one reading as definitive and to reject all others. In recent years such readings have come under attack, as the authority of Shakespeare, and indeed of all authors, has been questioned. The reasons for this change are complex, and too speculative to consider here, but no doubt have to do with a general crisis of confidence in other forms of authority. In effect, critical theory has shifted our attention from Shakespeare's plays as finished products, with a coherence of meaning and design that can be explicated, to the plays as process—indefinite, unstable, and impossible to pin down or ever finally comprehend. The attack on older assumptions about organic unity and integrity of meaning has come from at least five directions, all of which may be loosely associated with the concept of poststructuralism. One stems from the direct onslaught on structure by the advocates of deconstruction, a critical method best known from the writings of the French philosopher Jacques Derrida, and his impact on a group of faculty at Yale. These argue that texts are not concerned with external reality, but are open to an infinite play of signification, and since there is no end to this play, says Christopher Norris, "Deconstruction can never have the final word because its insights are inevitably couched in a rhetoric which itself lies open to further deconstructive reading."[12] Hence texts are always open to pluralist readings, as put with elegance by Stephen Booth in his book *King Lear, Macbeth, Indefinition and Tragedy* (1983); the very word "indefinition" could not have appeared in a title of a book on Shakespeare before the 1970s.

A second line of attack is that of the critics known as new historicists in this country, and an analogous group in Britain who call themselves cultural materialists. In some ways their approach is a counter to deconstruction, or at least to such propositions as Derrida's well-known dictum that there is nothing outside the text ("Il n'y a pas de hors-texte"),[13] inasmuch as they restore a historical context to their study of Shakespeare. They see the plays as sites of competing discourses within the culture and articulations of power in Shakespeare's age. But like the deconstructionists, who see the author as the subject of his work, which so to speak writes him, rather than as conscious creator, they have fostered the dismantling of the concept of individual authorship, asserting that plays should be seen as "the locus of a distinct, politically dynamic sequence of intersecting discursive practices, replete with competing ideologies."[14] So Shakespeare's plays, it is said, did not originate in a "pure act of untrammeled creation" by an artist, but as a "subtle, elusive set of exchanges, a network of trades and trade-offs, a jostling of competing representations, a negotiation between joint-stock companies."[15] Hence, according to Stephen Greenblatt, whose words these are, they are to be interpreted in terms of the circulation of social energy. The plays can in this way be demoted from their ranking as masterworks, and Shakespeare's cultural authority is undermined, since all texts become equivalent (including presumably those produced by the critics), and interesting only as negotiations between intersecting discourses, or in Greenblatt's revealing phrase, between "joint-stock companies." The project of new historicism and cultural materialism has been described as aiming to "dissolve the modern privileged notion of 'literature' altogether," applying a particular sociopolitical agenda which is designed to "merge literary texts back into the historical milieu from which academic studies such as 'English' have irresponsibly prised them."[16]

There is an important difference between the new historicists and cultural materialists, in that the former are politically neutral; that is to say, they proclaim their deep concern with the concept of power in relation to subversion, and with literature as part of a social process, but do so in relation to Shakespeare not in order to effect political change, but simply as registering a political sensibility. So, if in depriviliging literature and equating it with other forms of discourse new historicism seems daringly modern, in its apparent neutrality it appears resolutely old-fashioned. Cultural materialism, by contrast, has a political agenda, and is committed to changing the political order in Britain. New historicism seems born out of despair, or at least dismay with the status quo,[17] whereas cultural materialism is born out of political commitment and a belief that change must come. The critics associated with these two movements are amongst the most vocal and influential at the moment in relation to Shakespeare.

A third line of attack has come from feminists, who have made good use of psychoanalytic techniques to probe questions about the cross-dressing of boy-actors, the nature of subjectivity, and the play of sexuality and gender in Shakespeare's theater. They have drawn attention, for example, to the thread of misogyny in some of the major plays, and to the constrictions of their patriarchal view of the world. They have contributed to the deconstruction of the idea of Shakespeare as a figure to be reverenced, as the great teacher and philosopher. So too have performance critics, a group who have reacted against the powerful influence of the "new critics" of the 1950s, and to some extent against deconstructionists, who have a kinship with the new critics in focussing on the language of plays as poetry. The performance critics insist that the plays should be considered as scripts for performance. So Stephen Orgel, in search of what he calls the "authentic Shakespeare," argues that "the acting text of a play always was different from the written text," because actors and directors add elements like tone, stage action, and interpretation, so that the play comes into being as a practical collaboration between a playwright and other parties to the performance.[18] Properly, then, a play should be thought of as an anthology of performances, each one different from the others. Thus, "Shakespearean texts are produced by a multitude of determinations that exceed a criticism bent on controlling the text or assigning it determinate meanings or structures. Although all we have to go on are the texts, we must go on knowing that they do not make the Shakespearean text *proper*. No one can own the text. No one can clean it up."[19] Since all we have to go on are the texts, it is not clear how we might recover the "scripts" of Shakespeare, but this kind of argument has been hailed as dismantling the notion of the author and the text. "The author-god of traditional humanism doesn't exist," cries one critic in a book published in 1990.[20]

The fifth and last way in which the authority of Shakespeare and the unity of the texts have come under scrutiny is through a minor revolution in textual criticism. For decades a consensus of eminent bibliographical scholars held that where there existed more than one early text of a play (as in the case of eighteen of Shakespeare's plays), one text, usually the First Quarto, was likely to be closest to Shakespeare's manuscript, to a lost original (no manuscripts survive), and the differences from it in other printed texts of the play could be attributed to corruptions introduced in the theater or in the printing house. This conventional wisdom was challenged by one or two perceptive scholars beginning in 1931, but it is only since about 1978 that wide acceptance has been won for a new perspective. The analysis of the two texts of *King Lear* (Quarto 1608; Folio 1623) begun then and developed in Gary Taylor and Michael Warren's *Division of the Kingdoms* (1983) has shown that these do not represent a good text and a corrupted text, but two different versions of the play, which was revised, probably by Shakespeare himself, since some of the revisions are minute yet significant— e.g., the change in King Lear's lines in 1.4, "Who is it that can tell me who I am? Lear's shadow" (Q); these become in the Folio, "Who is it that can tell me who I am? *Fool.* Lear's shadow." It makes quite a difference if, instead of Lear recognizing that he is merely a shadow of himself, he has no glimmer of self-knowledge and the phrase "Lear's shadow" becomes another savagely ironic comment by the Fool on Lear's inability to see the truth.

In other words, editors and textual critics had been concerned to determine "what Shakespeare wrote," or what he "evidently preferred,"[21] and so in all standard editions of *King Lear* until the 1980s the text presented was a conflation of the Quarto and Folio, in order to include for the reader all those lines regarded as authentic by the editor. In the latest one-volume edition of the plays, the *Oxford Shakespeare* (1987), the two versions of *King Lear* are printed for the first time in sequence. It is now being recognized that many other plays may have been revised, and that the differences between the three texts of *Hamlet*, the two texts of *Othello*, and the variant texts of many other plays, also show the plays going through a process of revision or of adaptation for the stage or for print. So if the plays could be reworked by Shakespeare or someone in a continuing process of adaptation, the idea of the canonical text, first established by Shakespeare's original editors in the First Folio, his fellow actors Heminge and Condell, is seriously undermined. They claimed that "where (before) you were abus'd with diverse stolen, and surreptitious copies, maimed and deformed by the frauds and stealths of injurious impostors, that expos'd them: even those, are now offer'd to your view cur'd, and perfect of their limbs; and all the rest, absolute in their numbers, as he conceived them"—a claim that seemed to guarantee the authority of the Folio texts. Now no one would assert that we have a "perfect" text of any play, and if texts for the theater evolve by a process of interaction with other people and with forces in the theater and printing house, then once again the notion of the unitary work of art, related to an ideal concept of the author and his works as established not for an age but for all time (as Ben Jonson put it), goes by the board.

What all these approaches have in common is a displacement of the idea of the text of a Shakespearean play as embodying a finite structure and meaning. Instead the plays are problematized, and the text, conceived in

terms proposed by Roland Barthes, as a "score" asking the reader to col-
laborate with it,[22] provokes the claim that "only the critic executes the
work," and hence that "all types or forms of literary activity, whether
'primary' (literature) or 'secondary' (criticism), become indistinguishable
and are experienced only as forms of production."[23] The critic or director
becomes superior to the play, which can generate an infinite variety of
meanings through his or her realization of it. For students the result of this
dismantling of textual authority can be bewildering, for it leads to a multiplicity of critical discourses, and gives critics a sanction to parade their
own idiosyncrasies in however marginal relation to a play. But in many
ways these poststructuralist developments have been healthy. They have
made us recognize that all readings relate to the time of the critic as much
as they do to the play itself, that all interpretation is relative, that plays need
to be apprehended as scripts for performance as well as reading texts or
dramatic poems, and that an instructor in teaching Shakespeare is also
scripting a performance that is different each time he or she stages it. The
effect of all this can be seen in those occasional issues of *Shakespeare
Quarterly* devoted to teaching Shakespeare. In 1974 it was still much concerned with language, and battling the idea of the plays as dramatic poetry;
in 1984 it was largely concerned with teaching the plays as performance
texts, or through performance in the classroom; in 1990, it could be best
categorized by sampling the titles of its essays—on teaching differences,
on interrogating the scene of learning, on problematizing the instruction of
Shakespeare, on the politics of teaching *King Lear,* and on teaching para-
doxes.[24] Many of the 1984 and 1990 essays tie in with one or another of the
five poststructuralist moves I have been sketching.

While destabilizing Shakespeare, the practitioners of these new modes
of criticism often seem to be asserting that their approach is the correct one,
although the general effect of poststructuralist criticism is to reject any
determinacy of approach or of meaning. Some, for instance, fall into a
polemical style of criticism that may result in dogma or gobbledegook that
becomes either impenetrable or absurd. Let me give you an example: in *A
Midsummer Night's Dream*, Bottom, who loves to domineer, but in an
innocent and harmless way, since he has no power, wants to play all the
parts in *Pyramus and Thisbe,* the play the comic workmen are to stage for
the Duke's wedding. He is especially keen to play Lion, though Quince, the
director, has given it to Snug:

> *Snug.* Have you the lion's part written? Pray you, if it be, give it me,
> for I am slow of study.

> *Quin.* You may do it extempore, for it is nothing but roaring.
>
> *Bot.* Let me play the lion too. I will roar, that I will do any man's heart good to hear me. I will roar, that I will make the Duke say, "Let him roar again; let him roar again."
>
> *Quin.* And you should do it too terribly, you would fright the Duchess and the ladies, that they would shrike, and that were enough to hang us all.
>
> *All.* That would hang us, every mother's son.
>
> *Bot.* I grant you, friends, if you should fright the ladies out of their wits, they would have no more discretion but to hang us; but I will aggravate my voice so that I will roar you as gently as any sucking dove; I will roar you and 'twere any nightingale.
>
> (*MND* 1.2.66–78)

This delightful episode, in which Bottom instantly changes his heroic roar for the men into a cooing roar for the ladies, is treated by poststructuralist critics as exemplifying a deep anxiety about the instability of human identity:[25]

> This dialogue functions as a kind of internal commentary on Shakespearean ideological practice. The problematic of proto-professional ideological production denied autonomous political weight in a society struggling to preserve the hegemony of an aristocratic class-ideology is here displayed in order to be ridiculed. Shakespeare's artisans pose the issues quite clearly in their discussion: for *us* to assert an effective ability to manipulate their sense of reality . . . would be an unacceptable usurpation of ideological power, possibly punishable by death.

This is problematizing with a vengeance, as a superbly comic joke about the nature of dramatic illusion focussed in Bottom's naïve assumption that he can, like Laurence Olivier, do everything, becomes a solemn critique of "proto-professional ideological production" denied political weight, whatever that means (production of wealth by workers, or production of the play?).

Alternatively, those who argue for treating the play-text as a score or script may go overboard in a different way. So in the new enthusiasm for taking seriously what scholars used to regard as actors' interpolations in the texts of some plays, these may be accorded a special status. In *Hamlet,* for example, the prince dies in the Quarto with the words, "The rest is silence," but the Folio text adds "O, o, o, o," a conventional marker for a groan, or a sigh, as for dying or orgasm. Now it is true that all three editors of major editions of the play since 1982 omit these "O"s, though one, the 1987 Oxford editor, adds a stage direction he has invented: "He gives a long sigh and dies."[26] How does one represent a dying groan in print? For Terence Hawkes, these "O"s exhibit an "involving and implicating musical power beyond ordinary words," which loosens "the signifier-signified ligaments whose network usually seems to determine the boundaries of meanings within which the play operates"; so they subvert order, disrupt sequence," and "impede the ordinary linear flow of meaning," destabilizing the text. This is an extraordinary claim. To assign to the textual representation of a groan a "musical power beyond words" is to make it more important than the poetry Shakespeare gave to Hamlet.[27]

Because they have abolished the controlling parameters of traditional criticism, i.e., the idea of an authoritative text and a determinate meaning and structure, poststructuralist approaches to Shakespeare encourage the critic to take for granted his superiority to the text, which is open to whatever play of signification he or she can invent; the interpretive results are often heady, wild, excessive, eccentric. At the same time, they have guided us towards the important recognition that no commentary on Shakespeare can be final. They have also brought about a radical change by generating methods of interpreting Shakespeare that open up the plays rather than close them down. The significance of this change for the teaching of Shakespeare is in guiding us to the recognition that it is better to lead students and readers to make their own choices and explorations, than to try to coerce them into accepting one determinate point of view. If this seems obvious enough, let me remind you of where I started, with the confidence expressed by Harold Jenkins in 1982 that he knew Shakespeare's intentions in *Hamlet*. A later editor, Philip Edwards (the Cambridge Shakespeare, 1985) is equally confident; he writes, "There is no mistaking the plain sense of the Ghost's words," and says the Ghost gives Hamlet a "directive, a commission that is also a mission."[28] G. R. Hibbard (the Oxford Shakespeare, 1987) also speaks of Hamlet's "duty" to revenge.[29] Such confidence in a single determinate reading of the confrontation between the Ghost and Hamlet is what poststructuralist theory undermines.

Let me talk briefly about how this issue might be addressed in teaching. The focus here is on revenge, and I would want to consider the nature of revenge to start with. Why was it a topic of such interest in Shakespeare's age? Perhaps because it was widely practiced even though, as Eleanor Prosser has shown at length in a book entitled *Hamlet and Revenge*,[30] it was forbidden by law, and widely condemned, on the authority of the New

Testament. (The Old Testament, recording a much older world, advocated an eye for an eye and a tooth for a tooth.) Is revenge a natural human instinct, which in modern societies is controlled by law? We would like to think we have it under control, even as we flock to watch films like the *Godfather* series portraying the vendettas practised by the Mafia. About the time *Hamlet* was written, Francis Bacon began an essay on revenge that said, "Revenge is a kind of wild justice, which the more men hearken unto it, the more ought the law to weed it out."[31] Just so, but what if the law fails, or does not seem adequate protection? Here it might be appropriate to introduce two modern examples. I could have the class watch a movie like, say, *Death Wish* (1973). In it Charles Bronson, an unassuming little New York architect who incongruously (in view of Bronson's usual roles) calls himself a "bleeding-heart liberal," finds his wife and daughter beaten and raped, and his wife subsequently dies. Given a gun by a gun-toting friend from Arizona, he learns to shoot and turns himself into a vigilante; he takes to haunting the side streets and subways of the city with a hidden weapon, blazing away at those who take his apparently meek and humble figure to be an easy target for mugging or robbery. The police begin to get anxious about the trail of corpses he leaves, but in the end they merely invite him to leave town, and off he goes to Chicago, maybe to start all over again. This film was so successful it spawned three follow-ups: *Death Wish 2*, etc. Its effect is strange, for watchers are simultaneously glad to see him get revenge and sickened by what he does. The police, and the law, are pilloried as ineffectual in the film (the lieutenant in charge has a permanent sniffle), so where does justice lie? To focus the problem more sharply, you may remember an incident in the summer of 1989, when, after Israeli soldiers kidnapped an Arab sheik, an American hostage in Lebanon, Lt. Col. William Higgins, was executed. The *Los Angeles Times* reported on 1 August, "President Bush was last night already facing pressure from public opinion and right-wing members of Congress not to take the killing of Colonel Higgins lying down. 'It is time the United States, without regard to what anybody else thinks, goes to the root of the evil in the Middle East. We need revenge, we need justice,' a Republican, Mr. George Gekas, said." We need revenge, we need justice; but are these the same thing? In *Death Wish*, Bronson's revenge becomes more horrible than the initial act of rape that provoked it. There are more immediate analogies with what has been happening in Iraq recently.

Revenge is a frequent theme of classical drama, as mediated through the works of Seneca in Shakespeare's time, and refers back to a heroic age.

In heroic societies, as imagined in Homer's *Iliad* or in the *Oresteia* of Aeschylus, there are no cities or societies with an apparatus of law as in the modern world; Troy was a village. In such a society the key structures are those of household and kinship, and obligations are built up accordingly; the central idea of virtue is linked to what the Greeks called *arete* or excellence in action; "a man in heroic society is what he does," writes Alasdair MacIntyre,[32] not, as in our world, what he is (movie star, lawyer, etc.). In the heroic age life was fragile, men vulnerable; and "in heroic societies life is the standard of value. If someone kills you, my friend or brother, I owe you their death, and when I have paid my debt to you their friend or brother owes them my death. The more extended my system of kinsmen and friends, the more liabilities I shall incur of a kind that may end in my death."[33] In other words, revenge is not distinguished from justice, and is the normal and expected way to deal with, say, a murderer, since there is no other form of justice. A population explosion during Shakespeare's lifetime in London may have triggered a rise in dueling and lawlessness, but there was no effective policing anyway; and our age has similar problems, in that many do not trust the law, or see it as ineffectual because it takes years to bring a serial killer to justice. So our society, like Shakespeare's, is two-faced about revenge. It is popular as a theme in films and on television, and disreputable at the same time. The instinct to retaliate for an injury is natural, but also natural is our social concern in modern societies to keep that instinct in check.

How does all this help with *Hamlet?* Well, we like to think that justice and revenge have little to do with one another in a law-abiding society, and yet they are constantly being confused, as in *Death Wish*, and by Congressman Gekas—and, we might, add, by the Ghost in *Hamlet:*

> *Ghost.* If thou didst ever thy dear father love—
> *Ham.* O God!
> *Ghost.* Revenge his foul and most unnatural murther.
> *Ham.* Murther?
> *Ghost.* Murther most foul, as in the best it is,
> But this most foul, strange, and unnatural.
>
> (1.5.23–28)

The Ghost calls on Hamlet to revenge, which is as much as to say, "Kill Claudius"; and then, in his next words, adds, "Murther most foul, as in the best it is": what difference is there between Claudius killing old Hamlet, and Hamlet now killing Claudius? Can we say, with the editors I cited, that

Hamlet has a "duty" to carry out revenge? If this were a heroic society, we might answer yes. And perhaps this is why Shakespeare gives us little information about old Hamlet, but locates him imaginatively in an ancient world. Unlike Claudius, who deals in diplomacy like a modern ruler, old Hamlet fought wars, or solved disputes by single combat. Hamlet always sees his father in terms of a heroic world, linking him with classical deities like Mars, Hyperion, Hercules, Mercury; and he idealizes that world, in contrast to the one he belongs to, the modern world in which, like many young men now, instead of going to war, he goes to college.

Old Hamlet appears to belong in a heroic world in which courage is the central virtue, and every time the warrior fights he courts the death that lies in wait for him. In that simpler, masculine world, revenge would be required as a virtuous act. But the old Hamlet we hear about, and whom young Hamlet idealizes, is not the same as the figure we see when the Ghost speaks, for he confounds these simplicities by combining a heroic stance which assumes revenge as normal and necessary, with a Christian morality that defines virtue primarily in terms of sexual relations:

> But virtue, as it never will be moved,
> Though lewdness court it in a shape of heaven,
> So lust, though to a radiant angel link'd
> Will sate itself in a celestial bed,
> And prey on garbage.
>
> (1.5.53–57)

The opposite of virtue here is not cowardice, but lust. The Ghost demands revenge, but preaches a morality that expressly forbids it; "Leave her to heaven" for appropriate punishment, he says of Gertrude, but if this is right for her, why not for Claudius? "Vengeance is mine. I will repay, saith the Lord" according to St. Paul. Hamlet reveals his Christian bent in his first soliloquy when he expresses his concern "that the Everlasting had not fixed / His canon 'gainst self-slaughter." Another kind of slaughter, that identified with in revenge, loses the moral imperative it had in heroic societies, and takes on a barbarous and hellish aspect; this is seen in the revenge of Pyrrhus for the death of his father Achilles, as described by the First Player in a speech requested by Hamlet.

The heroic ideal in the play is thus tarnished by the mindless atrocity of Pyrrhus "mincing" old Priam with his sword, chopping him into bits, and also by strong-in-the-arm Fortinbras marching into Poland just to make war for a dubious "honor." And, perhaps suggesting an analogy with our own time, the court of Denmark pays lip service to a Christian morality, but practices intrigue, adultery, spying, and murder when required, so that the Christian ideal does not come off too well, either. So what then of the notion of Hamlet's "'duty"? According to the heroic code, he has a duty to get revenge; according to the Christian code, he is required to forego his revenge. What is he to do? That question might be seen as a leading issue in the play, which problematizes it in a way that allows no easy solution, as Hamlet's soliloquies testify. You can sidestep the problem by making a film with Mel Gibson playing Hamlet in an energetic style, having him see all that is hidden from him in the play, and cutting out most of the soliloquies; but I would want to highlight it in teaching the play, have students think about it, and make up their own minds.

If the instructor problematizes a play, or shows how Shakespeare has problematized an issue, what then does the student take away? She will, I hope, come to appreciate that Shakespeare does not provide us with determinate meanings, that the plays do not offer us simple messages or morals. Rather they explore the complexities of many-sided situations, often of an archetypal kind, as here in *Hamlet* in the dramatic confrontation of father and son who belong to different worlds; in the comedies, with wooing, cross-dressing, sexual and social relations, the generation gap between children and parents, and marriage; in the tragedies and history plays, with power structures and relations, the corrupting effects of power, the clash between private and public interests, the impact of sexuality on government, conflicts between generations, and between differing political and moral codes. All of these are of permanent interest, and you will notice that in speaking of revenge, I tried to bring out how this has been a difficult issue since the written origins of Western societies in the world of the ancient Greeks, and how it remains a difficult issue to this day. The issues Shakespeare raises reach out almost always to his own age, to our own time, and often into other periods of history as well, and his work remains of permanent interest because no author has more subtly and dynamically sounded out the deeper problematics and complexities of such matters. To bring these complexities into teaching enhances the immediacy and relevance of the plays for students. Teaching in this way is an exploration for instructor and student, in which what happens in the classroom ideally illuminates issues of interpretation and puts them in a wider context, but leaves the student free to draw her own conclusions. In recent years the once-idolized figure of Shakespeare, bard divine, has been cut down to size by postmodern critics, and in such reworkings of his life as that in Edward

Bond's play, *Bingo* (1973), in which he is shown as a grasping landowner, concerned in his retirement with enclosing lands, and hating his family. In some ways Shakespeare has become more interesting and accessible as a result, and these new perspectives, however mystified in some theoretical writings, or overpitched in some criticism, offer ways to improve and enhance what goes on in the classroom in the teaching of his plays.[34]

Notes

1. Lawrence Levine, *Highbrow/Lowbrow: The Emergence of Cultural Hierarchy in America* (Cambridge: Harvard University Press, 1988), p. 23.

2. Ibid., p. 41.

3. Charles Dickens, *Great Expectations* (1861), New Oxford Illustrated Dickens (London: Oxford University Press, 1953), p. 240.

4. Levine, *Highbrow/Lowbrow*, p. 78, citing A. A. Lipscomb, "Uses of Shakespeare Off the Stage," *Harper's New Monthly Magazine* 65 (1882): 431–38. Lipscomb was chancellor of the University of Georgia, 1860–74, and a professor at Vanderbilt University, Tennessee.

5. Bernard Shaw, *Our Theaters in the Nineties*, 3 vols. (London: Constable, 1932), 3:201.

6. Levine, *Highbrow/Lowbrow*, p.72, citing an advertisement for the New International Shakespeare, published in 1903.

7. Cited by Stephen Brown, "The Uses of Shakespeare in America: A Study in Class Domination," in *Shakespeare's Pattern of Excelling Nature*, ed. David Bevington and Jay Halio (Newark: University of Delaware Press; London and Toronto: Associated University Presses, 1978), pp. 230–31.

8. Cited in Levine, *Highbrow/Lowbrow*, p. 80.

9. Harold Jenkins, ed., *Hamlet*, The Arden Shakespeare (London and New York: Methuen, 1982), pp. 139–40.

10. Ibid., pp. 154, 157.

11. Ibid., p. 124.

12. Christopher Norris, *Deconstruction: Theory and Practice* (London and New York: Methuen, 1982), p. 84.

13. Cited in ibid., p. 41.

14. John Drakakis, "Theater, Ideology, and Institution: Shakespeare and the Roadsweepers," in *The Shakespeare Myth,* ed. Graham Holderness (Manchester: Manchester University Press, 1988), pp. 24–41, citing p. 36.

15. Stephen Greenblatt, *Shakespearean Negotiations: The Circulation of Social Energy in Renaissance England* (Oxford: Clarendon Press, 1988), p. 7.

16. Terence Hawkes, "Lear's Maps: A General Survey," *Deutsche Shakespeare Gesellschaft West Jahrbuch*, 1989, p. 135.

17. See the subtle analysis by Alan Liu, "The Power of Formalism: The New Historicism," *ELH* 56 (1990): 721–71.

18. Stephen Orgel, "The Authentic Shakespeare," *Representations* 21 (1988): 7.

19. Jonathan Goldberg, "Textual Properties," *Shakespeare Quarterly* 37 (1986): 216.

20. Michael Bristol, *Shakespeare's America, America's Shakespeare* (London and New York: Routledge, 1990), p. 115.

21. Gary Taylor and Michael Warren, eds., *The Division of the Kingdoms, Shakespeare's Two Versions of King Lear* (Oxford: Clarendon Press, 1983), citing Stanley Wells, "The Once and Future King Lear," p. 20.

22. Roland Barthes, "From Work to Text," in *Textual Strategies: Perspectives in Post-Structuralist Criticism,* ed. Josué V. Harari (Ithaca, N.Y.: Cornell University Press, 1979), pp. 73–81, citing p. 80.

23. Harari, "Critical Factions/Critical Fictions," in *Textual Strategies,* p. 40.

24. These are titles or subtitles of essays in *Shakespeare Quarterly* 41 (Summer, 1990).

25. James H. Kavanagh, "Shakespeare in Ideology," in *Alternative Shakespeares,* ed. John Drakakis (London and New York: Methuen, 1985), pp. 144–65, citing p. 154; this is cited in all seriousness by Edward Pechter in "Teaching Differences," *Shakespeare Quarterly* 41 (1990): 163.

26. G. R. Hibbard, ed., *Hamlet,* The Oxford Shakespeare (Oxford and New York, 1987), p. 352.

27. Terence Hawkes, *That Shakespeherian Rag: Essays on a Critical Process* (London and New York: Methuen, 1986), p. 88.

28. Philip Edwards, ed., *Hamlet,* The New Cambridge Shakespeare (Cambridge: Cambridge University Press, 1985), pp. 43, 45.

29. G. R. Hibbard, *Hamlet,* p. 48.

30. Eleanor Prosser, *Hamlet and Revenge* (Stanford, Calif.: Stanford University Press, 1967).

31. Francis Lord Bacon, *The Essayes or Counsells, Civill and Morall,* ed. Michael Kiernan (Cambridge: Harvard University Press, 1985), p. 11.

32. Alasdair MacIntyre, *After Virtue: A Study in Moral Theory* (London: Duckworth; Notre Dame, Ind.: University of Notre Dame Press, 1981), p. 115.

33. Ibid., p. 117.

34. For an excellent account of the impact of recent theoretical criticism on the teaching of Shakespeare, tempered by a "healthy skepticism about the idea that theory is necessarily closer to truth and virtue than practice is," see Robert N. Watson, "Teaching 'Shakespeare': Theory versus Practice," in *Teaching Literature: What Is Needed Now,* ed. James Engell and David Perkins (Cambridge, Mass., and London: Harvard University Press, 1988), pp. 121–50.

Making a Start
on *King Lear*

R. A. FOAKES

Workshop

Yesterday I outlined all too briefly five current approaches to Shakespeare: deconstructive, new historicist, feminist, performance, textual. Each is inclined on its own to become defensive, polemical, and shrill, so as to assert itself as especially important. But what they have all shown us is that Shakespeare's plays are problematic; in other words, they have shown the inadequacy of an older critical tradition that assumed each play had a determinate meaning, and they have opened up the plays to new kinds of exploration in the recognition that each reader or critic makes a new reading, and that there can be no final interpretation. They have also made us aware that all readings must relate to our own time as well as to the period when the play was written, since we make our own relationship to a play in the act of reading it. Thus the plays of Shakespeare are released from bondage to time; we recognize that they no longer need to be thought of as like ancient monuments, written in an archaic language and buried in footnotes, so that each has to be, as it were, excavated in order to be understood. In fact, we can only make sense of the issues raised by Shakespeare when we see them in relation to our own age and our own problems. Hence relating them to our own time is not a matter of looking for some kind of spurious "relevance" to ourselves, but an inescapable condition of studying the plays at all.

This is not to say that we can make the play mean anything we like. One obvious function of the instructor in teaching is to energize the class through his or her knowledge of Shakespeare's age, the conventions of the Elizabethan theater, the nuances of the dramatist's language, and nature of the playtexts, so that some guidelines are established. For instance, certain basic questions have to be addressed. A play needs to be understood as a drama, not as a novel; many students find it hard to adjust to works which do not have a "point of view," which lack an authorial voice, and which unfold in time on the stage, where the pages cannot be turned back as in a work of fiction. Shakespeare's plays are written mainly in verse; and the function of poetry in opening up imaginative vistas, and in releasing his dramatic world from the shackles of realism or naturalism, needs to be understood. In an age dominated by the camera in film and TV, and by the novel as a written form, students may need help in appreciating the power of poetry to create an imaginary world that can occupy several times and places at once (as in *A Midsummer Night's Dream* the characters seem to straddle an ancient and a modern age, and see "a wood" near "Athens gates" as a desert, a jungle, a hawthorn copse, or a pastoral landscape, according to their state of mind). The conventions of staging in Shakespeare's plays also may need to be explained—how stage directions should be read, how scenes flow into one another, how the settings were created through poetry at a time when there was no stage lighting, and actors and audience were crowded intimately together sharing the same light. Shakespeare's rich and inventive language, too, does have its pitfalls for the unwary student, who needs to be alert to wordplay, and to slippages in the meaning of some common words.

It might seem that I am taking back with one hand what I've given with the other, in claiming that new approaches to Shakespeare release us from bondage to the past, but arguing at the same time that we must pay attention to that past. This is not really a contradiction. Let me illustrate my point from *Macbeth*. At the center of this play is the great invocation of darkness by Macbeth as he rouses himself to carry out the murder of Banquo:

> Come, seeling night,
> Scarf up the tender eye of pitiful day,
> And, with thy bloody and invisible hand,
> Cancel and tear to pieces that great bond
> Which keeps me pale!—Light thickens, and the crow
> Makes wing to the rooky wood.
>
> (3.2.46–51)

Here the word "seeling" relates to hawking, a sport long replaced by flying and football; literally it means sewing up the eyes of a bird in order to train it. There is also a pun on "sealing," as a seal is affixed to a deed or bond in a legally binding agreement; so Macbeth calls on forces of darkness to blind the forces of good, of the day and pity, and to destroy the bond of nature that links human beings to one another and to God; he is, so to speak, suppressing his own conscience in order to fire himself up for an act of murder. But then, what of "Light thickens, and the crow / Makes wing to the rooky wood"? The note on the word "rooky" in the respected Arden edition reads:

> rooky] i.e., black and filled with rooks. There have been many attempts to save Shakespeare from writing this excellent line, which is regarded as tautological—"murky" (Roderick), "roky" = misty (various), "rouky" = perching, i.e. where the crow settles for the night (Cuningham), "reeky" = steamy (Wilson), "rooky" = foggy, misty (Scots and northern dialect), "rouky" = chattering (from "rouk," talk privately), "rucky" = multitudinous. With the last two suggestions, cf. Meredith, *Modern Love*, "multitudinous chatterings."

This seems to give us every possibility of meaning without illuminating the lines at all, and is what I would call an archaeological footnote. The image vividly imagines a solitary black bird, the crow, winging its way (for plunder or attack?) to the gregarious society of rooks, who live in groups in a rookery, and so conveys a sense of Macbeth's stealthy attack, in the darkness associated with evil, on the peaceful society of his court; he is turning himself into one of night's black agents seeking its prey.

Here the words "seeling" and "rooky" need explaining, not simply as archaic terms, but in ways that bring them to life for a modern reader, so that we sense Macbeth casting a spell in order to silence his conscience, the bond that keeps him pale, and we see into the mind of a murderer, who has to overcome the better part of himself, and blind himself to what he is doing in order to do it. Among the functions of the instructor, then, are two important ones. One is to bring out and interrogate the imaginative resonances of the text without archaeologizing it. Another is to show that current critical approaches have not drawn us into a giddy method of making the play say anything we please; we have to establish some parameters within which the new freedoms can operate. But these freedoms allow many perspectives to be brought into play at once, in the recognition that all interpretations are relative and incomplete, and what we see now in terms of our own time may be as significant as what we can reconstruct of the past.

I would like to turn to *King Lear* now to illustrate my argument at more length. [For the text of *King Lear* 1.1.33–283, see pp. 94–97.] In the time we have it will only be possible to deal with a few aspects of such a complex play, and I would like to involve you in a discussion of what is at the heart of it, Lear himself and his relations with his daughters. First let me briefly provide a setting for our discussion. Until 1960 or so this play was usually interpreted as a play of redemption, in which Lear "loses the world and gains his soul" in a spiritual pilgrimage;[1] one well-known essay on it was called "The Golden World of King Lear."[2] The emphasis was very much on Lear as a type of ordinary man passing through a vale of suffering, but saved at the end; everything else in the play was subordinated to his personal feelings, and his relationship with Cordelia. The apparently gratuitous death of Cordelia was something of a problem, but could be dealt with by converting her into a kind of saint who is already saved; critics emphasized the way in the later part of the play she is associated with Christian love and mercy. In the 1960s *King Lear* began to be seen as a play of despair, Shakespeare's bleakest drama of desolation, notably in Peter Brook's production (1962) and film (1971), which were influenced by Jan Kott's *Shakespeare our Contemporary,* translated into English in 1964, but known to Brook in an earlier French translation. In this book the chapter on the play was headed *"King Lear* or *Endgame,"* as if it could be identified with Samuel Beckett's nightmare vision. But there were many critical interpretations, too, which stressed the grim pagan world of the play, and the way all hints of consolation are eroded and undercut in the final scenes.[3] Now not only was King Lear's own suffering seen as unrelenting to the end, but the death of Cordelia became another example of pointless cruelty, outdoing the blinding of Gloucester. Since the 1970s no one has returned to a redemptive reading, but many have questioned interpreting the play merely as nihilistic. Poststructuralist criticism has tended to point to the instability of the play, or what Stephen Booth calls its "indefinition";[4] then it becomes possible to argue that the end of the play allows more than one perspective, and can be bitter and sweet at the same time. Even such a brief glance at the play's critical history thus helps to release us from bondage to any notion of a fixed interpretation.

King Lear is based on a story of events that took place about 800 B.C., and a long stage tradition extending to the 1960s has set the play in a primitive world of megaliths, often with visual echoes of Stonehenge. The effect has been to distance the play from the audience; but Brook and later directors have created settings that suggest European landscapes devastated after a great war, the Thirty Years' War of the seventeenth century, or the Europe of World War I or II. A play that had seemed primitive, located in a remote past, began in the 1960s to speak like no other to our own times.

Then, as the anxieties of the 1960s diminished, the play was returned to Shakespeare's own age when, in the 1970s and 1980s, it was staged with a Jacobean setting and costumes, relating it to the world of James I. The new historicists were doing the same in their criticism, though they differed as to whether Shakespeare was supportive of patriarchal power structures or speaking for the poor and dispossessed.[5]

How does Shakespeare's play allow such a range of historicizing and such contradictory readings? Although the story relates to a primitive world, and the characters throughout refer to the gods (that is to say, to classical deities if they are identified at all, not the Christian God), the text is not located in time, and we have to go to the sources to discover the dating. So, in a play apparently set in a pre-Christian age, Shakespeare could make Cordelia at one point use a phrase from Christ's words to his father in the Gospel according to Luke; she says with reference to Lear in 4.4., "O dear father, / It is thy business that I go about." So far as we know, the play was staged in front of a Jacobean facade at the Globe, and so was a contemporary play for its audience then. Apart from some vague references to Dover, near where the final battle is fought, the play is not located in space, other than somewhere in England. So we are left free to relate it to the time of James I, or to our own time, too. But why does it seem so much a play for our age, being now generally regarded as Shakespeare's "greatest" play[6] and more often staged than ever in its history?[7] Is it because our world is obsessed with violence, and often dominated by old men who cling on to power?

One other factor we need to take into account is the existence of two texts of the play, the Quarto of 1608 and what appears to be Shakespeare's revised version in the Folio of 1623. In reworking about three hundred lines were omitted from the Folio text, and nearly one hundred new ones added, and these changes can have an important effect on interpretation, though they do not consistently support either an upbeat or a bleak reading of the play. Let's see what answers we come up with, by looking at some crucial episodes in the main action of the play that begins with the entry of King Lear in the opening scene. We need to imagine the play in performance to notice that the entry is a ceremonial one: a sennet sounds (Quarto), a flourish (Folio) on trumpets, announcing the entry of "one bearing a coronet" (Quarto) (on a cushion?), preceding Lear and all the court; Gloucester, Kent and Edmund are already onstage for a crowd scene, a state occasion. And Lear's first purpose is to settle the marriage of Cordelia with the King of France or Duke of Burgundy, who have been hanging about the court for some time as suitors. Lear combines this determination of Cordelia's marriage—she appears to have no choice in the matter—with a "darker purpose," a secret plan, to divide the kingdom. Notice that he has already fixed the new boundaries, and he, or perhaps Gloucester, who knows about it, has a map showing the division.

Now I wonder if some students would volunteer to help me, because I find this scene difficult and problematic. It's hard to get inside each of the characters, so perhaps some would help me by standing in for the three daughters and Kent. I shall not ask you to act the part, but to act for, or be a representative of, one character, and see how you would answer questions the audience throws at us. I say "us" because I will act as spokesman for Lear himself, since I'm the only one here old enough. [*At this point, with some cajoling, four students came down and sat in front of the class to speak for the four characters.*] Let me then invite the rest of you to join me in questioning them as to what they think they are doing. But first, you may like to begin with Lear himself, and to lead off, I will grill myself as king. I would first ask Lear why he divided the kingdom, and why he gave this business precedence over the marriage bids for Cordelia. My answer, for Lear, might run as follows: As Shakespeare first conceived of me, I come on stage and announce that I (or "we"—I like to use the royal plural, to show what I decide is good for all) have divided the kingdom with the intention of retiring to "shake all cares and business from our age." Please keep in mind that I am a very old man, over eighty as I confess later on, and this sudden decision I have made entirely myself, as has long been my habit. Notice the strangest feature of my reign: it has no memory of the past. I've been in power so long that I can't remember who my father was. If you ask me who was my queen—I don't recall her; my daughters certainly had a mother, but she must have died some time ago, and no one mentions her. I had no children when I was young; I must have married very late, and as a result I have this awkward situation with three young daughters, one still unmarried. Two have married noblemen, and I'm a bit bored with the way they all stick around the court. The third is a teenager, not much older than Juliet in *Romeo and Juliet* or Viola in *Twelfth Night*, who are about fourteen, and of marriageable age. I want to do what I see as the best for her, and get her off my hands; but I have had to deal with the division of the kingdom first to establish Cordelia's dowry. Speaking more generally, I've been in power so long I can't even remember who had it before me. It is extraordinary that there is no one in this play who remembers the past, or is it that not one dares to remind me of my own history?

Anyway, I love power, but I'm weary of all the affairs I have to manage, and I have decided to retire.

That's all there is to it in the Quarto, but Shakespeare seems to have had second thoughts, for he revised the opening of the play in the Folio of 1623, and added a bit more explanation for what I do; in the later version I announce my wish to "unburdened crawl toward death." Then I tell my sons-in-law Cornwall and Albany, "We have this day a constant will to publish, / Our daughters' several dowers, that future strife / May be prevented now." You see how Shakespeare wanted me to show that I am making a kind and generous gesture in sharing the kingdom; I want to prevent quarrels in the future about who should inherit. You must admit it is hard to have daughters and no son, no man to rule by force if necessary. In the circumstances, sharing the kingdom seemed best. And I am becoming anxious about dying, crawling toward death—there isn't much else for me to look forward to. Only, of course, I want to hang on to the title and dignities I'm used to, and keep a retinue of knights to attend on me, all men who can join me in hunting, my favorite sport. Does this seem reasonable? Have you warmed to me a little bit?

Aud.: But why have you decided to make your daughters compete for the best share of the country by declaring their love for you?

Lear: A good question. You see, I have been used to power for a long time, and as an absolute monarch I have to stage my major decisions in public so that everyone will acknowledge them; it's my way of announcing them to the world. So I thought up a little ceremony in which I would ask them each to say how much they loved me; they knew in advance, of course, that they would be on public display.

Aud.: But how could you divide the kingdom on the spot, and . . . talk of giving a bigger share, your "largest bounty," to the daughter who has most "merit"?

Lear: Oh, that was all a setup. I had divided the kingdom already into more or less equal thirds; I consulted Gloucester about it, as he quite improperly reveals to Kent in the opening lines of the play (often missed by latecomers and people in the audience still cracking hazelnuts!). I wanted a big public occasion, and I wasn't expecting anyone to tell the truth; that's not what ceremonies are for, and I love ceremony. You wouldn't expect to speak the truth, and tell him what you really think of his policies, if you were introduced to the President at the White House, would you? You would find the appropriate formulae for the occasion, say the expected thing; that's all I wanted.

Aud.: Don't you ever consider the feelings of other people? You say what you did was "reasonable." Do you think others might not see it as reasonable?

Lear: That's also a good question. No; I don't consider the feelings of other people. Why should I? I run the show, and my power is absolute only as long as I always let them know who is in charge.

Aud.: But you are also a father; doesn't this affect you?

Lear: Yes. But feelings should not interfere in matters of state; when you have been king as long as I have, you don't have much time for feelings. When I staged the show of asking each daughter to say how much she loved me, it was all for the public record, a way of ratifying the division. But let's see what the daughters think about this. Goneril and Regan, you made some fine statements when asked to express your love. How do you feel about that? Were you treating the occasion as mere ceremony? Were you, as many now say, merely flattering me?

Goneril: Oh, no, certainly not.

Lear: How would you defend what you said?

Goneril: Well, for my part, I really did love you. My speech was rehearsed, but I meant what I said.

Aud. [to Lear]: You said you were not really concerned about feelings, yet you now ask how Goneril and Regan felt.

Lear: Well, I was thinking of the occasion as a public ceremony, but you have heard Goneril saying that she meant what she said. I wonder what Cordelia has to say?

Cordelia: I think your question was unfair. Love is not something it is easy to express in words; after all, you have known me through my fifteen years (or however many), and actions speak louder than words—you should know that I love you. Our relationship means more to me than using flowery words to get a bigger share of the kingdom.

Aud. [to Lear]: I still don't see how you can justify this ceremonial business. Can you explain further?

Lear: Let me just point to one thing that Cordelia said—that we had a special sort of relationship. Now, I was as surprised as anyone at the way she behaved. She says we have this special thing going, and yet she stands up in public and humiliates me. She knows perfectly well the whole business was ceremonial, and there was no question of a bigger share, for they were all equal in size. I'm old enough to be her grandfather, after all. I was amazed that a girl so young could confront me, an all-powerful king, and say nothing when I asked her to speak. And when she did open her mouth, it was to measure her love for me as though it could be quantified: "I love you according to my bond, nor more nor less."

Cordelia: Well, as I told you, I was taken aback at having to express publicly something I thought you and I had as a mutual understanding. Beyond that, I feel my integrity was involved as well, and you didn't take that into account when you asked me to put on a mask and say what you wanted to hear. True love doesn't show itself in the way Goneril and Regan spoke.

Lear: Well, as to truth, when I remarked on how uncharitable you were being, "So young and so untender," you retorted, "So young my lord, and true"; but you were not speaking truth then, were you? Because now you say you really love me.

Cordelia: But the parent-child bond is so strong it should not be questioned; you falsified the relationship first—you were the one who asked me to quantify my love by saying how much I loved you.

Aud.: I'm tired of hearing Lear's point of view.

Lear: I'm tired too; all this talk wears out an old man.

Aud.: What has Kent to say about all this?

Kent: I think Lear's pride got in his way, and made him deny Cordelia's love and truth; but although I was banished when the old king got angry, I decided out of loyalty to stick around and try to serve him, and maybe save his soul.

Lear: I can see that you wanted to serve me, but could you explain why, the moment you came to me in Goneril's court and I took you on, you made a nuisance of yourself by beating and tripping up Oswald, who was Goneril's steward and an important officer? And a bit later, when I sent you with a message to Regan, you abused Oswald again, chased him with a sword and wanted to kill him. What was all this violence for?

Kent: I thought you were in danger of losing control, and things were getting pretty chaotic in Goneril's house. You did a stupid thing in dividing the kingdom, and abandoning the rights of primogeniture, and that made me angry; then it made me more angry to see you treated with disrespect.

Lear: Goneril and Regan may have something to say about your behavior.

Goneril: I thought it was outrageous. I had no peace in my own house. It's easy to blame Regan and me for the way we treated you, but everyone seems to forget the way you treated us, as if we were your servants, with all your rowdy knights creating mayhem in my house.

Lear: Perhaps you would remind us of your complaints—Shakespeare strengthened them in revising the play in the Folio. Let's hear what you say there.

Goneril:

> This man hath had good counsel—A hundred knights!
> 'Tis politic and safe to let him keep
> At point a hundred knights; Yes, that on every dream,
> Each buzz, each fancy, each complaint, dislike,
> He may enguard his dotage with their pow'rs
> And hold our lives in mercy.

(1.4.322–27)

There's more, too, and added lines for Regan; we really were genuinely afraid these armed knights might take over and throw us out.

Lear: I liked having an armed guard "at point" around me, to give me a sense of security, and I couldn't bear to give everything up. After being in power so long, I suppose I got into the habit of authority, as when I returned from hunting and expected to be served right away: "Let me not stay a jot for dinner." As king I was used to making this kind of demand, and I couldn't bear insubordination. That's why I struck that insolent steward for criticizing my Fool. Kent backed me up, as usual, a bit too vigorously.

Regan: I really did love my father, but he made the situation impossible. Also I admit it wasn't just the riots of his followers that bothered me—I was greedy, like him I suppose—I wanted the power he said he was giving us as well as control in my own house.

Aud. [to Goneril and Regan]: But he's been really generous to you. Why do you have to take away his last shred of pride and throw him out? There's no evidence the knights were so troublesome.

Regan: You are overdramatizing the situation. We were not trying to kick him out. We just wanted to have what he said he had given us, but he went on making impossible demands on us; if he meant to give us the kingdom, he should have given it completely, not tried to keep control.

Cordelia: You are lying, you have no respect or love for your father. [To the audience:] Don't believe a word she says.

Goneril: If you really loved your father, you wouldn't have a problem in saying so.

Regan: Cordelia, you are supposed to be the smart one; now you are just revealing how jealous of us you are.

Lear: Cordelia, you seem to despise your sisters, and feel pretty hostile towards them. Do you feel an urge to retaliate?

Cordelia: Yes, in a way; not that I'm a vengeful kind of person—but I do feel that for your sake, and for the sake of tradition, I have a responsibility to fight back against the wrong that has been done.

Lear: You found me when I was mad, you restored me to sanity again, and really did show you loved me then, and I'm more than grateful; but something very odd happened in that scene. If you remember, when I came round I managed to stand after a little while, and walk a bit. You were very affectionate, in a deferential manner, asking, "Will it please your highness to walk?"—"highness" sounded strange after I had been brought so low, and I was now seeing you as my daughter, not my subject. I replied, "Pray you now, forget and forgive: I am old and foolish." I was thinking not only of myself, and you, but of others, too; after all that I had been through, I had come to the recognition that the right course was to "forget and forgive." But this is what you were not prepared to do; you were loving to me, but hating towards your sisters. You seemed to think you had to restore me to the throne, the last thing I wanted at my age. Indeed, when, as I thought, you woke me up, you may remember I said, "You do me wrong to take me out o' the grave"—I would have been happy to die then, but you insisted on fighting for my rights.

Cordelia: I thought when you came round you were conscious at first of your past misery, and so spoke the way you did. You have to admit that you were always in love with power, and I supposed that you would want to recover your authority.

Lear: Okay, but here you are in England leading a French army, and you insist on fighting; the next thing I know after being restored to sanity is that I'm being led into battle. You were obviously not prepared to "forget and forgive," but insisted on dragging me, old and foolish as I am, onto the battlefield—there I am, being marched over the stage at the beginning of 5.2, "Enter with drum and colours, Lear, Cordelia and their forces" (Folio text), or "Enter the powers of France over the stage, Cordelia with her father in her hand" (Quarto); does she pull me here, or merely support me because I am so frail? Either way, I don't like it. Why didn't you just send me back to Dover, or take me back to France with you?

Cordelia: I thought you were asking my forgiveness, and there was really nothing to forget, in the sense that I never held a grudge against you. But I think you have forgotten what Goneril and Regan did to you. I was not prepared to forget that. Besides, I have my pride in the traditional way of doing things, which you broke with by dividing the kingdom.

Regan: But we were running the kingdom properly, and keeping order; the only problems were caused by our father.

Cordelia: You brutally drove him out.

Goneril: Not at all. He gave us the kingdom, but wouldn't let us rule.

Cordelia: But you said you loved him, and you failed to take care of him; consider his age.

Goneril: He chose to rush out into the storm; it wasn't *our* doing. And you were so anxious about him, we were content to leave to you the job of caring for him. I wonder if you came back with an army because you were so upset at not getting a share of the kingdom, and wanted to gain control of England not for Father, but for yourself?

Cordelia: No, no. Absolutely not.

[*At this point Cordelia, Goneril and Regan might have begun to fight in earnest, and it was time to call a halt, except for one last audience question to Lear.*]

Aud.: Were you able at the end, surrounded by the devastation you caused, to accept some responsibility for it?

Lear: No, I don't think I ever come to that kind of awareness. I realized that the power I had possessed was a kind of role-playing, one I had become so used to, I could not shed it at first, but only through the process of going half-mad, "dying" into a sleep of oblivion, and being brought back, as it were, to life. When I tried to take my clothes off, symbolically I was shedding my role as monarch. I learned to feel for others by the end, not just for Cordelia; it is tragic that she misunderstood my urge to "forget and forgive" as directed solely to her. But after being released from prison, and when I entered carrying her, I was thinking only of her. You might say that the selfishness of a monarch who ignored the feelings of everyone else at the beginning of the play is replaced at the end by another kind of selfishness, a possessiveness that is really rather self-centered—clutching Cordelia alone, and ignoring the rest of the world: "We two will sing like birds in the cage." And at the end all my attention is focussed on her, as if I hope for a word, any word—even perhaps the terrible word "nothing," which was all she would say when she first opened her lips:

> Do you see this? Look on her, look, her lips!
> Look on her lips, look there.

But death is all I want, and perhaps no one would want to deny me the right to die in the delusion that she may be alive (as in the Folio text; in the Quarto, these last two lines are not present, and I die of a broken heart).

This truncated report hardly does justice to a lively debate, which of necessity in the time available could not deal with all aspects of the play. Hardly anything was said about Gloucester, Edgar and Edmund, for instance, but some of the central issues in the play emerged, and the emphasis on the daughters was, I think, valuable. One well-known feminist essay on this play argues that it endorses the ideology of a patriarchal society, and displays the "representation of patriarchal misogyny," in a demonstration that "the institution of male power in the family and the State is . . . the only form of social organization strong enough to hold chaos at bay."[8] Such an argument misses the point, even if in general Shakespeare, like other male writers of his age, assumed as natural a patriarchal order derived ultimately from God. For *King Lear* is dominated by its women, and when they are in power Goneril and Regan turn out to be as hard and tough as their father. They show they have the courage and strength of character to rule and compete with men. Lear's preference is for a male society; he surrounds himself with his hundred knights on giving up rule, and his later misogyny may be attributed to the shock of discovering that Goneril and Regan, whom he seems not to have known except as adornments of his court, are just like him in their imperiousness. And Cordelia also has the obstinacy to face down her father at the start, and later insists on fighting to put him back in power, which is not what he wants. I said early on that one reason we find the play so important now may be because of the analogy between Lear and the old men who have held sway in the centers of power in our world in recent times. Peter Brook saw the "politics of sclerosis" in Lear, comparing him to Stalin.[9] But there is another way to see the play, not in terms of what Lear does, but rather in terms of what happens to him.

Here I am not thinking of the rather sentimental idea of Lear's personal progress to some kind of self-discovery; I am not sure that he does discover much by the end. Let's consider instead the process by which Lear is reduced from an all-important figure at the center of power to a nobody. After Lear goes out into the storm at the end of act 2, Regan and Cornwall say to Gloucester, "Shut up your doors," closing off the old man and the storm outside. This marks the point at which they succeed in marginalizing Lear so that he no longer matters as a force to be reckoned with. The encounter of the blind Gloucester and the mad old king in act 4 is so poignant in part because they are reduced to parodic images of what they once were:

> *Gloucester:* Is't not the king?
> *Lear:*   Ay, every inch a king!
> When I do stare, see how the subject quakes.

The power struggles in the realm now go on without them, and indeed, Lear is offstage between act 3, scene 6 and act 4, scene 6. We attend instead to the growing threat of civil war between Goneril on the one hand, perhaps backed by Edmund, and Regan on the other, reluctantly supported by Albany; and the even greater concern about an invasion by a French force to aid Lear. Action, so to speak, swirls around the two old men in the buildup to the clash between British and French forces. All Lear and Gloucester want is to die, but they are kept alive by the ministrations of their children, Cordelia and Edgar, and are left aside as spectators of the battle. Lear is captured and sent off as a prisoner, while Goneril and Regan quarrel to the death; then Edgar in disguise challenges Edmund, and they fight hand to hand on stage until Edmund is mortally wounded. In the heat of these events, just as Albany is calling for the bodies of Goneril and Regan to be brought on stage, Kent enters, unregarded at first by Albany, who has more immediate concerns on hand:

> *Albany:* Produce the bodies, be they alive or dead.
> This judgment of the heavens, that makes us tremble,
> Touches us not with pity. [To Kent:] O, is this he?
> The time will not allow the compliment
> Which very manners urges.
>   *Kent:* I am come
> To bid my king and master aye good night.
> Is he not here?
>   *Albany:* Great thing of us forgot!
>
>   (5.3.231–37)

On one level forgetting Lear is to forget "a great thing," for he has been the center of attention through the first three acts. But on another level the sudden mention of the old king after a long sequence of hectic action in which he has been an irrelevance reminds us of his insignificance in rela- tion to the events we have been witnessing. Often an audience laughs nervously at this point, I think because they respond to the double perspective on Lear here. He is at once the great thing in the play and of no importance any longer.

Albany has the bodies of Goneril and Regan brought on stage, and the body of Edmund carried off, so that in the last scene of the play, when Lear carries on Cordelia, he is in the presence of the dead bodies of all his children. He has lost everything, and outlived all his family, as a result of his own initiative in dividing the kingdom, and there is nothing left for him except death with dignity. In personal terms we respond to the pathos of his situation here, but what reinforces the tragedy of Lear is that at the same time it can be seen as related to our own society. For we live in a society that simultaneously encourages us to feel that each person counts, and the individual is all-important; and yet our society marginalizes us at the same time. So the play may be seen as exposing the contradiction between the importance we attribute to individual expression and fulfillment on the one hand, and on the other hand, the way the individual is reduced by the workings of our society to a cipher, an entry in a bank of computerized information, a part of the mass, a social security number, a face on a driving license, a fingerprint in a police file. This contradiction is reflected in what happens to Lear, and may be one of the most urgent things the play has to say to us today.

Notes

1. Kenneth Muir, ed., *King Lear*, The Arden Shakespeare (London: Methuen, 1952), p. 1.

2. Geoffrey Bickersteth, "The Golden World of *King Lear*," *Proceedings of the British Academy* 32 (1946).

3. As in, for example, N. S. Brooke, *King Lear* (London: Edward Arnold, 1963), and William R. Elton, *King Lear and the Gods* (San Marino, Calif.: Huntington Library, 1966).

4. In *King Lear, Macbeth, Indefinition and Tragedy* (New Haven: Yale University Press, 1983). More precisely, Booth seeks to bring out "the simultaneously fixed and unfixed quality of the whole of *King Lear*" (p.43).

5. See, for the first point of view, Leonard Tennenhouse, *Power on Display: The Politics of Shakespeare's Genres* (London and New York: Methuen, 1986), and Kathleen McLuskie, "The Patriarchal Bard: Feminist Criticism and Shakespeare's *King Lear* and *Measure for Measure*," in *Political Shakespeare*, ed. Jonathan Dollimore and Alan Sinfield (Manchester: Manchester University Press; Ithaca: Cornell University Press, 1985); and for the second, see Annabel Patterson, *Shakespeare and the Popular Voice* (Oxford and Cambridge, Mass.: Blackwell, 1989).

6. So, for example, Stephen Booth can begin his account of the play as follows: "*The Tragedy of Lear*, deservedly celebrated among the dramas of Shakespeare, is now com-

monly regarded as his greatest achievement" (*King Lear, Macbeth, Indefinition and Tragedy*, p. 5).

7. Between 1681 and 1834, when William Macready restored much of Shakespeare's text, the play was performed only in the sentimentalized reworking by Nahum Tate, in which Lear and Gloucester remain alive to witness the marriage of Edgar and Cordelia. In the numerous productions since the 1960s the play has often been trimmed or reshaped to make a contemporary point, as in Peter Brook's 1962 production and his film made in 1971, in which the setting in Jutland, and cuts made in the text, emphasized the harsh, wintry nature of the world of the play as Brook saw it.

8. McLuskie, "The Patriarchal Bard," pp. 98–99.

9. "Politics of Sclerosis: Stalin and Lear" (Peter Brook interviewed by A. J. Liehm), translated by Richard Seaver, *Theatre Quarterly* 3, no. 10 (1973): 13–17.

King Lear, 1.1.33–283

(With permission from Houghton Mifflin, *The Riverside Shakespeare,* ed. G. Blakemore Evans, 1974.)

Enter [one bearing a coronet, then] KING LEAR, CORN-
WALL, ALBANY, GONERIL, REGAN, CORDELIA, *and*
ATTENDANTS.

Lear. Attend the lords of France and Burgundy,
    Gloucester.

Glou. I shall, my lord. *Exit [with Edmund].* 35

Lear. Mean time we shall express our darker pur-
    pose.
Give me the map there. Know that we have divided
In three our kingdom, and 'tis our fast intent
To shake all cares and business from our age,
Conferring them on younger strengths, while we 40
Unburthen'd crawl toward death. Our son of Cornwall,
And you, our no less loving son of Albany,
We have this hour a constant will to publish
Our daughters' several dowers, that future strife
May be prevented now. The princes, France and Bur-
    gundy,   45
Great rivals in our youngest daughter's love,
Long in our court have made their amorous sojourn,
And here are to be answer'd. Tell me, my daughters
(Since now we will divest us both of rule,
Interest of territory, cares of state),   50
Which of you shall we say doth love us most,
That we our largest bounty may extend
Where nature doth with merit challenge? Goneril,
Our eldest-born, speak first.

Gon. Sir, I love you more than [words] can wield
    the matter,   55
Dearer than eyesight, space, and liberty,
Beyond what can be valued, rich or rare,
No less than life, with grace, health, beauty, honor;
As much as child e'er lov'd, or father found;
A love that makes breath poor, and speech unable: 60
Beyond all manner of so much I love you.

Cor. [Aside.] What shall Cordelia speak? Love,
    and be silent.

Lear. Of all these bounds, even from this line to
    this,
With shadowy forests and with champains rich'd,
With plenteous rivers and wide-skirted meads, 65
We make thee lady. To thine and Albany's [issue]
Be this perpetual. What says our second daughter,
Our dearest Regan, wife of Cornwall? [Speak.]

Reg. I am made of that self metal as my sister,
And prize me at her worth. In my true heart 70
I find she names my very deed of love;
Only she comes too short, that I profess
Myself an enemy to all other joys
Which the most precious square of sense [possesses],
And find I am alone felicitate   75
In your dear Highness' love.

Cor. [Aside.] Then poor Cordelia!
And yet not so, since I am sure my love's
More ponderous than my tongue.

Lear. To thee and thine hereditary ever
Remain this ample third of our fair kingdom, 80
No less in space, validity, and pleasure,
Than that conferr'd on Goneril.—Now, our joy,
Although our last and least, to whose young love
The vines of France and milk of Burgundy
Strive to be interested, what can you say to draw 85
A third more opulent than your sisters'? Speak.

Cor. Nothing, my lord.

Lear. Nothing?

Cor. Nothing.

Lear. Nothing will come of nothing, speak again.

Cor. Unhappy that I am, I cannot heave 91
My heart into my mouth. I love your Majesty
According to my bond, no more nor less.

Lear. How, how, Cordelia? Mend your speech a
    little
Lest you may mar your fortunes.

Cor.   Good my lord, 95

You have begot me, bred me, lov'd me: I
Return those duties back as are right fit,
Obey you, love you, and most honor you.
Why have my sisters husbands, if they say
They love you all? Happily, when I shall wed, 100
That lord whose hand must take my plight shall carry
Half my love with him, half my care and duty.
Sure I shall never marry like my sisters,
[To love my father all].

    Lear. But goes thy heart with this?
    Cor. Ay, my good lord. 105
    Lear. So young, and so untender?
    Cor. So young, my lord, and true.
    Lear. Let it be so: thy truth then be thy dow'r!
For by the sacred radiance of the sun,
The [mysteries] of Hecat and the night; 110
By all the operation of the orbs,
From whom we do exist and cease to be;
Here I disclaim all my paternal care,
Propinquity and property of blood,
And as a stranger to my heart and me 115
Hold thee from this for ever. The barbarous Scythian,
Or he that makes his generation messes
To gorge his appetite, shall to my bosom
Be as well neighbor'd, pitied, and reliev'd,
As thou my sometime daughter.

    Kent.   Good my liege— 120
    Lear. Peace, Kent!
Come not between the dragon and his wrath;
I lov'd her most, and thought to set my rest
On her kind nursery. [*To Cordelia.*] Hence, and avoid
    my sight!—
So be my grave my peace, as here I give 125
Her father's heart from her. Call France. Who stirs?
Call Burgundy. Cornwall and Albany,
With my two daughters' dow'rs digest the third;
Let pride, which she calls plainness, marry her.
I do invest you jointly with my power, 130
Pre-eminence, and all the large effects
That troop with majesty. Ourself, by monthly course,
With reservation of an hundred knights
By you to be sustain'd, shall our abode
Make with you by due turn. Only we shall retain 135
The name, and all th' addition to a king;
The sway, revenue, execution of the rest,
Beloved sons, be yours, which to confirm,
This coronet part between you.

    Kent.   Royal Lear,
Whom I have ever honor'd as my king, 140
Lov'd as my father, as my master follow'd,
As my great patron thought on in my prayers—
    Lear. The bow is bent and drawn, make from

the shaft.
    Kent. Let it fall rather, though the fork invade
The region of my heart; be Kent unmannerly 145
When Lear is mad. What wouldest thou do, old man?
Think'st thou that duty shall have dread to speak
When power to flattery bows? To plainness honor's
    bound,
When majesty falls to folly. Reserve thy state,
And in thy best consideration check 150
This hideous rashness. Answer my life my judgment,
Thy youngest daughter does not love thee least,
Nor are those empty-hearted whose low sounds
Reverb no hollowness.
    Lear. Kent, on thy life, no more.
    Kent. My life I never held but as [a] pawn 155
To wage against thine enemies, ne'er [fear'd] to lose it,
Thy safety being motive.
    Lear. Out of my sight!
    Kent. See better, Lear, and let me still remain
The true blank of thine eye.
    Lear. Now, by Apollo—
    Kent.   Now, by Apollo, King, 160
Thou swear'st thy gods in vain.
    Lear.   O vassal! miscreant!
                 [*Starts to draw his sword.*]
    Alb., Corn. Dear sir, forbear.
    Kent. Kill thy physician, and [the] fee bestow
Upon the foul disease. Revoke thy gift,
Or whilst I can vent clamor from my throat, 165
I'll tell thee thou dost evil.
    Lear.   Hear me, recreant,
On thine allegiance, hear me!
That thou hast sought to make us break our [vow]—
Which we durst never yet—and with strain'd pride
To come betwixt our sentence and our power, 170
Which nor our nature nor our place can bear,
Our potency made good, take thy reward.
Five days we do allot thee, for provision
To shield thee from disasters of the world,
And on the sixt to turn thy hated back 175
Upon our kingdom. If, on the tenth day following,
Thy banish'd trunk be found in our dominions,
The moment is thy death. Away! By Jupiter,
This shall not be revok'd.
    Kent. Fare thee well, King; sith thus thou wilt
    appear, 180
Freedom lives hence, and banishment is here.
[*To Cordelia.*] The gods to their dear shelter take thee,
    maid,
That justly think'st and hast most rightly said!
[*To Regan and Goneril.*] And your large speeches
    may your deeds approve,

That good effects may spring from words of love. 185
Thus Kent, O princes, bids you all adieu,
He'll shape his old course in a country new. *Exit.*
Flourish. Enter GLOUCESTER *with* FRANCE *and* BUR-
   GUNDY, ATTENDANTS.
   [*Glou.*] Here's France and Burgundy, my noble
      lord.
   Lear. My Lord of Burgundy,
We first address toward you, who with this king 190
Hath rivall'd for our daughter. What, in the least,
Will you require in present dower with her,
Or cease your quest of love?
   Bur.   Most royal Majesty,
I crave no more than hath your Highness offer'd,
Nor will you render less.
   Lear.   Right noble Burgundy, 195
When she was dear to us, we did hold her so,
But now her price is fallen. Sir, there she stands:
If aught within that little seeming substance,
Or all of it, with our displeasure piec'd,
And nothing more, may fitly like your Grace, 200
She's there, and she is yours.
   Bur.   I know no answer.
   Lear. Will you, with those infirmities she owes,
Unfriended, new adopted to our hate,
Dow'r'd with our curse, and stranger'd with our oath,
Take her, or leave her?
   Bur.   Pardon me, royal sir, 205
Election makes not up in such conditions.
   Lear. Then leave her, sir, for by the pow'r that
      made me,
I tell you all her wealth. [*To France.*] For you, great
      King,
I would not from your love make such a stray
To match you where I hate; therefore beseech you
T' avert your liking a more worthier way   211
Than on a wretch whom Nature is asham'd
Almost t' acknowledge hers.
   France.   This is most strange,
That she, whom even but now was your [best] object,
The argument of your praise, balm of your age, 215
The best, the dearest, should in this trice of time
Commit a thing so monstrous, to dismantle
So many folds of favor. Sure her offense
Must be of such unnatural degree
That monsters it, or your fore-vouch'd affection 220
Fall into taint; which to believe of her
Must be a faith that reason without miracle
Should never plant in me.
   Cor.   I yet beseech your Majesty—
If for I want that glib and oily art   224
To speak and purpose nor, since what I [well] intend,

I'll do't before I speak—that you make known
It is no vicious blot, murther, or foulness,
No unchaste action, or dishonored step,
That hath depriv'd me of your grace and favor,
But even for want of that for which I am richer—230
A still-soliciting eye, and such a tongue
That I am glad I have not, though not to have it
Hath lost me in your liking.
   Lear. Better thou
Had'st not been born than not t' have pleas'd me better.
   France. Is it but this—a tardiness in nature 235
Which often leaves the history unspoke
That it intends to do? My Lord of Burgundy,
What say you to the lady? Love's not love
When it is mingled with regards that stands
Aloof from th' entire point. Will you have her? 240
She is herself a dowry.
   Bur.   Royal King,
Give but that portion which yourself propos'd,
And here I take Cordelia by the hand,
Duchess of Burgundy.
   Lear. Nothing. I have sworn, I am firm.   245
   Bur. I am sorry then you have so lost a father
That you must lose a husband.
   Cor.   Peace be with Burgundy!
Since that [respects of fortune] are his love,
I shall not be his wife.
   France. Fairest Cordelia, that art most rich
      being poor,   250
Most choice forsaken, and most lov'd despis'd,
Thee and thy virtues here I seize upon,
Be it lawful I take up what's cast away.
Gods, gods! 'tis strange that from their cold'st neglect
My love should kindle to inflam'd respect.   255
Thy dow'rless daughter, King, thrown to my chance,
Is queen of us, of ours, and our fair France.
Not all the dukes of wat'rish Burgundy
Can buy this unpriz'd precious maid of me.
Bid them farewell, Cordelia, though unkind, 260
Thou losest here, a better where to find.
   Lear. Thou hast her, France, let her be thine,
      for we
Have no such daughter, nor shall ever see
That face of hers again. [*To Cordelia.*] Therefore be
      gone,
Without our grace, our love, our benison.— 265
Come, noble Burgundy.
   Flourish. Exeunt [all but France, Goneril,
      Regan, and Cordelia.].
   France. Bid farewell to your sisters.
   Cor. The jewels of our father, with wash'd eyes
Cordelia leaves you. I know you what you are,

And like a sister am most loath to call   270
Your faults as they are named. Love well our father;
To your professed bosoms I commit him,
But yet, alas, stood I within his grace,
I would prefer him to a better place.
So farewell to you both.   275
    Reg. Prescribe not us our duty.
    Gon.   Let your study
Be to content your lord, who hath receiv'd you

At fortune's alms. You have obedience scanted,
And well are worth the want that you have wanted.
    Cor. Time shall unfold what plighted cunning
      hides,   280
Who covers faults, at last with shame derides.
Well may you prosper!
    France. Come, my fair Cordelia.
             Exeunt France and Cordelia.

Disestablishing Shakespeare

Leah Marcus

Disestablish Shakespeare? Why would anyone want to disestablish Shakespeare? More particularly, why would anyone want to do it in a lecture series like this one, which is devoted to the theory and practice of teaching Shakespeare, with the idea that Shakespeare should be disestablished? By the idea of "disestablishing Shakespeare" I refer not to some demonic plot to throw the Bard and his works out the window, or (worse yet) out of a canon of Great Books, but rather to a process that is going on right now within the classroom and outside it and certainly within the parameters of the present lecture series—a process by which Shakespeare is being separated from some of the literary, philosophical, political, and broadly cultural institutions with which he has come to be associated over the centuries, or at least during our own twentieth century.

When we use the magical name Shakespeare, we are not, in fact, likely to be referring to the historical figure alone—a man about whom we know little. We know that he was baptized on 26 April 1564 at the Church of the Holy Trinity in Stratford-upon-Avon (his traditional birth date of 23 April is conjectural). We know that he was granted a marriage license on 27 November 1582 to wed Anne Hathaway (eight years his senior), that a daughter Susanna was born to them six months later and christened on 26 May 1583, followed by twins—Hamnet and Judith—in 1585. We know that by 1592 Shakespeare was a player in London and had begun writing plays, that he became a shareholder in the dramatic company called at first the Lord Chamberlain's Men and, after 1603, the King's Men. We know that he became increasingly prosperous during the 1590s, invested in Stratford real estate, retired back to Stratford sometime around 1610, and died there on 23 April 1616 at the relatively young age of fifty-two.

No, that skeleton of a life and career is only part of what we mean when we refer to "Shakespeare"—and this time I have put the name in quotation marks. Shakespeare is not only a historical figure for us, but a name by which we designate a vast terrain of cultural activities. Shakespeare is the greatest English writer, some would say the greatest writer of all times and in any language. Students study Shakespeare in the classroom, from grade school onward in some school systems. A few hardy souls actually read Shakespeare for pleasure. Many more attend performances of Shakespearean plays in the theater, where his work is highly popular at present. There are numerous Shakespeare festivals throughout the United States, with more seeming to pop up all the time. Shakespeare is performed by professional companies, amateurs, schools: in Texas, there is an annual contest at which Texas high school students prepare forty-five-minute versions of a Shakespeare play of their choosing and perform it to compete for statewide honors.

Shakespeare is regularly used as a cultural shibboleth, at least in some circles. If you have "brushed up your Shakespeare" you may pass as an attractive, well-versed person; if not, then not. His name is constantly invoked in the present national wars over multiculturalism and political correctness, usually but not always by those who wish to emphasize the continuing importance of the canonical great authors. William J. Bennett, for example, argued in a 1985 article entitled "To Reclaim a Legacy" that Shakespeare should head the list of works that "Should be Read" in American schools. Similarly, in *The Closing of the American Mind,* Allan Bloom recommends Shakespeare as one important component of a liberal education. Shakespeare figures heavily on E. D. Hirsch's encyclopedic list in *Cultural Literacy* entitled "What Every American Needs to Know."[1] If you wish to pass as cultured in the eyes of these authors, you have to know more than a little Shakespeare.

But "Shakespeare" is not only used to grace cocktail conversations and reports on American higher education. In the same way that Shakespeare is popular in the theater, Shakespeare can be used to sell commercial items. His name, face, or lines from the plays, have been used in modern advertising to market products from canned tuna to condominiums. The name of Shakespeare works magic in more modest ways: in some states high schools have begun doing "Shakespeare marathons" in which students take turns in offering a continuous reading through all of the plays as a fund-raising technique. As anyone who has ever visited Stratford-upon-Avon knows, people will buy almost any plastic object that has the name or face of Shakespeare affixed to it—as though through a kind of talismanic magic, such items acquire instant value by being imprinted with our chief cultural symbol of greatness in literature. Having visited the shrine, the pilgrims return with a sacred relic. The phenomenon exists at a more local level. If you were to visit my office in the Department of English at the University of Texas, you would find taped to the glass-windowed door a dish towel bearing a reproduction of the First Folio title page; it was brought to me by a student who had just returned from Stratford. At the English Department office at Texas, you can buy T-shirts showing Shakespeare in a ten-gallon hat (souvenirs of the university's annual Shakespeare at Winedale Festival). But this is still small potatoes. Louis Marder, the editor of the *Shakespeare Newsletter,* has amassed a gargantuan collection of Shakespeare memorabilia of all kinds: plates, cups, cigarette lighters, doorstops, everything imaginable printed with the sacred effigy.

Why do I have that dish towel on my office door, I wonder? Could it be that I, too, am using Shakespeare to sell something to students, namely my own expertise, the high significance of what I do? Am I signaling toward another vast arm of the Shakespeare enterprise—the dozens of scholarly and more popular books and articles published on Shakespeare each year? If you want to succeed with a scholarly book in some area of Renaissance literature, you are well advised to write about Shakespeare: your work will probably be noticed by the vast corps of scholar-teachers of Shakespeare, but it will also stand a good chance of appealing to nonspecialists.

My characterization of the vast and amorphous cultural terrain we call Shakespeare could go on and on, but probably doesn't need to. What does need to be emphasized is that in the last half-decade, this territory we call "Shakespeare" has come to appear less and less a single, unified thing. It is instead a vast set of different, and sometimes contradictory, social and cultural forces better characterized through a plural—Shakespeares—than as a singular Shakespeare. The first time I recall encountering Shakespeare used as a plural in this way was in the British collection *Alternative Shakespeares,* edited by John Drakakis (London: Methuen, 1985). Drakakis's collection was intended, in part, as a showcase of new and mostly poststructuralist methodologies with a strong emphasis on cultural materialism. He states in his introduction that the book will offer "a variety of perspectives upon Shakespeare and the criticism which sustains his reputation, through new work in post-structuralism, deconstruction, psychoanalytic criticism, continental semiotics, structural marxism, feminism, the analysis of discursive practices, and cultural materialism" (p. 24). The book could easily have been titled *Alternative Versions of Shakespeare,* but what Drakakis had in mind was a bit more disruptive: by using the plural "Shakespeares" he called attention to Shakespeare as not a man, but a cultural construct remade in different ways by different human agents with competing critical and social agendas. The charismatic power of Shakespeare in Anglo-American culture—particularly as invoked by conservatives like Bennett, Hirsch, and Bloom—has depended to significant degree on the culture's perception of its unitary nature. If we are to invoke Shakespeare as an important element of our common heritage as English-speaking Westerners, then Shakespeare has to be a single (albeit complex), identifiable entity imagined usually as a historical personage who transcended his own era. He was "not of an age, but for all time," including ours. Drakakis's volume, and poststructuralist revaluations of Shakespeare more generally, have taken aim at this cultural icon by denying its underlying premises of unity. To deny the self-sameness of "Shakespeare" is, in a variety of interesting ways, to disestablish Shakespeare. Not that such a disestablishment is original to our period. The Lamont Lecture Series has been advertised with a poster showing, behind the individual titles of the talks, the figure of Sarah Bernhardt performing the role of Hamlet. Hamlet with discernible woman's breasts beneath his rich doublet! In its time, that was a disruptive image indeed; earlier "disestablishings" like Bernhardt's lie behind those of our own era. What I would like to do here is to survey recent critical trends in order to explore some of the forms very recent "disestablishing" has taken—particularly as they affect the teaching of Shakespeare. I will close by attempting an assessment. What has been gained by disestablishing Shakespeare? What, if anything, has been lost?

I have spoken thus far as though the disestablishment of Shakespeare were a purely academic phenomenon. That is far from being the case. There are presently, as there have no doubt been at diverse times in the past, strong signs of broad cultural reaction against the iconicity of Shakespeare. These are more evident in Britain than in the U.S. Over there, the reading and interpretation of Shakespeare are much more closely and materially tied to social and economic success than they are in our country, in that the exams British students must survive in order to attend university include questions on Shakespeare which must (according to critics of the system) be answered in traditional, predetermined ways in order to qualify as correct. The learning of Shakespeare in Britain has a coercive quality about it that is far less evident here. In Britain, support for Shakespeare as a common cultural symbol seems to be eroding in visible ways. Sam Wanamaker's project for restoring the Globe Theater has not received the expected support from Britain itself; the enterprise has been much more enthusiastically received in the U.S. and former colonies than in the motherland of the Bard. The vigilance of cultural materialists like Drakakis, Jonathan Dollimore, Kate Belsey, Terry Eagleton, and Alan Sinfield,[2] has helped to insure that national cultural institutions like the Royal Shakespeare Company function in a lively and sometimes hostile environment of critique. Indeed, the academic critique was preceded and influenced by a strong tradition of British theatrical practice. Alternative stagings of Shakespeare like those by Peter Brook and Michael Bogdanov in the decades prior to our own have kept before the British public haunting reimaginings of Shakespeare that tease out subversive elements within the plays and profoundly challenge Shakespeare's traditional status as a guarantor of cultural orthodoxy.

As this paper is being written, *I Hate Hamlet* is about to open on Broadway. In general in the United States, however, reaction against Shakespeare has been more muted, much more diffuse than in Britain, just as "Shakespeare" is a less centralized construct here than in Britain. There is no national exam for which we have to know Shakespeare in order to pass. The appeal to Shakespeare is therefore less materially grounded, or at least less obviously so; it carries many of the same associations with elite culture as in Britain, but without the same degree of uniformity. Indeed, it is perhaps because "Shakespeare" has lost some of its elite associations in the U.S. that conservative educators are so anxious to restore the name to an earlier preeminence. Shakespeare in this country is more of a popular phenomenon than in Britain. It may be that emphasis on "Shakespeares" in the U.S. will have a very different and less unsettling political impact than in the U.K., since here the idea of a diversity of Shakespeares may confirm rather than challenge some specifically American cultural ideals—our cherished self-description as a "melting pot," our theoretical tolerance for and celebration of our polyglot and polymorphous origins. It has been my experience that American students—particularly those from disadvantaged economic backgrounds—usually like Shakespeare. I doubt whether this is any longer true in Britain.

Nevertheless, the British critique has entered American classrooms. One of the most successful forms this has taken can be characterized as "Tillyard bashing." E. M. W. Tillyard, when he wrote his *Elizabethan World Picture* during World War Two, little thought he was creating a monster. What he hoped to accomplish was to give students and other readers basic familiarity with Tudor cultural myths that get reflected in Shakespeare's plays—the idea of a Great Chain of Being, the interdependence and mutual reflection of macrocosm (the universe) and microcosm (an individual man). What his book also communicated was a vision of basic order and coherence to which Shakespeare and other Elizabethans were held to subscribe. His book offered students a vocabulary by which they could analyze key speeches and metaphors involving ideas about order and degree; it has been uncommonly useful to students in the past—I will never forget what a feeling of historical enablement it gave me as an undergraduate struggling with Shakespeare. Judging by the fact that it is still in print, it may be just as useful today. Nevertheless, the book has been broadly attacked by British cultural materialists and American new historicists for its normative assumptions. Order is preferable to disorder; the world is basically settled in shape, and can be seen as an aesthetic whole, a "picture." To enlist Shakespeare in the service of such a vision is, to Tillyard bashers, automatically to privilege traditional institutions—the monarchy, the Anglican church from whose homilies Tillyard quoted widely in assembling his "picture"—at the expense of elements within the plays (and within Elizabethan culture more broadly) that challenged such orthodoxies.

For the Tillyard bashers, among whom Jonathan Dollimore in *Radical Tragedy: Religion, Ideology, and Power in the Drama of Shakespeare and His Contemporaries* (Chicago: University of Chicago Press, 1984) may be taken as an able spokesman, *The Elizabethan World Picture* was bound up with a prewar and postwar positioning of Shakespeare to support the political status quo.

> His alleged conformity to received ideas was constantly proclaimed, ideas which expressed confident belief in order, degree, constituted authority, obedience to rulers and a corresponding contempt for the populace, and so on. (P. 59)

British cultural materialists openly enlist Shakespeare for an alternative Marxist social vision in which traditional authority is decentered and disempowered groups are given a voice. Characteristically, these critics proceed by discrediting Tillyard's vision of cultural unity and providential design. In the history plays, for example, Tillyard is blamed for confusing the Tudor myth with the whole picture:

> We find that there was not one but several, rival providentialist accounts of history, Lancastrian, anti-Lancastrian and Yorkist. Depending on which was advanced the monarch was seen either as agent or transgressor of God's plan. In the light of this we see not just that most of Shakespeare's history plays fail to substantiate this (non-existent) unitary myth, but also

that some of them have precisely the opposite effect of revealing how myth is exploited ideologically. (Dollimore, p. 90)

Here, as in cultural materialist work generally, Shakespeare is redefined as a site of conflicting ideological imperatives whose plays do not so much support a single conservative "picture" as explore its political workings as institutionalized myth within Elizabethan culture. Both by undermining Tillyardesque interpretation of the plays and by using the plays' multiple voices to undermine the idea of a unitary Shakespeare, British cultural materialists have helped to disestablish "Shakespeare" even while appropriating some of the power of the mythos for more radical political and social goals.

American new historicists like Stephen Greenblatt, Louis Montrose, or Annabel Patterson (a British scholar in this series who has become American by association)[3] are usually grouped together with British cultural materialists. Even though the Americans do not generally harness their interpretation of Shakespeare to an overt political agenda, they, too, have worked to decenter earlier normative historical interpretation. The *bête noire* for American new historicists, perhaps even more than Tillyard and the stabilities he enshrined, has been the New Criticism, with its guiding presupposition that literature has not, and doesn't need to have, any function beyond the aesthetic—that Shakespeare, like other great masters, far transcends the petty exigencies of his own society and ours and speaks to us on a more transcendent plane of pure art. As with Tillyard-bashing, the new historicist attack on the New Critical isolation of art has linked it with postwar circumstances—particularly, in the U.S., with a broad cultural anaesthesia during the fifties and early sixties that could envision no role for the university beyond that of the "ivory tower" dedicated to the conservation and consolidation of detached, positivist modes of analysis. The new historicist redefinitions of Shakespeare have been aimed less against social injustice at large, more against the insularity of the academy under New Critical assumptions about the proper place of art.

New historicists relentlessly historicize the plays in ways that evacuate their "transcendent" messages: *The Merchant of Venice* is about conflicts between mercantile and earlier aristocratic notions of honor, value, and friendship; *The Tempest* is about the dilemmas of the colonizer, confronted with intransigent "others" like the slave, Caliban; *King Lear* is about exorcism, the crisis of the aristocracy, and the evacuation of transcendent meaning itself, insofar as the play portrays a world in which one after another system for the assertion of universal truth is laid bare and dismembered. American new historicists are usually less insistent than their British counterparts on the multiplicity of Shakespeare: quite often, in a critical maneuver that has been likened to American cold war strategies of the fifties, they emphasize the drama's containment of its own subversive impulses, thus fashioning Shakespeare into a willing or unwilling agent of centralized Elizabethan authority. Nevertheless, their work, like that of the British cultural materialists, has provoked new debate about the nature of Shakespeare's political vision and opened Shakespeare up to a competing array of historical modes of understanding, none of which has either the clarity or the stability of the earlier "picture."

This new work has entered the university classroom via direct and indirect paths. Not only are essays by the revisionist critics frequently assigned as supplemental reading (perhaps along with Tillyard), but the questions raised by new historicists and cultural materialists have filtered into discussion in ways that would have been unthinkable a generation ago. How might *Measure for Measure* reflect the actual workings of royal absolutism? What does the critique of "ceremony" do to the idea of monarchy in *Henry V?* What is the effect of the strong undercurrent of "common" voices—citizens, clowns, grave diggers, thieves, pimps and bawds, court fools, country charlatans—on audience perception of the higher social orders within Shakespeare? These are questions we are finding it harder and harder to avoid in our classroom teaching of the plays. The name of the Bard in our classrooms is becoming as strongly associated with the articulation of these other voices as with the communication of any single Renaissance orthodoxy.

In the new work, not only can Shakespeare not be associated with a coherent "world picture," but he can no longer be expected to offer us realistic characters who are psychologically comprehensible, who exemplify universal elements of human nature. In 1904, A. C. Bradley published his monumental *Shakespearean Tragedy,* which demonstrated the artistic power and unity of *Hamlet, Othello, King Lear,* and *Macbeth* by focussing largely on the psychology of the tragic protagonist in each play. The book, which originated in Bradley's English lectures at Oxford University and elsewhere, can be regarded as one of the founding documents of the discipline of English as we know it: in explicating Shakespeare at Oxford, Bradley was acting as that university's first chair of English as opposed to classical literature; he was asserting for Shakespeare the same status as an object for academic scholarly inquiry as had long been granted to the great works of Greece and Rome.[4] The keystone of his method was interpretation through psychological insight. Of *Hamlet*, for example, he asserted that "the whole story turns upon the peculiar character of the hero. For without this character the story would appear sensational and horrible; and yet the actual *Hamlet* is very far from being so. . . . [I]f we had no knowledge of this character, the story would hardly be intelligible" (*Shakespearean Tragedy* [reprinted New York: Fawcett, 1965], p. 79). He proceeds through several chapters to analyze Hamlet as though he were an actual person in the grip of a devastating, disabling melancholy. Bradley, like Tillyard, has been enabling for many generations of university students. At age nineteen I found him almost as useful as Tillyard, though I note that, unlike Tillyard, Bradley is no longer available in paperback in the United States as of the writing of this essay. Perhaps *Shakespearean Tragedy* has run its course as a teaching aid at the undergraduate level. For the first several decades of the twentieth century, scholars could call upon Bradley as the basis for their own psychological or more explicitly psychoanalytic interpretations of the works of the Bard. Freudian readings of the plays saw Bradley as authorizing their own psychological studies of the characters as "real people." Shakespearean personalities seemed to possess a universality and transparency that made them available for study almost like a patient on a couch.

Within the last decade or so, psychoanalytic study of Shakespeare has become more complicated: now we are not only confronted with an array of competing methodologies for dealing with the analysis of the character, but the methods many of us favor no longer purport to "explain" human personality with the same assurance that earlier Bradleyan interpretation did. New historicists and cultural materialists take almost as much pleasure in Bradley-bashing as in Tillyard-bashing, on the grounds that there is no universal human nature, that Shakespeare's characters are constructs, not personalities, and that even if they were understood as personalities or "subjects," they would have to be understood within the parameters of their own quite alien culture, from which we are so distant that we cannot hope for complete understanding even if that were desirable. Practitioners of different modes of psychological criticism now construct such different "Shakespeares" that they can no longer be seen as talking within the same basic discursive field. As a case in point, we might contrast two just-published books with strong psychoanalytic methodological underpinnings: *Bargains with Fate: Psychological Crises and Conflicts in Shakespeare and His Plays*, by Bernard J. Paris, Ph.D. (note the use of the academic title)

(New York: Plenum Press, 1991), and *Staging the Gaze: Postmodernism, Psychoanalysis, and Shakespearean Comedy,* by Barbara Freedman (who also happens to have a Ph.D. degree but does not use the title) (Ithaca, N.Y.: Cornell University Press, 1991). Both books are post-Freudian in terms of methodology. Paris defends Bradley's character analysis and seeks to update it by using the psychoanalytic theories of Karen Horney; Paris's book is, in the manner of older Freudian studies, as much a showpiece for the advancement of his chosen interpretive method as it is an analysis of Shakespeare. The book aims at clarity—in terms of its own method, in terms of its capacity to enlighten readers about the motives and conflicts of Shakespearean heroes. In Paris's interpretation, the latter all make psychologically adaptive "bargains with fate" that establish rules for their interactions with the universe. When these bargains are broken, the tragic heroes adopt one or more of the defensive postures described in the writings of Horney.

Freedman's book could not be more different, based as it is on the theory of Jacques Lacan, and on the conviction that psychoanalytic inquiry can never lead to insight along the positivist lines of *Bargains with Fate.* Freedman asserts early on, "Putting to one side the issue of therapeutic value, let us assume that psychoanalysis is not a science and does not function like one. Rather than seek to secure a *place* for psychoanalysis, we might find value in its ability to *displace.* Since psychoanalytic theory studies that which by definition cannot be known (the unconscious), it holds philosophical interest as a self-subversive methodology in search of an object. As a critique of knowledge which subverts itself, psychoanalysis works through the problematics of the place of its own scene as a means of generating an awareness of blindness" (p. 37). Freedman's Shakespeare, accordingly, is an endless staging of the absence of self-presence, of blindness and erasure; the Renaissance stage itself cannot achieve the magic of presence. Shakespeare's comedies, Freedman's particular subject, rely on models of *"staging misrecognition* and on *staging* as *misrecognition"* (p. 110), on games of loss and retrieval at the perceptual level. Where Paris finds certainties, Freedman critiques the previous field of psychoanalytic interpretation of Shakespeare (by implication including Paris) in terms of the array of places in which different schools find their certainties—certainties which are, for Freedman, always illusory. *Bargains with Fate* and *Staging the Gaze* have nothing to say to each other. Shakespeare—even Shakespeare as psychoanalytic subject—is irretrievably split between the two critical views (not to mention others), forcing us, yet once more, to posit an array of Shakespeares constructed not only out of methodological difference, but out of a denial of the concept of self-identity by which we could imagine Shakespeare as a recognizable, single entity.

To what extent does or should such revisionist psychoanalysis find its way into the classroom? That will depend, of course, on the extent to which either the professor or the students are devotees of one or another psycho-analytic method. My own experience is that Bradleyan (or even Freudian) character analysis is, for now at least, too empowering an interpretive tool for students to be expected to give it up. Being able to "read" Shakespearean characters in terms of motives and underlying conflicts allows students to feel instantly more at ease with texts that may seem overwhelmingly alien at first: Only after a sense of dizzying historical distance has been over-come through their recognition of "common humanity" with the characters in the plays are students likely to be interested in exploring methodologies that presuppose a rejection of psychological verisimilitude. Nevertheless, the new methodologies hover about the edges of classroom discussion, in that it is much harder now than it used to be to psychoanalyze Shakespearean characters without asking hard historical questions. To what extent might the custom of arranged marriage, for instance, alter the presuppositions with which either partner would approach the bond of wedlock in *The Taming of the Shrew?* To what extent are oedipal readings of *Hamlet* or other Shakespearean plays anachronistic in that they are posited on post-Renaissance family models? To what extent might King Lear be displaying precisely the type of narcissistic personality structure that would be expect-ed in a successful Renaissance monarch? (One might think, for example, of Henry VIII, who had a similar tendency to banish wives and favorites for small derelictions of what he perceived as their duty.)

It is one of the seeming oddities of the recent critical scene that charac-ter study and psychoanalytic interpretation in a more-or-less traditional mode were being taken up by one prominent group of critics at just the moment when these methodologies were being rejected for their ahistoricity or deceptive aura of positivism by other groups of critics. I referring to feminist interpreters of Shakespeare like Coppélia Kahn, Janet Adelman, and some of the authors represented in the pioneering anthology *The Woman's Part: Feminist Criticism of Shakespeare,* ed. Carolyn Lenz, Gayle Green, and Carol Neely (Urbana: University of Illinois Press, 1980).[5] These feminist critics also belong among the "disestablishers" of Shakespeare in that they demonstrate the significant degree to which traditional construc-tion of Shakespeare has omitted women and gender issues from consideration—as though Shakespeare, being a white male, could only be approached from a white, male point of view. The first wave of Shakespearean feminist critics around 1980 were, like British cultural materialists, interested in appropriating Shakespeare for the woman's movement. Many of the essays in *The Woman's Part* find in Shakespeare all of the empathic traits that we women hoped to find in our men as we struggled to liberate ourselves and them from stereotyped sex roles. In his comedies, some of the essays contend, Shakespeare "attempts to move his male characters to a more mature level of functioning in which a woman may be loved as a complete human being" (p. 83); Shakespeare's *Taming of the Shrew* "does *not* preach the subjection of woman" (p. 67); Gertrude in *Hamlet* is "nurturant and loving" rather than the sexual monster portrayed by previous male criticism (p. 195). Given their task of bringing into prominence a whole vast area of the plays that had been passed over in previous criticism, it is not surprising that feminist Shakespeareans found character study in a seemingly old-fashioned mode essential to their project. In order to repair decades of neglect of woman characters and woman's issues in the plays, they had to make Shakespeare's women as real for their readers and students as Bradley and others had previously made the men.

More recent feminist work on Shakespeare has swung away from some of the first-wave optimism about Shakespeare's protofeminism. In more recent work by scholars like Patricia Parker (who also contributes in this series), Lynda Boose, Linda Woodbridge, Karen Newman, Dympna Callaghan, and Phyllis Rackin, Shakespeare is less hospitable towards women.[6] Recent work analyzes patriarchy in the plays along with its mechanisms for female suppression and explores sets of configurations by which women become purveyors of anti-culture. They are associated with matter as opposed to form and spirit, chaos and formlessness as opposed to structure; they are the object of considerable male anxiety on the part of Shakespeare and his culture about the containment of their subversive energies. Most devastatingly of all, in books like Mary Beth Rose's *The Expense of Spirit: Love and Sexuality in English Renaissance Drama* (Ithaca, N.Y.: Cornell University Press, 1988), Shakespeare as a historical figure is asserted to be highly conservative rather than liberated, by comparison with other dramatists of the period, in his portrayal of woman's roles and potentialities. Much recent feminist work is aimed squarely at the traditional idea of Shakespeare as a Universal. He can look that way, feminists argue, only from a perspective that assumes male dominance to be natural and universal. Instead, recent work in the area of gender studies is reducing

Shakespeare to one voice among many within Renaissance culture. And that voice is, more often than not, split—an array of different but overlapping voices.

The value of interrogating Shakespearean drama in terms of its portrayal of women can scarcely be overestimated in the classroom. It provides an almost instant recipe for successful discussion because it opens up the plays to ideological investigation of a kind that is immediately accessible to our students. Two-thirds or more of our English majors these days are women, and few of them have been untouched by modern feminism. Male students are scarcely less affected by recent alterations in expected gender roles, although their attitudes toward the present fluid situation are often frankly ambivalent. The multiplicity of recent feminist approaches to Shakespeare provides students with a rich interpretive matrix from which they can come to their own conclusions about the patterning of gender roles both within the plays and outside them.

A significant group within each of the critical movements we have considered so far emphasizes the importance of Shakespeare's historical milieu, the London theater—or rather the London playhouse, since the term *theater* suggests for us a high cultural status that the playhouse did not possess. There have, of course, been theater historians in every decade, but only within the last few years has the academic world begun to assimilate the implications of the fact that Shakespeare was a player, playwright, and businessman—not an author at all in our usual sense of the term. How could someone who wrote For All Time write for money? Yet that is what Shakespeare did. He wrote, and helped to write, plays for an institution that was essentially collaborative in nature. Our image of Shakespeare, drawn in large part from high modernist notions of artistic creativity, is of a heroic figure penning immortal verses in solitude, then releasing them to his company, where they might be mangled and sullied in performance. What we know about Renaissance theatrical practice, however, suggests that this image is a chimera. The Bard is likely to have worked collaboratively with other dramatists far more often than not. He is unlikely to have exerted strong proprietary control over his work at any stage: the scripts belonged to the company, and he seems to have made no effort to publish them himself or otherwise control their revision. He may have revised them himself, but less with an eye towards achieving some preconceived idea of perfection than with a desire to adapt to exigencies of the moment's casting problems, shifts in audience tastes and box office revenues, official displeasure, and threatened or actual censorship. I will not dwell on the mercurial, unstable Shakespeare—or rather Shakespeares—that emerge from a consideration of theatrical practices of the period, because issues of performance versus text emerge in this Lamont Shakespeare Series in the lectures by R. A. Foakes and John Wilders. What I would like to emphasize, however, is the impact of recent work on our conception of the Shakespearean text.

One of the most interesting ways in which Shakespeare has been "disestablished" is at the level of the very texts we read. In the late nineteenth century, perhaps as part of a broader desire for codification represented in such Herculean efforts as the creation of the *Oxford English Dictionary,* it began to be possible to speak of Shakespeare's texts as fixed and immutable, except for very minor variations between one edition and the next. E. D. Hirsch's list of Shakespeareana as part of "What Every American Needs to Know" is predicated on the fixity of the text: we can know what Shakespeare created. But that fixity has been more a product of gentlemanly agreement among scholars than of historical certainty about what Shakespeare wrote or intended. It has also been a product of a time-honored theory of copytext by which editors are free to combine substantive features from different authoritative early versions in order to create the "best" possible text, the text Shakespeare "intended." But what if Shakespeare never intended a single, fixed text? What we know about theatrical practice suggests he did not (and here, obviously, I am speaking of Shakespeare the shadowy historical personage, not "Shakespeare" the cultural institution). Recently, editors and other scholars have begun looking closely at the early Quarto and Folio texts of the plays with an eye toward discerning differences rather than creating an amalgamated whole. What they have been finding is that, even at the level of the texts, there are Shakespeares rather than Shakespeare—different versions of many of the plays. They appear to have been revised quite deliberately in order to meet different circumstances—changing climates of opinion or exigencies of performance.

The recent interrogation of traditional editorial practice began with the texts of *King Lear.* The Quarto published in 1608 is significantly different from the Folio version of 1623; the scholarly work of Steven Urkowitz, Michael Warren, and Gary Taylor makes a strong case for keeping the two versions separate and distinct, as indeed they are in Stanley Wells and Gary Taylor, eds., *William Shakespeare: The Complete Works* (Oxford: Clarendon Press, 1986).[7] Wells and Taylor reportedly would have liked to print two texts for several other plays in the Oxford edition if financial considerations had allowed. Although many new single-play editions look much like their older composite-text precursors, we can expect, indeed hope, that future editions will afford more respect to the integrity of the different early versions of the plays.

Why should we want to complicate the Shakespearean text in ways I have suggested? And how would we cope with ensuing complexities in the classroom? The attraction of the multiple-text critical movement is that it feels liberating to many Shakespearean scholars and editors. We have lived too long with the same old texts. To reinvestigate their origins and history is to throw off some of the hoary, if venerable, load of tradition that has come to feel burdensome in our consideration of Shakespeare. In all likelihood, as we blithely throw off the past we will also repeat the past. Anyone who has studied previous "disintegrators" of the Shakespearean text will recognize that the present movement has venerable antecedents, although previous "disintegrations" were concerned with preserving nuggets of "pure Shakespeare" in a way that recent editorial revisionists are not. The goal now is more and more to recognize the fecund multiplicity of what earlier scholars wanted to make unitary.

That is not to say that our standard composite texts of Shakespeare have lost their utility. In the undergraduate classroom particularly, we will continue to rely on them. My experience has been that while undergraduate students are captivated and intrigued by the idea that there may be more than one way for Hamlet to deliver "To be or not to be," or for *The Taming of the Shrew* to end, they cannot be expected to cope with dual versions of all the plays they read unless they read very few plays. A more successful way to introduce the idea of Shakespearean textual instability is by injecting bits and pieces of variant versions at key points in the discussion in a way that frees students to develop confidence in their own powers of interpretation, since they see that even the composite text itself does not possess the ultimate authority we tend to credit it with.

What has been gained by "disestablishing Shakespeare" in the ways I have discussed (among many others I could also have discussed)? I have already mentioned some specific ways in which disestablishing Shakespeare can influence work in the classroom, where our goal, presumably, is to get students to become familiar with and enjoy Shakespeare, but also to carry more than just Shakespeare away with them. Usually, the new approaches help make those things happen. Recently, however, some students have rebelled against the anti-idealizing tendency of much of the new critical work. They read Shakespeare, they say, in order to be uplifted; the new work does not help with that at all. Uplifted from what? I am always tempted to ask, thereby revealing my own skepticism about either the possibility or desirability of an art that is purely transcendent. But it never works to tell such students they are wrong. Rather, we need to respect their need to idealize, particularly to the extent that it signifies a desire for cultural empowerment. Much as early feminists found the grounds for subjectivism swept from beneath their feet by poststructuralist theory just at the moment that they wished to insert women's subjectivity and subjection into an ongoing discussion, so, by questioning students' appropriations of Shakespeare, we who "disestablish" Shakespeare in the classroom risk creating a new critical elitism that is just as exclusionary as the old.

What about the world outside the classroom? I am not at all certain that academic disestablishing of Shakespeare has had any impact upon society at large, or upon very real social problems, although I would like to think that it can and should, albeit not with the gratifying directness we would like. The scholarly movement to disestablish Shakespeare in the U.S. may be both cause and effect of the American democratization of Shakespeare to which I referred early on. But the movement (or movements) has also provoked a reactive reattachment on the part of some cultural critics to comfortable, traditional ways of conceptualizing Shakespeare. So long as no single group achieves a hegemonic voice on the subject, the atmosphere of vigorous contestation in which we find ourselves at present should be regarded as a sign of cultural health. The institutionalization of a "Disestablishment Shakespeare"—without the saving grace of the plural— would be as stultifying for intellectual and social growth as its opposite. Our hope should be that if "Shakespeare" continues to play the visible cultural role it plays at present, its effect will be to further the process of cultural democratization with which it seems to be associated just now. Our fear should be that there may be not a direct but an inverse relationship between the democratization of Shakespeare we are witnessing and broader social reform.

Notes

1. William J. Bennett, "To Reclaim a Legacy," *American Education* 21, no. 1 (1985): 19; Allan Bloom, *The Closing of the American Mind: How Higher Education has Failed Democracy and Impoverished the Souls of Today's Students* (New York: Simon & Schuster, 1987); E. D. Hirsch, *Cultural Literacy: What Every American Needs to Know* (New York: Vintage Books, 1988). For this specific assemblage of citations, I am indebted to Richard

Watkinson, "Shakespeare and Education—Texas Style," a paper submitted to my University of Texas graduate seminar "Reconstructing Shakespeare" in May 1991.

2.   See, in addition to the books cited in my text, Catherine Belsey, *The Subject of Tragedy: Identity and Difference in Renaissance Drama* (London: Methuen, 1985); Terry Eagleton, *William Shakespeare* (Oxford: Basil Blackwell, 1986); and Jonathan Dollimore and Alan Sinfield, eds., *Political Shakespeare: New Essays in Cultural Materialism* (Ithaca, N.Y.: Cornell University Press, 1985).

3.   For representative work, see Stephen Greenblatt, *Shakespearean Negotiations: The Circulation of Social Energy in Renaissance England* (Berkeley: University of California Press, 1988); Louis Montrose, "The Purpose of Playing: Reflections on a Shakespearean Anthropology," *Helios,* n.s. 7 (1980): 51–74, and "'Shaping Fantasies': Figurations of Gender and Power in Elizabethan Culture," *Representations* 1 (1983): 61–94; and Annabel Patterson, *Shakespeare and the Popular Voice* (Oxford: Basil Blackwell, 1989).

4.   See Terence Hawkes, *That Shakespeherian Rag: Essays on a Critical Process* (London: Methuen, 1986), 27–33.

5.   See in particular Coppélia Kahn, *Man's Estate: Masculine Identity in Shakespeare* (Berkeley: University of California Press, 1981); Janet Adelman, "'Anger's My Meat': Feeding, Dependency and Aggression in *Coriolanus,*" in *Shakespeare: Pattern of Excelling Nature,* ed. David Bevington and Jay Halio (Newark: University of Delaware Press, 1978), 108–24, reprinted in *Representing Shakespeare,* ed. Murray M. Schwartz and Coppélia Kahn (Baltimore: Johns Hopkins University Press, 1980), 129–49; and "'Born of Woman': Fantasies of Maternal Power in *Macbeth,*" in *Cannibals, Witches, and Divorce: Estranging the Renaissance,* ed. Marjorie Garber (Baltimore: Johns Hopkins University Press, 1987), 90–121.

6.   See, for example, Patricia Parker, *Literary Fat Ladies: Rhetoric, Gender, Property* (London: Methuen, 1987); Lynda Boose, "The Father and the Bride in Shakespeare," *PMLA* 97 (1982): 325–47; Linda Woodbridge, *Women and the English Renaissance: Literature and the Nature of Womankind 1540–1620* (Urbana: University of Illinois Press, 1984); Karen Newman, *Refashioning Femininity and English Renaissance Drama* (Chicago: University of Chicago Press, 1991); Dympna Callaghan, *Women and Gender in Renaissance Tragedy: A Study of King Lear, Othello, The Duchess of Malfi, and The White Devil* (New York and London: Harvester Wheatsheaf, 1989); Phyllis Rackin, "Women as Anti-Historians: Women's Roles in Shakespeare's Histories," *Theater Journal* 37 (1985): 329–44.

7.   Stephen Urkowitz, *Shakespeare's Revision of King Lear* (Princeton: Princeton University Press, 1980); Gary Taylor and Michael Warren, eds., *The Division of the Kingdoms: Shakespeare's Two Versions of King Lear* (Oxford: Clarendon Press, 1983); and Stephen Orgel's influential general article, "The Authentic Shakespeare," *Representations* 21 (1988): 1–26.

Teaching Textual Variation:
Hamlet and *King Lear*

LEAH MARCUS

Workshop

Last night in my lecture, "Disestablishing Shakespeare," I addressed the idea that there is not one set text for many of Shakespeare's plays, but instead an array of early texts. Depending on which early text we happen to read, we may end up interpreting Shakespeare quite differently. I would like to explore this subject further today by looking at short passages from *Hamlet* and *King Lear*. Part of the point of our little exercise will be to demonstrate ways in which our reaction to a given text may depend in part on the form in which it is presented to us.

For *Hamlet,* let us look at two versions of "To be or not to be" from *The Riverside Shakespeare,* edited by G. Blakemore Evans (Boston: Houghton Mifflin, 1974). The first one (figure 3) offers you the soliloquy as it appears in the text. The second one (figure 4) is taken from the textual notes to the same Riverside edition; it offers you "'To be, or not to be" again, but this time from the 1603 Quarto—the so-called "Bad" Quarto of the play. You will note immediately that the "Bad" Quarto version is given without verse lineation and in the Quarto's original spelling, while the standard text is properly printed as blank verse, and in a much more standardized spelling. The 1603 Quarto's very presentation in the textual notes makes it appear less trustworthy, less "right" than the authoritative version of the speech.

Let me describe a little of what people have thought in the past about these two different versions of Hamlet's famous soliloquy. Until around the turn of the twentieth century, there was fairly wide critical and editorial consensus that the 1603 version was an early text of the play—Shakespeare's rough draft or earliest attempt. What happened according to this scenario is that Shakespeare gradually refined the text and made it longer and more complex, coming up with the Second Quarto version, which was published

Enter HAMLET.

Ham. To be, or not to be, that is the question: 55
Whether 'tis nobler in the mind to suffer
The slings and arrows of outrageous fortune,
Or to take arms against a sea of troubles,
And by opposing, end them. To die, to sleep—
No more, and by a sleep to say we end 60
The heart-ache and the thousand natural shocks
That flesh is heir to; 'tis a consummation
Devoutly to be wish'd. To die, to sleep—
To sleep, perchance to dream—ay, there's the rub,
For in that sleep of death what dreams may come, 65
When we have shuffled off this mortal coil,
Must give us pause; there's the respect
That makes calamity of so long life:
For who would bear the whips and scorns of time,
Th' oppressor's wrong, the proud man's contumely, 70
The pangs of despis'd love, the law's delay,
The insolence of office, and the spurns
That patient merit of th' unworthy takes,
When he himself might his quietus make
With a bare bodkin; who would fardels bear, 75
To grunt and sweat under a weary life,
But that the dread of something after death,
The undiscover'd country, from whose bourn
No traveller returns, puzzles the will,
And makes us rather bear those ills we have, 80
Than fly to others that we know not of?
Thus conscience does make cowards [of us all],
And thus the native hue of resolution
Is sicklied o'er with the pale cast of thought,
And enterprises of great pitch and moment 85
With this regard their currents turn awry,
And lose the name of action.—Soft you now,
The fair Ophelia. Nymph, in thy orisons
Be all my sins rememb'red.

Fig. 3. "To be or not to be" from *The Riverside Shakespeare* **(Courtesy of Houghton Mifflin)**

55-89 To . . . rememb'red.] *This soliloquy appears in the following form in Q1:* To be. or not to be, I there's the point, /: To Die. to sleepe, is that all? I all: / No, to sleepe, to dreame, I mary there it goes, / For in that dreame of death, when wee awake, / And borne before an euerlasting Iudge, / From whence no passenger euer retur'nd, / The vndiscouered country, at whose sight / The happy smile, and the accursed damn'd. / But for this, the ioyfull hope of this, / Whol'd beare the scornes and flattery of the world, / Scorned by the right rich, the rich curssed of the poore? / The widow being oppressed, the orphan wrong'd, / The taste of hunger, or a tirants raigne, / And thousand more calamities besides, / To grunt and sweate vnder this weary life, / When that he may his full *Quietus* make, / With a bare bodkin, who would this indure, / But for a hope of something after death? / Which pusles the braine, and doth confound the sence, / Which makes vs rather beare those euilles we haue, / Than flie to others that we know not of. / I that, O this conscience makes cowardes of vs all, / Lady in thy orizons, be all my sinnes remembred. (*Q1 places this soliloquy, and the interview between Hamlet and Ophelia which follows, in II.ii after the equivalent of ll. 169-70;* Der bestrafte Brudermord, *though it omits the soliloquy, also places the Hamlet-Ophelia interview essentially as in Q1*)

Fig. 4. "To be or not to be," "Bad Quarto" version, from *The Riverside Shakespeare* (Courtesy of Houghton Mifflin)

in 1604, only a year after the First or "Bad" Quarto appeared in print. The Second Quarto, according to its title page, offered the play "enlarged to almost as much againe as it was, according to the true and perfect Coppie." There is yet another early version of *Hamlet* different from the two quartos, the First Folio version of the play, published in 1623. As I'm sure your regular instructor has made you aware, Shakespeare quartos are small, easily carried texts of single plays—rather like modern paperbacks. The First Folio was large and impressive—it offered Shakespeare's complete dramatic works and helped to create the veneration for Shakespeare that has lasted until the present. Nevertheless, for *Hamlet*, the Folio version is not the preferred text. Most editors have traditionally regarded it as inferior to the Second Quarto. The standard Riverside text that you have here is based primarily on the Second Quarto version, with some readings borrowed from the First Folio and from later editions of the play.

As I mentioned a minute ago, the idea that the 1603 version of the play was Shakespeare's first crack at *Hamlet* was predominant even as recently as the beginning of the twentieth century. In 1904 A. C. Bradley was able to write about *Hamlet* in his highly influential book *Shakespearean Tragedy* as though everybody agreed that the 1603 Quarto was indeed an early version of the play. During the next thirty years, though, something interesting happened. By the time John Dover Wilson published his equally influential book *What Happens in Hamlet* in 1935, he was able to assume that everyone agreed with his opinion that the 1603 Quarto was not Shakespeare's original version of the speech, but instead a corrupt copy put together by inferior players as a way of making a bit of extra money by performing and/or publishing the play without the author's consent.

This may seem like a small difference to you, but its implications are far-reaching. An early Shakespearean draft is of much greater interest than a mere stolen and corrupted copy. You can say that an early version is valuable because it gives us the author's first thoughts on a subject, and allows us to see how his ideas develop. A corrupt copy, on the other hand, at least in the view of most editors since Wilson, is practically worthless. So much critical energy during the last fifty years has gone into "proving" the inferiority of the 1603 quarto version that we may wonder why it hasn't been thrown out. *The Riverside Shakespeare* is unusual among modern classroom editions because it at least gives you the text of the 1603 version of "To be, or not to be" in the notes. But compared to the polished, standard text in the play itself, the 1603 version as printed in the notes looks like a hodgepodge, which makes it hard to regard the text as anything else but a hodgepodge, a corrupt copy. Recently, though, there has been a revival of interest in the so-called "Bad" Quarto of *Hamlet*. It has been performed quite successfully. Readers have begun to notice that it is not quite so incoherent as editors since Wilson have liked to suggest. Today, I would like us to experiment with reading both versions of "To be, or not to be" as parallel rather than "better" and "worse" texts. We will nobly suspend aesthetic judgment and not worry too much about which version is earlier and which later. How "bad" will the 1603 Quarto look then?

Let's begin by comparing the two versions. You'll notice that the first line from the 1603 version goes "To be, or not to be, I [aye] there's the point." Everyone knows that the famous line "should" read, "To be, or not to be, that is the question," as in the standard text. If you were to stand up on stage during a performance of the standard text and declaim, "To be, or not to be, I there's the point" the audience would probably laugh heartily at your expense. But what would they be laughing at? How much of our traditional derision toward the 1603 text is a matter of convention—based on our own social and aesthetic expectations built up over several centuries—about what Hamlet is supposed to sound like? Why doesn't everybody take five minutes or so to look over the two versions of the soliloquy? I warn you that if you read the 1603 version with the expectation of getting it to look like the standard text, you will be disappointed. You should feel completely free to consult with each other. Please take into account the fact that the 1603 text is in old spelling, whereas the other is neatly polished and modernized.

Okay, has everybody had enough time? Yes?

Aud.: It seems that the very first line "To be, or not to be . . . " is a question. It seems like a corruption to say that it is a "point" as in the 1603 version.

Marcus: Aha! So "To be, or not to be" is a question Hamlet is asking himself, not a statement?

Aud.: Well, if that's true, I'm wondering why there isn't a question mark after "not to be" in the standard text, if it is definitely a question.

Marcus: Yes, that's interesting. Why not? We can't assume that Shakespeare put a question mark there, and there is no question mark in either the Second Quarto or Folio versions, on which the Riverside text is based. The Second Quarto has a comma and the Folio has a colon. Often these early texts do not have a question mark when we would expect one, but that certainly leaves open the status of the line. Is it a question or not?

Aud.: I disagree with the idea that the line has to be a question. How could there be a question mark there? When it goes on it says [in the standard text] "whether 'tis nobler in the mind to suffer / The slings and

arrows of outrageous fortune, / Or to take arms against a sea of troubles
. . . " He is providing a dual argument. Both sides are expressed. Because
he says "To be, or not to be, that is the question" doesn't mean he is asking
a question. He's developing the argument, making the point that you can
go both ways, being and not being, and he hasn't decided which way to go.
On the other hand, I think that in the Quarto of 1603, when he says, "To be,
or not to be, I there's the point," he is clearly making a statement. It's not a
question whether one is better than the other. You can only do one, and
Hamlet has to decide.

Marcus: You're providing a good argument in defense of the wording
of the "Bad" Quarto of 1603. If you wanted to defend this version of "To
be, or not to be," Hamlet's need to decide could be the issue. In the 1603
version, Hamlet has to make up his mind one way or the other. You could
call the first line a question, as Hamlet does in the later version, or you
could call it the "point" of the problem, as he terms it in the 1603 version.

Aud.: Yes, but see, I'm still undecided between the two texts. I think
it's important that the "To be, or not to be" argument is kept open. I think
the 1603 version is too closed.

Marcus: Yes. One of Hamlet's problems throughout much of the play
is whether or not to act to avenge his father's murder, and also whether or
not to commit suicide. Later on in both versions of the soliloquy, he considers whether "he himself might his quietus make / With a bare bodkin." The
bodkin is, of course, a dagger—he seems to be entertaining the possibility
that he can solve his own problems of existence by doing himself in. What
interests me particularly, however, is that his arguments against suicide are
quite different in the two versions. For example, what image of the afterlife
do we get in the two versions?

Aud.: One is dread and one is hope.

Marcus: Yes indeed. One is dread and one is hope. Which is which?

Aud.: Hope is in the corrupt [1603] version. And dread is in the standard version.

Marcus: So if the afterlife is imagined differently in the two versions,
then the whole argument Hamlet is making might need to be different in
the two. Right? Why don't you see if you can figure that out? In the earlier
version, we learn the contents of Hamlet's dream. In the standard version,
the dream is left mysterious. The "Bad" Quarto reads,

> For in that dreame of death, when wee awake,
> And borne before an euerlasting Iudge,
> From whence no passenger euer retur'nd,

> The vndiscouered country, at whose sight
> The happy smile, and the accursed damn'd.

The standard version reads,

> For in that sleep of death what dreams may come,
> When we have shuffled off this mortal coil,
> Must give us pause . . .
> . . . the dread of something after death,
> The undiscover'd country, from whose bourn
> No traveller returns, puzzles the will,
> And makes us rather bear those ills we have,
> Than fly to others that we know not of?

Aud.: In one conception of the afterlife, there is a God who punishes those who sin with hardships and self-slaughter, and in the other, there is a God who rewards those who endure the hardships of life.

Marcus: You're saying that the God who rewards . . .

Aud.: . . . the God who rewards is the one in the corrupt version. In its conception of the afterlife, there is a much more promising implication—that it's worth bearing all "the scorns and flattery" and so on because there *is* a reward.

Marcus: Yes, indeed. "But for this, the ioyfull hope of this, / Whol'd beare the scornes and flattery of the world, / Scorned by the right rich, the rich curssed of the poore?" So it goes on.

Aud.: What's funny is the way the hope changes in the corrupt version. It's very positive at first: "The happy smile" because they know where they are going, and the cursed are damned. And with "this, the ioyfull hope of this" they gear their actions. But then you get to the hope further down: "But for a hope of something after death?" Why would we endure all this for hope of something after death? Then you get into the statement "which pusles the braine"—which I assume refers to the hope. But I'm not positive. And with "doth confound the sence," the hope begins to be undercut.

Marcus: I think you need to read "But for" in its common Renaissance sense of "Except for." He's arguing that it is better to bear the ills of this life than risk unknown evils in the afterlife. The hope is undercutting something else, such as the possibility of sinning further by taking one's own life.

Aud.: Okay. And then there is this funny kind of conclusion: "Which makes vs rather beare those euilles we haue / Than flie to others that we know not of." I think that's where the most puzzling parts of the soliloquy come. And then, of course, conscience—"O this conscience"—becomes something very different, because you're almost willing at this point to associate with hope the thing that "makes cowardes of vs all."

Marcus: I think so. The 1603 text offers a more straightforward picture: you have a more visibly Christian universe in which good people are rewarded and bad people are damned. What you do on this earth relates to what happens to you in the afterlife. In this version, the lines "Which makes vs rather beare those evilles we haue, / Than flie to others that we know not of" refer to the possible evil consequences of our actions. Hamlet is musing, "If I act, if I do this dreadful deed of killing Claudius, what I will be doing is putting myself in mortal jeopardy for no particular gain." So the uncertainty relates to this life. When it comes to the afterlife, Hamlet envisions almost total certainty. That is, he does in the "corrupt" version of the speech.

Aud.: In the standard version, the polished version, he seems to be getting more of that sense of uncertainty throughout: he says not "I there's the point," but "There's the question," as if there's a problem. The other passage seems to be all very cut and dried. I definitely sense that clearcutness in the less polished [1603] version, while in the polished version I sense more a focus on puzzling the will as the problem.

Marcus: What it comes down to in part in choosing between the two is the matter of uncertainty. How do we feel about certainty and uncertainty? With the First Quarto version, the more you look at it, the more answers you get. In the standard version that we're used to reading, all Hamlet says is "For in that sleep of death what dreams may come, / When we have shuffled off this mortal coil, / Must give us pause." We are left in total uncertainty, as he is.

Aud.: He says, "Must give us pause."

Marcus: "Must give us pause." And what kind of dreams is he talking about?

Aud.: In the standard version it's a "sleep of death." It's not just any old dream, but a sleep of death.

Marcus: Yes. And what happens after the death—the dreaded something after death? It is "The undiscover'd country, from whose bourn / No traveller returns." I don't want to call this version pagan, necessarily, but it is totally uncertain about the afterlife. Totally undecided. Does that make it more defensible or less so in your view? How do you feel about undecidability?

Aud.: Is the undecidability the question of whether or not to commit suicide or what? I'm not really sure what he's undecided about: his attitude towards suicide or his attitude towards something else?

Marcus: That's certainly an important distinction. The answer is, both. Particularly if you compare the standard text with the more decisive Hamlet of the 1603 version, in the standard text there seems to be very little that he is not undecided about. What I'm concerned with is the strong probability that we have tended to prefer the more polished version because it fits in with our twentieth-century agnosticism, our doubt, and because, in fact, it has represented the essence of *Hamlet* for fifty years in our culture. It's precisely that sense of doubt that has made *Hamlet* seem so modern to us, and it was during the heyday of modernism as a literary movement that the general consensus shifted from regarding the 1603 version as Shakespeare's earliest version to regarding it as a totally corrupt text. So when we get a Hamlet who suddenly understands the basic pattern of the universe, we say, "Wait, that can't be Hamlet. That's no Hamlet that I recognize."

Aud.: I think the unpolished [1603] version is more personal to the individual. As you read that first line "To be, or not to be, I" maybe if this punctuation hasn't been worked on, that "I" is really on the other side of the comma. Now you're not talking necessarily about death, but about identity.

Marcus: You're saying that instead of mentally translating "I" to "Aye," we might be able to interpret it as the first-person singular pronoun. It's not a strong possibility, but certainly worth exploring. One of the interesting things about working with the early texts is that such multiple possibilities for meaning based on Renaissance orthography suddenly emerge.

Aud.: It makes the speech more interesting in general: instead of a question of life versus death, it's a question of "Who am I?"

Marcus: Would you do the same thing with the next "I": "To Die, to sleepe, is that all? I all"?

Aud.: Well, you can look at it that way. If he is the measure of all things —if as a person he is everything—then, to die is to be completely gone. To change his identity, he's losing a great deal: the name, the identity, is the most important thing. So to get rid of his identity, will all, then, be worthless?

Marcus: And what you're saying then is that in a way, this orthography, which looks like a terrible mistake—spelling A-Y-E as I—is allowing you the possibility of that reading?

Aud.: Right.

Marcus: Yes, that's one of the really interesting things that people have been suggesting in general about the so-called corrupt texts. That sometimes what appear to be mistakes in spelling, if you regard them instead as interesting puzzles, open up other possibilities for meaning. In the Stephen Booth edition of *Shakespeare's Sonnets* (New Haven: Yale University Press, 1977), for example—which gives the modern spellings on one side and the old spellings on the other side—exactly that kind of thing happens. You see other possibilities for meaning that got edited out when editors decided that the text had to have modern spelling or even consistent spelling.

As a result of all of this discussion, are you starting to like the poor, homely old First Quarto of *Hamlet* a little bit better? Is there anybody here who gets impatient with people who are always muddling about indecisively? Anyone here who would really prefer to see a little more action and definition? That's the way *Hamlet* reads in the 1603 version, and there seems to be a tendency recently to value this version more highly than in the heyday of Modernism. I know many of my graduate students at the University of Texas and previously at the University of Wisconsin have thought the 1603 version is more successful dramatically: in terms of larger patterns of action, as in terms of the single soliloquy we've looked at today, the "corrupt" *Hamlet* gets straight to the point while the standard version dithers around. What a heretical thing to say! But that's a view that I see emerging. As a matter of fact, in actual theatrical productions of the play, the order of scenes is often changed from that of the standard version to an order much closer to that of the "corrupt" 1603 text. Indecisiveness doesn't necessarily work well on stage. But rather than explore the interesting differences among versions of *Hamlet* further, we need to move on to *King Lear*.

For our brief discussion of *King Lear*, I'm offering you handouts showing the First Quarto and First Folio versions of the last scene of the play arranged as parallel texts (figure 5). You'll notice that this time the case is not weighted in favor of either version as it was with the Riverside *Hamlet*—the two texts receive the same treatment, and both are in old spelling with the original punctuation and line divisions. You will have trouble at first with the long *s* [ʃ] which is a bit of a pain, but otherwise I hope you will find the two fairly legible, particularly since you are already familiar with the play. This parallel text edition is almost a hundred years old: its full title is *King Lear: Parallel Texts of the First Quarto and the First Folio, Edited for the Use of University Classes, &c.*, ed. Wilhelm Vietor, revised ed. (Marburg: N. G. Elwert'sche Verlagsbuchhandlung, 1892). It's interesting that after a hundred years, such a grizzled old teaching aid might become useful once again. I thought that, given the shortness of our time, an edition using modern typography might be easier for you to work with than the Quarto and Folio texts themselves, although I think you will discover, if you ever do look at them in facsimile, that you can read them fairly easily. Try it some time!

Just a word about the two versions of *King Lear*, which I discussed in very general terms in last night's lecture. The text on the left is the First Quarto, published in 1608; the text on the right is the First Folio version (1623). Neither is presently considered a "bad" text, although they are certainly different. As I mentioned last night, there has been a recent movement to regard both versions as Shakespearean, the Folio version as revised by Shakespeare himself from the Quarto version of the play. What we will be looking for here is, again, variation in meaning. How is reading the play in two parallel versions different from reading the standard text of the play, which conflates the two?

Has everyone had a chance to look at both versions? What differences do you see here?

Aud.: Differences in punctuation.

Marcus: Yes. In general the Quarto version is much less actively punctuated. It tends to separate everything with commas, which some editors used to view as a sign of textual corruption, although the First Quarto of *King Lear* is much more highly regarded by most editors than the "Bad" Quarto of *Hamlet*. More recently, scholars have interpreted sparse punctuation of this kind as deliberate on Shakespeare's part, and as giving more freedom to the actors. It gives you the words, but it leaves up to you where you want to put the intonation and emphasis—how you want to shape the speech. Why don't we talk about Kent first. In the Quarto version, we get this image of Kent:

> He fastened on my necke and bellowed out,
> As hee'd burst heauen, threw me on my father,
> Told the most pitious tale of *Lear* and him,
> That euer eare receiued, which in recounting
> His griefe grew puissant and the strings of life,
> Began to cracke twice . . .

Excuse me—"Began to cracke," period. I think in delivering the lines, you would want to put your imaginary punctuation after "cracke" and then say, "twice then the trumpets sounded / And there I left him traunst [tranced]."

V. iii.

Make inftruments to fcourge vs tho darke and vitious
Place where thee he gotte, coft him his eies.

    Baſt. Thou haft fpoken truth, tho wheele is come
full circled I am heore.
    Alb. Me thought thy very gate did prophecie,
A royall nobleneffe I muft embrace thee.
Let forow fplit my heart if I did euer hate thee or thy father.

    Edg. Worthy Prince I know't.   [78
    Alb. Where haue you hid your felfe?
180 How haue you knowne the miferies of your father?
    Edg. By nurfing them my Lord,
Lift a briefe tale, and when tis told
O that my heart would burft the bloudy proclamation
To efcape that followed me fo neere,
O our liues fweetnes, that with the paine of death,
Would hourly die, rather then die at once.
Taught me to fhift into a mad-mans rage
To affume a femblance that very dogges difdain'd
And in this habit met I my father with his bleeding rings,
190 The precious ftones new loft became his guide,
Led him, beg'd for him, fau'd him from difpaire,
Neuer (O Father) reueald my felfe vnto him,
Vntill fome halfe houre paft, when I was armed,
Not fure, though hoping of this good fucceffe,
I aſkt his bleffing, and from firft to laft,
Told him my pilgrimage, but his fluwd heart,
Alacke too weake, tho conflict to fupport,
Twixt two extreames of paffion, ioy and griefe,
Burft fmillingly.
    Baſt. This fpeeoh of yours hath moued me,
200 And fhall perchance do good, but fpeake you on,
You looke as you had fomething more to fay,
    Alb. If there be more, more wofull, hold it in,
For I am almoft ready to diffolue, hearing of this,

    Edg. This would haue feemd a periode to fuch
As loue not forow, but another to amplifie too much,
Would make much more, and top extreamitie
Whil'ft I was big in clamor, came there in a man,
Who hauing feene me in my worft eftate,
210 Shund my abhord fociety, but then finding

Fig. 5. Parallel Texts of *King Lear* from the Vietor edition (1892)

Make inftruments to plague vs:
The darke and vitious place where thee he got,
Coft him his eyes.

    Baft. Th'haft fpoken right, 'tis true,
The Wheele is come full circle, I am heere.

    Alb. Me thought thy very gate did prophefie
A Royall Noblenesse: I muft embrace thee,
Let forrow fplit my heart, if euer I
Did hate thee, or thy Father.

    Edg. Worthy Prince I know't.

    Alb. Where haue you hid your felfe?

180 How haue you knowne the miferies of your Father?

    Edg. By nurfing them my Lord. Lift a breefe tale,
And when 'tis told, O that my heart would burft.
The bloody proclamation to efcape
That follow'd me fo neere, (O our liues fweetneffe,
That we the paine of death would hourely dye,
Rather then die at once) taught me to fhift
Into a mad-mans rags, t'affume a femblance
That very Dogges difdain'd: and in this habit
Met I my Father with his bleeding Rings,

190 Their precious Stones new loft: became his guide,
Led him, begg'd for him, fau'd him from difpaire.
Neuer (O fault) reueal'd my felfe vnto him,
Vntill fome halfe houre paft when I was arm'd,
Not fure, though hoping of this good fucceffe,
I ask'd his bleffing, and from firft to laft
Told him our pilgrimage. But his flaw'd heart
(Alacke too weake the conflict to fupport)
'Twixt two extremes of paffion, ioy and greefe,
Burft fmilingly.

    Bast. This fpeech of yours hath mou'd me,

200 And fhall perchance do good, but fpeake you on,
You looke as you had fomething more to fay.

    Alb. If there be more, more wofull, hold it in,
For I am almoft ready to diffolue,
Hearing of this.

Who twas that fo indur'd with his ftrong armes
He faftened on my necke and bellowed out,
As heed burft heauen, throw me on my father,
Told the moft pitious tale of *Lear* and him,
That euer eare receiued, which in recounting
His griefe grew puiffant and the ftrings of life,   [79
Begun to cracke twice, then the trumpets founded.
And there I left him traunft.
    Alb. But who was this.

220   *Ed.* Kent fir, the banifht *Kent,* who in diguife,
Followed his enemie king and did him feruice
Improper for a flaue.
          Enter one with a bloudie knife,
    Gent. Helpe, helpe,   (knife?
    Alb. What kind of helpe, what meanes that bloudy

    Gent. Its hot it fmokes, it came euen from the heart of-

    Alb. Who man, fpeake?
    Gent. Your Lady fir, your Lady, and her fifter
By her is poyfoned, fhe hath confeft it.
    Baft. I was contracted to them both, all three
Now marie in an inftant.

230   *Alb.* Produce their bodies, be they aliue or dead,

This Iuftice of the heauens that makes vs tremble,
Touches vs not with pity.   *Edg.* Here comes *Kent* fir.
    Alb O tis he, the time will not allow   *Enter Kent*
The complement that very manners vrges.
    Kent. I am come to bid my King and maifter ay good night,

Is he not here?
    Duke. Great thing of vs forgot,
Speake *Edmund,* where the king, and where *Cordelia*
Seeft thou this obiect *Kent.*   *The bodies of Gonorill and*
    Kent. Alack why thus.   *Regan are brought in.*
    Baft. Yet *Edmund* was beloued,
240 The one the other poyfoned for my fake,
And after flue her felfe.   *Duke.* Euen fo, couer their faces.

Enter a Gentleman.

Gen. Helpe, helpe: O helpe.

Edg. What kinde of helpe?

Alb. Speake man.

Edg. What meanes this bloody Knife?

Gen. 'Tis hot, it fmoakes, it came euen from the heart
of —— O fhe's dead.

Alb. Who dead? Speake man.

Gen. Your Lady Sir, your Lady; and her Sifter
By her is poyfon'd: fhe confeffes it.

Baſt. I was contracted to them both, all three
Now marry in an inftant.

Edg. Here comes *Kent*.

Enter Kent.

230   *Alb.* Produce the bodies, be they aliue or dead;

Gonerill and Regans bodiesbrought out.

This iudgement of the Heauens that makes vs tremble.
Touches vs not with pitty: O, is this he?
The time will not allow the complement
Which very manners vrges.

Kent. I am come
To bid my King and Mafter aye good night.
Is he not here?

Alb. Great thing of vs forgot,
Speake *Edmund*, where's the King? and where's *Cordelia*?
Seeſt thou this obiect *Kent*?

Kent. Alacke, why thus?

Baſt. Yet *Edmund* was belou'd:

240   The one the other poifon'd for my fake,
And after flew herfelfe.

Alb. Euen fo: couer their faces.

V. iii.

Baſt. I pant for life, ſome good I meane to do,
Deſpight of my owne nature, quickly ſend,
Be briefe, int toth' caſtle for my writ,
Is on the life of *Lear* and on *Cordelia*,
Nay ſend in time.   *Duke.* Runne, runne, O runne.

Edg. To who my Lord, who hath the office, ſend
Thy token of repreeue.

250   *Baſt.* Well thought on, take my ſword the Captaine,
Giue it the Captaine?   *Duke.* Haſt thee for thy life. [80

Baſt. He hath Commiſſion from thy wife and me,
To hang *Cordelia* in the priſon, and to lay
The blame vpon her owne deſpaire,
That ſhe fordid her ſelfe.
    Duke. The Gods defend her, beare him hence a while.
       Enter Lear with Cordelia in his armes.
    Lear. Howle, howle, howle, howle, O you are men of ſtones,
Had I your tongues and eyes, I would vſe them ſo,
That heauens vault ſhould cracke, ſhees gone for euer,
260 I know when one is dead, and when one liues,
Shees dead as earth, lend me a looking glaſſe,
If that her breath will miſt or ſtaine the ſtone,
Why then ſhe liues.   *Kent.* Is this the promiſt end.

Edg. Or image of that horror.   *Duke.* Fall and ceaſe.

Lear. This feather ſtirs ſhe liues, if it be ſo,
It is a chance which do's redeeme all ſorowes
That euer I haue felt.   *Kent.* A my good maiſter.

Lear. Prethe away?   *Edg.* Tis noble *Kent* your friend.

Lear. A plague vpon your murderous traytors all,
270 I might haue ſaued her, now ſhees gone for euer,
Cordelia, Cordelia, ſtay a little, ha,
What iſt thou ſayoſt, her voyce was euer ſoft,
Gentle and low, an excellent thing in women,
I kild the ſlaue that was a hanging thee.
    Cap. Tis true my Lords, he did.
    Lear. Did I not fellow? I haue ſeene the day,
With my good biting Fauchon I would
Haue made them skippe, I am old now,

Baſt. Ipant for life: ſome good I meane to do
Deſpight of mine owne Nature. Quickly ſend,
(Be briefe in it) to'th' Caſtle, for my Writ
Is on the life of *Lear*, and on *Cordelia*:
Nay, ſend in time.

Alb. Run, run, O run.

Edg. To who my Lord? Who ha's the Office?
Send thy token of repreeue.

250   *Bast.* Well thought on, take my Sword,
Giue it the.Captaine.

Edg. Haſt thee for thy life.

Baſt. He hath Commiſſion from thy Wife and me,
To hang *Cordelia* in the priſon, and
To lay the blame vpon her owne diſpaire,
That ſhe for-did her ſelfe.

Alb. The Gods defend her, beare him hence awhile.

Enter Lear with Cordelia in his armes.

Lear. Howle, howle, howle: O your are men of ſtones,
Had I your tongues and eyes, Il'd vſe them ſo,
That Heauens vault ſhould crack: ſhe's gone for euer.

260   I know when one is dead, and when one liues,
She's dead as earth: Lend me a Looking-glaſſe,,
If that her breath will miſt or ſtaine the ſtone,
Why then ſhe liues.   [309a

Kent. Is this the promis'd end?

Edg. Or image of that horror.

Alb. Fall and ceaſe.

Lear This feather ſtirs, ſhe liues: if it be ſo,
It is a chance which do's redeeme all ſorrowes
That euer I haue felt.

Kent. O my good Maſter.

Lear. Prythee away.

Edg. 'Tis Noble *Kent* your Friend.

Lear. A plague vpon you Murderors, Traitors all,

270   I might haue ſau'd her, now ſhe's gone for euer:
Cordelia, Cordelia, ſtay a little. Ha:
What is't thou ſaiſt? Her voice was euer ſoft,
Gentle, and low, an excellent thing in woman.
I kill'd the Slaue that was a hanging thee.

Gent. 'Tis true (my Lords) he did.

Lear. Did I not fellow?
I haue ſeene the day, with my good biting Faulchion
I would haue made him skip: I am old now,

V. iii.

And thefe fame croffes fpoyle me, who are you?
Mine eyes are not othe beft, ile tell you ftraight.

280   *Kent.* If Fortune bragd of two fho loued or hated,
One of them we behold.   *Lear.* Are not you *Kent?*

Kent. The fame your feruant *Kent,* where is your feruant *Caius,*

Lear. Hees a good fellow, I can tell that,
Heele ftrike and quickly too, hees dead and rotten.
   Kent. No my good Lord, I am the very man.
   Lear. Ile fee that ftraight.
   Kent. That from your life of difference and decay,   [81
Haue followed your fad fteps.   *Lear.* You'r welcome hither.

290   *Kent.* Nor no man elfe, als chearles, darke and deadly,

Your eldeft daughters haue foredoome themfelues,
And defperatly are dead.   *Lear.* So thinke I to.

Duke. He knowes not what he fees, and vaine it is,
That we prefent vs to him.   *Edg.* Very bootleffe.   *Enter*
  Capt. *Edmund* is dead my Lord.   *Captaine.*

Duke. Thats but a trifle heere, you Lords and noble friends,
Know our intent, what comfort to this decay may come, fhall be
applied: for vs we wil refigne during the life of this old maiefty,
300 to him our abfolute power, you to your rights with boote, and
fuch addition as your honor haue more then merited, all friends
fhall taft the wages of their vertue, and al foes the cup of their deferuings, O fee, foe.

Lear. And my poore foole is hangd, no, no life, why fhould a
dog, a horfe, a rat of life and thou no breath at all, O thou wilt
come no more, neuer, neuer, neuer, pray you vndo this button,
thanke you fir, O, o, o, o.   *Edg.* He faints my Lord, my Lord.

And thefe fame croffes fpoile me. Who are you?
Mine eyes are not o'th'beft, Ile tell you ftraight.

280 *Kent.* If Fortune brag of two, fhe lou'd and hated,
One of them we behold.

Lear. This is a dull fight, are you not *Kent*?

Kent. The fame: your Seruant *Kent*,
Where is your Seruant *Caius*?

Lear. He's a good fellow, I can tell you that,
He'le ftrike and quickly too, he's dead and rotten.

Kent. No my good Lord, I am the very man.

Lear. Ile fee that ftraight.

Kent. That from your firft of difference and decay,
Haue follow'd your fad fteps.

Lear. Your are welcome hither.

290 *Kent.* Nor no man elfe:
All's cheerleffe, darke, and deadly,
Your eldeft Daughters haue fore-done themfelues,
And defperately are dead

Lear. I fo I thinke.

Alb. He knowes not what he faies, and vaine is it
That we prefent vs to him.   [309b

Enter a Meſſenger.

Edg. Very bootleffe.

Meſſ. *Edmund* is dead my Lord.

Alb. That's but a trifle heere:
You Lords and Noble Friends, know our intent,
What comfort to this great decay may come,
Shall be appli'd. For vs we will refigne,
During the life of this old Maiefty

300 To him our abfolute power, you to your rights,
With boote, and fuch addition as your Honours
Haue more then merited. All Friends fhall
Tafte the wages of their vertue, and all Foes
The cup of their deferuings: O fee, fee.

Lear. And my poore Foole is hang'd: no, no, no life?
Why fhould a Dog, a Horfe, a Rat haue life,
And thou no breath at all? Thou'lt come no more,
Neuer, neuer, neuer, neuer, neuer.
Pray you vndo this Button. Thanke you Sir,

310 Do you fee this? Looke on her? Looke her lips,
Looke there, looke there.   *He dis.*

Edg. He faints, my Lord, my Lord.

V. iii.

 Lear. Breake hart, I prethe breake. *Edgar.* Look vp my Lord.

 Kent. Vex not his ghoſt, O let him paſſe,
He hates him that would vpon the wracke,
Of this tough world ſtretch him out longer.
 Edg. O he is gone indeed.
 Kent. The wonder is, he hath endured ſo long,
He but vſurpt his life.
 Duke Beare them from hence, our preſent buſines
Is to generall woe, friends of my ſoule, you twaine
220 Rule in this kingdome, and the goard ſtate ſuſtaine.
 Kent. I haue a iourney ſir, ſhortly to go,
My maiſter cals, and I muſt not ſay no.
 Duke. The waight of this ſad time we muſt obey,
Speake what we feele, not what we ought to ſay,
The oldeſt haue borne moſt, we that are yong,
Shall neuer ſee ſo much, nor liue ſo long.

F I N I S.

Kent. Breake heart, I prythee breake.

Edg. Looke vp my Lord.

Kent. Vex not his ghoſt, O let him paſſe, he hates him,
That would vpon the wracke of this tough world
Stretch him out longer.

Edg. He is gon indeed.

Kent. The wonder is, he hath endur'd ſo long,
He but vſurpt his life.

Alb. Beare them from hence, our preſent buſineſſe
Is generall woe: Friends of my ſoule, you twaine,
320 Rule in this Realme, and the gor'd ſtate ſuſtaine.

Kent. I haue a iourney Sir, ſhortly to go,
My Maſter calls me, I muſt not ſay no.

Edg. The waight of this ſad time we muſt obey,
Speake what we feele, not what we ought to ſay:
The oldeſt hath borne moſt, we that are yong, .
Shall neuer ſee ſo much, nor liue ſo long.

                                   Exeunt with a dead March.

FINIS.

In this Quarto version, we have the image of Kent as having behaved in a really extraordinary fashion. What happens to the last scene of the play if this description of Kent is absent, as it is from the Folio? How might that change the other things that Kent says? I don't think there are very many differences between his actual lines after this, but I am interested in what happens to those later lines if you think of him as a man who has been on the brink, and who seems to be halfway towards death himself: the "strings of life" have begun to "crack."

Aud.: Well, what I'm thinking about is I see Kent as being portrayed as some type of truth-teller by Edgar. By omitting this description of his telling "the most pitious tale of *Lear* and him" you don't know that Kent understands what Lear is going through, that he can, like the Fool, speak the truth. And by omitting that, you may lose the sense and wonder, "Does he know Lear?" Yes, he does know him. But if the image of Kent is omitted, it opens the scene up to—well, not a whole different interpretation, but we've lost the sense: you don't know that he told the "pitious tale" of *Lear*, so why does he hold Lear in high regard? He does understand the energies that he's losing, and he can feel the pangs of aging also, though he's not as old as Lear.

Marcus: And he can feel that sense of being pushed beyond the limit.

Aud.: And he's doing it as a much younger man, which makes the truth even more important—you know, as a truth-teller. Omitting that—I'm trying to think of the rest of the text.

Marcus: Do you think you get a much stronger sense of Lear's despair with the description of Kent's grief?

Aud.: Yes.

Marcus: Why, thank you very much. That was exactly what I was getting out of it, too. If you don't have this description of Kent from the Quarto, the things that Kent says throughout the final scene may sound grim enough—"I am come / To bid my King and Master aye good night. / Is he not here?"—but you might think that the idea of bidding Lear forever good night simply meant that Kent was going away; whereas if you have this other version where he has almost died as a result of the strong emotion he's been through—"the strings of life / Began to cracke"—then you're much more likely to take that "come / To bid my King . . . good night" in its darker meaning of his own moving towards death and also as a prognostication of Lear's death and despair that we don't get nearly so strongly in the Folio version.

Aud.: I still think there's a lot of reconciliation, as in the reunion of

Lear and Cordelia in the end. Kent is the younger man aging himself through emotional strain rather than through the years, and his pangs can be felt a lot deeper. I sense that this dark inner feeling is in Kent, but I don't think it's a dark picture of Lear at the end. I think it's a bright ending for him. As a younger person, Kent saw things more darkly, but I don't think that ought to relate to Lear. He can understand Lear, but it's much deeper for Kent as a younger person.

Marcus: Oh, okay. So maybe we should talk about Lear, because you've led directly into that. What you're arguing is that there doesn't have to be a parallel between these two people.

Aud.: No, there doesn't, not in the sense that Kent understands. He can speak the truth of Lear, but there's not a parallel between their sense of aging. I think for Lear it's dark at first, but the reconciliation in the end brings out a brightness, and there's a sense of hope. Whereas for the younger Kent, experiencing the pangs of suffering and realizing them as a younger man, they're much darker. You don't want to think of those things.

Marcus: Of course, he's not a young man, but forty-eight . . .

Aud.: Well, middle-aged.

Marcus: Yes, middle-aged, and I do agree that for us at least, middle age is too early to be preparing for death, unless your life has become unbearable. In any case you certainly get the image that Kent is preparing for death in a way that you and I would not. I guess I tend to see him more as identifying with Lear. He wants to go with him: "I am come / To bid my King and Master aye good night," but then later on, in the Folio wording, he says "My Master calls me, I must not say no." You can interpret the "Master" to mean God, or you can interpret it to mean Lear. If you imagine Kent as assuming that King Lear is on the brink as well, it becomes a kind of joint venture—they're heading off into the sunset together, some kind of unknown afterlife together.

What about that question of whether King Lear dies redeemed? He has that famous and mysterious speech, which I marked for you. It all seems to hinge on Cordelia. On pages 166–67 of the handout the two versions are virtually identical except for the punctuation: "This feather stirs, she liues: if it be so, / It is a chance which do's redeeme all sorrowes / That euer I haue felt." You can say—or at least some people have suggested—that he's arguing, "If she is alive, then I feel redeemed." This moment of despair is a chance to express redemption. I think what you're arguing is that he does feel redeemed.

Aud.: At the beginning of this scene, he speaks about being in prison and it's very passionate. So at the end, the passion continues. He sees death; he's going to see life. There's a sense of passion that's continued from that beginning to the end of the play. Even in death he says "She lives!" and so even in death he sees life. He carries over the passion to the end. I feel he senses himself reconciled with his past. You know, he goes down and then back up. He's weathered the storm and he's uplifted by that. It's a swell of passion in the end, and it comes directly from Lear.

Marcus: I think that interpretation works extremely well for the composite version that you have used in discussing the play before today. That is, it works extremely well for the Folio, from which the speeches you are talking about are predominantly taken. But I'm not quite sure it works for the Quarto because I'm not sure that in the Quarto version he does die thinking that Cordelia is alive. Let's take a look at those lines. First of all, in line 293, I think it's interesting that the Quarto version has the Duke saying of King Lear, "He knowes not what he *sees* [my emphasis]." Of course, the Duke could be mistaken, but on a surface level, he isn't. You were just talking about Lear's vision, but here is a statement that seems to be denying Lear's powers of sight. The Folio version says, "He knowes not what he *saies* [my emphasis]." So that is a very interesting difference.

Aud.: Lear's "seeing" does not seem real to me. He's seeing not as we see, but I don't know, in the Quarto version, does he still bear Cordelia in his arms?

Marcus: Yes, according to the stage directions.

Aud.: . . . as an aged man, eighty years old, swelling up and carrying his daughter. I feel that just to see this action is amazing—you'd think he'd be dragging her on the sled behind him.

Marcus: Unnatural strength.

Aud.: Yes, and some of it is passing on. You know, I haven't really compared the scenes, but I still feel that what is important is the sense that other people, besides Kent, can't really see what Lear experiences. "He doesn't know" they say, "she's not alive." But to him, she is and that's what's important. He feels that way. He sees life and death, so it really doesn't matter exactly what he's really seeing. He could just be dreaming that and that's okay. At least he feels reconciled.

Marcus: Yes, but I'm not too sure in these two versions that, when he comes to the actual moment of death, he is still dreaming the same dream. Let's look at the rest of the speech. He says almost the same thing on both sides of the page: "no no no life? / Why should a Dog, a Horse, a Rat haue life, / And thou no breath at all? Thou'lt come no more. . . . " In one version it's "thou wilt come no more" and three "neuers." In the other it's five "neuers." Then he says, "Pray you vndo this Button," which is lovely and ambiguous. You don't know whose button it is. Is it a button on his own clothing? Is it a button on Cordelia's clothing? If it is a button on Cordelia's clothing, then you can imagine that he thinks she's alive. At the end, in the Folio version, he says, "Thanke you sir, / Do you see this? Looke on her? Looke her lips, / Looke there, looke there. " And, according to the Folio stage direction, "*He dis* [dies]." Lear dies believing that Cordelia is still alive, so that in terms of his own "bargain with fate," you could argue that he dies redeemed. But what about the other side, the Quarto version? It reads, "Pray you undo this button, thank you sir, O o o o." You have to imagine the "o"s as being groans. When Edgar says, "He faints my Lord, my Lord," we can imagine Edgar trying to revive him or some such thing, whereas in the Folio Edgar doesn't "see" the reality that Lear has already died. There's no stage direction saying exactly when Lear dies in the Quarto. Also, in the Quarto, Lear says "Breake hart, I prethe breake." Who says that in the Folio version?

Aud.: Kent.

Marcus: Kent. Very interesting. And then Kent says, "Vex not his ghost, O let him passe."

Aud.: In the Folio version, when he says "Looke on her, looke on her," he's not necessarily saying she's alive. He may just be seeing how beautiful she is or what he's lost or . . .

Marcus: It could be. I think of it as a reference back to the looking glass he called for earlier. You remember he wanted a mirror to see if he could detect her breath. Maybe now he thinks of her as beautiful or something like that, and you're right, you don't have to interpret the speech as a reference to her continuing life. If you don't, however, then you have a more bleak set of possibilities for both versions, don't you? In any case, on the left-hand side of the page in the Quarto version, King Lear's last words are "Breake hart, I prethe breake." On the right hand side of the page in the Folio version, they are "Looke, her lips, / Looke there, looke there," which certainly could be interpreted as some kind of mistaken belief.

Aud.: Also the question mark in the Folio version after "And thou no breath at all?" slightly opens it up a little bit, as it doesn't open it up in the Quarto version.

Marcus: Good point. The fact that the punctuation mark is just a comma in the Quarto version makes it look more like a statement than like a question he's asking her, such as, "Do you or do you not have breath?"

Aud.: So in the Folio version, is Kent referring to his own heart or is he referring to Lear's heart?

Marcus: I think Kent's referring to his own heart. And in the Quarto version, where the lines are given to Lear, Lear is referring to his own heart, too. But the fact that those lines would be transferred over to someone else really suggests that the Folio version is slightly more upbeat about the death. At least, it's a much easier version of the scene in which to make the traditional argument for redemption, especially if the argument is derived from the idea of seeing something that other people really cannot see. In the Quarto version, I don't think there's anything to be seen. At least he doesn't say, "Looke there, looke there," with the idea of something to be seen. He sees nothing.

Aud.: In going along with the argument that Shakespeare revised, that he's the reviser and the transformer . . .

Marcus: Yes, that's the argument in the ascendancy these days, although who knows?

Aud.: If so, from the earlier to the later *King Lear*, he's moving from a more questionable view of the afterlife and the possibility of redemption to a more positive assertion of that possibility. The two *Hamlet*s, however . . .

Marcus: Yes, isn't that interesting. The two *Hamlet*s do the exact opposite.

Aud.: In the revisions of the two *Hamlet*s, from the earlier Bad Quarto to the later Folio version, the sense of afterlife gets more uncertain, whereas in the revisions of the two *Lear*s, it appears to get more certain!

Marcus: Excellent observation. It's worth looking more closely at this kind of thing. It tends to fragment any sense you might have of Shakespeare as a coherent individual who moves from this position to that position with total psychological plausibility.

We've run out of time. Those of you who are interested are welcome to explore the different versions of the plays further on your own. To end, let me ask you whether it makes any difference in *King Lear* who's speaking the last lines of the play, Edgar or Albany? We won't have time to answer it here, but you can think about it for next time, and maybe also discuss it then with your regular instructor, because it is a major crux between the Quarto and Folio texts of *King Lear*. And perhaps you can see that difference going along with the greater despair, or the greater hope, depending on whether it's the Quarto or Folio version you're talking about.

Thanks very much for bearing with me during this experimental class.

You've convinced me even further that undergraduates can deal quite well with matters of Shakespearean textual difference. Whatever else you may have gotten out of today's discussion, I hope this class has made you more aware of the constructed nature of the standard texts we like to call Shakespeare.

Dramatic Structure and Dramatic Effect in *Julius Caesar*

JOHN WILDERS

No doubt there are large numbers of people all over the world who teach the plays of Shakespeare in the way I do, but since I created this method entirely on my own, the best way of describing it is to explain how I discovered it. It owes practically nothing to literary or dramatic criticism and during the course of this lecture I shall refer to very few critics. On the contrary, my method was devised in part to deal with those elements in the plays which the critics who influenced the way I read them—who told me what to look for, and therefore determined what I actually found—seemed unaware of, or at least ignored.

In the England in which I grew up there had recently been a conscious reaction against the character-analysis which had dominated Shakespearean criticism ever since Samuel Johnson had published the preface to his edition of Shakespeare's works almost two centuries earlier. This reaction had been most clearly signaled by L. C. Knights's article "How Many Children Had Lady Macbeth?" (1933) in which he argued that a Shakespearean play consists of much more than a set of psychologically consistent characters but is woven out of interrelated images which express cohesive themes. This preoccupation with themes and images—which is revealed in the title of Knights's major contribution to Shakespearean criticism, *Some Shakespearean Themes* (1959)—substituted for an emphasis on character an emphasis on language, and especially metaphor. The most eloquent and productive exponent of this approach, however, was Knights's near-namesake (with whom he was often confused, to the irritation of both men): G. Wilson Knight. In, for example, *The Shakespearean Tempest* (1932) the latter analyzed practically all the plays, drawing attention to the images of storm with which many of them begin and music with which many of them conclude.

These were the kind of critics who shaped my understanding of the plays in the late forties and early fifties when I was a student. But at the time I was really leading two different lives, as I became vividly aware. The student who spent his mornings hearing about Shakespearean metaphor and reading Wolfgang Clemen's *The Development of Shakespeare's Imagery* (1951) (published in my third year at Cambridge) spent his evenings taking part as an actor in the productions mounted by the student dramatic society, the Marlowe Society, the purpose of which was, and still is, to produce the plays of Shakespeare and his contemporaries. At the time I felt a sense of guilt that, instead of applying myself to my books, I was apparently wasting my life by acting in Greene's *Friar Bacon and Friar Bungay*, Jonson's *The Alchemist,* Shakespeare's *Henry VIII, Titus Andronicus, Love's Labour's Lost, Coriolanus* and a production by my contemporary John Barton of *Julius Caesar* with Elizabethan pronunciation. I no longer feel any guilt about these seemingly frivolous activities, because to take part in the plays is, of course, by far the best way to understand them in detail and in the form—performance in a theater before an audience—for which they were originally designed. To study Shakespeare's plays and not to take part in them or at least to see regular and frequent productions, is like studying Mozart and never actually hearing a note of his music.

As I took part in these productions, it became increasingly clear that the Shakespeare whose plays I was intimately involved with in the evenings had very little to do with the Shakespeare analyzed by the critics I was reading in the mornings. And this, I believe, is the opinion of audiences. Do you ever hear anyone leaving the theater after a production of *Hamlet* and exclaiming, "Weren't the image clusters magnificent!" or "What a superb treatment of the themes of purgation and disease"? What draws audiences to productions of Shakespeare's plays is first and foremost their dramatic effect, the way in which they engage, sustain and finally reward an audience's attention so that, as Johnson said, "the mind is carried irresistibly forward." This power, as I shall now argue, is derived in the first place from Shakespeare's grasp and control of dramatic structure. It is the dramatic construction of the plays which produces their dramatic effect.

The first example I shall give is in fact the scene from the plays in which I experienced this truth for the first time. The only way, I hope, in which I resemble Polonius is that both of us played the part of Julius Caesar at the university. I did so in John Barton's production with Elizabethan pronunciation I mentioned earlier. The production, incidentally, also involved the reconstruction of an Elizabethan thrust stage, with two entrance doors at the back and an upper stage, schoolboys in the women's roles and an auditorium lit throughout the performance so as to resemble the daylight of the Globe and other Elizabethan public theaters. The scene which most interested me was act 3, scene 1, the scene in which Caesar is assassinated. This is, of course, the central, pivotal scene of the entire play in that everything which occurs before then leads up to the assassination and everything which occurs after it does so as a consequence of the assassination. It is a long scene (of almost three hundred lines) and one which I came to know intimately, because Caesar enters at the very beginning and remains on the stage to the very end. I was also in a unique position to experience it because, for most of the scene, I was lying motionless on the ground, apparently dead. I was able to listen.

What, I suppose, initially excited me was the effect created by the entrances of three characters immediately after the murder: Mark Antony's servant, then Antony himself, and then the servant of Octavius. To begin with, the only sense I had was that these entrances were, during some performances, astonishing and at others unremarkable. Their success depended on the way in which the actors timed their entrances and this in turn depended on the pace and rhythm of the scene already created by the actors on stage—which was, in turn, dependent on the reactions of the audience and the speed with which they were capable of responding to the actors. All I can say is that, at the most successful performances, the actors timed their arrivals at precisely the right moment and the effect was magical, as though they had, for once, sensed what had been in the dramatist's mind, and done exactly what he wanted. The effect can best be compared to the performance of a piece of music in which the first notes of a new instrument or singer—the piano in a concerto or the soprano in the quintet from *Meistersinger*—are heard at what we instinctively know to be the right moment.

It was, roughly speaking, the tendency of nineteenth-century criticism to treat Shakespeare's plays as though they were novels, and the tendency of the New Critics like Wilson Knight to treat them as poems. My tendency is to treat them as works of music, and act 3, scene 1 of *Julius Caesar* in certain ways resembles a symphony. Like a symphony it can be divided into well-defined movements or sections, each one of which has its own pace and contrasts strongly with the other movements. The first two sections, which are dramatically very tense, depict the final moments before the assassination. In the first the conspirators, fearful that their plot may be uncovered at the last minute, finally group themselves round the central figure of Caesar; the second, which is dominated by Caesar himself, is slow, measured and formal. Instantly after the murder Shakespeare leads us to the third movement, which is very rapid, a combination of several different voices—Cinna's, Brutus's, Cassius's and others'. It was hard for me, as the dead Caesar, to visualize the scene. The voices seemed to rush uncertainly one way and another, full of half-lines and unfinished sentences, unlike the previous section which is composed chiefly of Caesar's own measured public statements. The fourth section is also a contrast: Brutus takes control of his fellow conspirators and, in an episode which is so slow and formal as to resemble a ritual, he invites them to gather round the corpse and bathe their hands in Caesar's blood. As this movement comes to an end, the conspirators behave as though the play were practically finished. The deed for which they have been preparing themselves is done, the moment towards which everything has been leading has passed, and they clearly intend to make an exit:

> *Decius.* What, shall we forth?
> *Cassius.* Ay, every man away.
> Brutus shall lead, and we will grace his heels
> With the most boldest and best hearts of Rome.

At this moment Shakespeare wrote one of the most chillingly dramatic of his stage directions: *Enter a Servant.* It is powerful because the servant has come from Mark Antony, with the request that he may be received by the conspirators and told why Caesar deserved to die. Brutus, of course, agrees. Antony now makes his entrance, is allowed to make his funeral oration and the assassination becomes not the beginning of a new era of "peace, freedom and enfranchisement," but a pretext for civil war. The entry of the servant is therefore immensely significant both dramatically and politically. It is dramatically stunning because the servant is a totally new character and one for which both the conspirators and the audience have been unprepared. Shakespeare, as a master of dramatic construction, knows exactly how to whet an audience's appetite and, after some delay, to satisfy it. He does that with the assassination, for which he has kept us waiting at least since the conclusion of the second scene. But he also knows how to arouse our expectations and then offer us the unexpected. Having led us to expect an ending, he gives us a new beginning, and that beginning is marked by the servant's entrance. Had the servant not entered, or had the conspirators been prepared for him, the civil war might never have broken out, Antony would not have become a triumvir, Octavius would not have become Caesar Augustus, Vergil would not have written the *Aeneid,* and our own lives would have been very different. Politically his entrance is therefore immensely significant too. This nameless character who has only twelve lines is one of the most important in the play.

But to return to our movements. The fifth movement has a special tension of its own. It is the episode in which Antony makes his peace with the conspirators only to reveal in his soliloquy (the sixth movement) his resolution to avenge the death of Caesar on the "butchers" who caused it. The seventh and final movement also has its interest because its beginning is matched by the arrival of another servant, this time from Octavius, whose entrance is also unexpected.

Shakespeare expresses in the succession of these movements the way in which history consists of the rise and fall of great men. Roman history depicted in *Julius Caesar* is controlled first by Caesar, then, briefly, by Brutus, then by Antony. Each one in turn is given a section or movement in this scene in which he is the focus of our attention. But, Shakespeare implies, there is already, waiting in the wings, an as yet unseen character, Octavius, who will finally overthrow Antony and will live to be the first Roman emperor. The division of the scene into movements or sections therefore reveals a great deal about Shakespeare's dramatic structure, but it also reveals something of his conception of the movement of history. I think I surprised a schoolteacher whom I met at a conference in Germany. He told me that he taught Shakespeare's plays by emphasizing their relevance to the lives of his students and asked me if I did the same. "No," I replied, "I split them into sections."

In our scene from *Julius Caesar* Shakespeare also uses a number of other structural and dramatic procedures which create their effects on an audience, and I shall now talk about them and relate them to similar procedures in his other plays. One of them I have, in effect, already described. To divide the scene into sections is to reveal how Shakespeare shifts the focus of our attention from one major character to another. As I have said, first Caesar, then Brutus, then Antony, then Octavius's messenger stand at the center of the action. Shakespeare was, of course, not only a playwright but an actor who wrote parts both for himself and for his colleagues and he took care to give all his leading actors a slice of the action, a chance to use their distinctive voices (for his is an aural and visual art as well as a verbal one). But, as a man who had been an actor before he became a playwright, he also knew from experience how to keep an audience's mind continually refreshed by offering them first one actor, then another, on whom to concentrate. This is so often his practice that it is hard to select from literally hundreds of examples a single illustration. In the *First Part of Henry IV* he distributes the action between three locations: the court, the tavern and the battlefield. The first, dominated by the king, the second by Falstaff and the third by Hotspur. Only the prince appears in all three and, while keeping the audience's attention by the simple expedient of variety, Shakespeare implicitly tells us something important about the prince, his adaptability, his multifaceted personality (a quality also shown by Hamlet), and the breadth and inclusiveness of his vision.

We can also notice how, as one section moves into another, the audience receives a number of different visual impressions. The full stage with which act 3, scene 1 of *Julius Caesar* begins gives way to a stage occupied only by the handful of conspirators and this, in turn, leads to a stage occupied by one single character, Antony. These changing visual impressions create dramatic variety but they also reveal something about Antony. In the preceding section we have observed him making his peace with the assassins to the extent of shaking their bloody hands, one by one, so that the blood which finally contaminates his hands as well as theirs becomes a manifestation of his alliance, his brotherhood, with the conspirators. It is only when they all leave him that he reveals how deceptive this evidence of brotherhood actually is and that his real determination is to take arms against them. The blood on his hands now takes on a totally new significance and becomes an emblem of the blood whose shedding he will avenge in the civil war he will himself initiate.

Antony's solitariness, and the contrast it affords with the group of people that preceded it, also expresses his apartness from the conspirators, and the secretiveness with which he hides from them the intentions he is resolved to carry out. This particular dramatic effect in which all the characters leave the stage except one who then confides in us, could be called "clearing the stage." When, two weeks ago, I was discussing an example of it in *A Midsummer Night's Dream,* my students supplied me with so many examples of it from other plays by Shakespeare that I had to tell them to stop. It occurs earlier in *Julius Caesar,* in the second scene, when after Caesar has crossed the stage in his processional walk to the games, Brutus and Cassius stay behind to discuss, necessarily in secret, their fears of Caesar's ambitions. The fact that they don't join the procession emphasizes their apartness, their unwillingness to join in the general adulation— an apartness reinforced by the repeated shouts of support for Caesar we hear from off stage. The apartness, the secretiveness, of Hamlet is also expressed visually when, in the second scene of the play, the stage clears and he is left alone and, like Antony, conveys his hostility to the regime in a soliloquy ("O that this too, too solid flesh would melt"). It is in episodes such as these that a character reveals to us that his inner thoughts, his true feelings, are not what we supposed them to be.

About my final example of this effect I should like to speak at a little more length. Some years ago I was coaching a group of students in the second scene of *Henry IV Part 1* in which, you will recall, Prince Hal is shown relaxing and joking with Falstaff and Poins, and is finally left alone to deliver his only soliloquy, "I know you all, and will awhile uphold / The unyok'd humour of your idleness." The student playing Prince Hal, in fact a graduate student of drama, gave an excellent performance on which I congratulated him. "Not at all," he retorted. "It's terrible. I can't make out what is in the man's mind." After some searching and discussion we finally made the discovery that this was the whole point of the scene before the soliloquy. Throughout the dialogue Falstaff makes scarcely concealed enquiries about the prospects ahead of him when Hal becomes king. Hal never replies to them but parries them by turning them into jokes or just ignores them:

> *Falstaff.* Shall there be gallows standing in England when thou art King? and resolution thus fubbed as it is with the rusty curb of old Father Antic the law? Do not thou, when thou art king, hang a thief.
> *Prince.* No, thou shalt.
> *Falstaff.* Shall I? O rare! By the Lord I'll be a brave judge!
> *Prince.* Thou judgest false already! I mean thou shalt have the hanging of thieves, and so become a rare hangman.

A man who jokes or refuses to answer such a leading question is probably hiding something and this, I believe, is one of the impressions an audience should receive. When, as the scene ends, Shakespeare clears the stage and leaves us alone with Hal, we are unusually grateful to hear his soliloquy, because it tells us what we have been anxious to know: what his real intentions actually are. He confides to us the information he had concealed from Falstaff and we view him throughout the rest of the play in the light of the information we have been exclusively privileged to hear. In this way the analysis of structure leads into the analysis of character and motivation.

Another dramatic device Shakespeare uses in relation to Mark Antony he employs frequently elsewhere and to similar effect. The soliloquy Antony delivers towards the end of our scene is the more astonishing because he has, hitherto, been a practically silent character. He has appeared only three times before—twice in the procession with Caesar, as he goes to and from the games, and once on the morning of the assassination when, with the conspirators, he comes to escort Caesar to the capitol. On his first appearance he speaks a line and a half, on his second two and a half, and on his third only half a line. His very silence can itself be worrying and though Shakespeare can do anything with language, he also knows when to use expressive silences. Moreover, the little we are told of the largely silent Antony induces us to consider him a trivial, irresponsible character who loves going to the theater and tends to sleep late in the morning. How much more unexpected and astonishing, therefore, is the sudden outburst of the soliloquy:

> Over thy wounds now do I prophesy
> (Which like dumb mouths do ope their ruby lips
> To beg the voice and utterance of my tongue),
> A curse shall light upon the limbs of men;
> Domestic fury and fierce civil strife
> Shall cumber all the parts of Italy;
> Blood and destruction shall be so in use,
> And dreadful objects so familiar,
> That mothers shall but smile when they behold
> Their infants quartered with the hands of war,
> All pity choked with custom of fell deeds.

The largely silent reveler of the first two acts suddenly displays a capacity for deep feeling, a vindictiveness, and a resolution of which we had not thought him capable. The sight of Caesar's corpse has transformed him into a political person. By making Antony almost entirely silent during the early part of the play, Shakespeare rouses our curiosity and then, with the soliloquy, satisfies it in abundance.

There are plenty of examples of significant and dramatically effective silences elsewhere in the plays. Hamlet's almost complete silence on his first appearance is an obvious example; so is the silence of Don John in the first scene of *Much Ado About Nothing*, a scene in which all the other characters express their sociability, their good-natured affection, their pleasure in welcoming the soldiers back from the war. Don John's silence is positively expressive, evidence that by nature he is antisocial, ill-natured, disaffected at the end of the war—and with good reason, for it is he who has just been defeated. He is one of those particularly unpleasant men who make a point of not laughing at other people's jokes, and when, in a later scene, he explains himself, he tells us what we have already suspected from his silence.

I should have explained earlier that my method of teaching Shakespeare is, in the first place, to get a group of students from the class to stand up and read the scene to be analyzed that day. I cast the scene during the previous class and, if possible, give the students a quick rehearsal so that they will have at least some preparation. Then we divide the scene into sections, a process which (as I hope I have demonstrated) not only reveals its dramatic construction, but leads on to other elements such as the way in which structure raises expectations, creates tension, offers a variety of aural and visual impressions, and also expresses character and relationships. I spend little or no time plodding word for word through the dialogue, a process I endured so painfully in high school. The student actors are compelled to understand the dialogue because they have to stand up and make sense of it in public, and a passage spoken by an actor who understands it can short-circuit the footnotes and make direct sense to the listener.

When we read a play silently instead of watching it we tend to be unaware of the presence on the stage of characters who don't speak. If, however, we watch the first scene of *Much Ado About Nothing* we may notice that another character, besides Don John, is also silent. Hero speaks only one line and her silence is, of course, the more striking because Beatrice and Benedick seem unable to keep quiet. She is, in fact, pretty silent through-out the play and this marks her out not only as an essentially passive character, lacking initiative and self-confidence, but also as a girl who may have any kind of personality: she could be the modest young lady who Claudio initially thinks she is or she could be the lascivious woman he later believes she is. Her very lack of words, her lack of any recognizable per-sonality, makes Claudio's reappraisal of her much more convincing.

There is one episode in *As You Like It* in which a character never utters a line. This is the episode in which first Rosalind, then Celia and then Touchstone, take it in turn to read aloud and parody Orlando's romantic verses. Corin, who has already established himself as a humble shepherd whose greatest pride is "to see [his] ewes graze and [his] lambs suck," stands silently throughout this performance, a mute, implied criticism of the literary antics engaged in by the sophisticated visitors from the court. Shakespeare had, incidentally, created a similar effect some years earlier when in *Love's Labour's Lost* the schoolmaster's verbal pyrotechnics are witnessed by the eloquently silent Constable Dull. And lest we should overlook his silence or fail to interpret it, Shakespeare gives him a single line, almost the final line of the scene. In response to the schoolmaster's comment, "Constable Dull, thou hast spoken no word all this while," the stolid policeman replies, "Nor understand none neither."

To return to our scene from *Julius Caesar,* we can discover in the last two sections Shakespeare practicing an art in which he was unusually skillful and which he used, I believe, in every scene he wrote: the art of preparation. The elements I have been discussing are little mentioned by literary critics, but this particular element has been excellently treated by Wolfgang Clemen in his *Shakespeare's Dramatic Art* (1974). Described briefly, Shakespeare always takes care as he concludes one episode to prepare his audience for what is likely to happen in the next. Thus, in *Julius Caesar,* no sooner has the first part of the play concluded with the murder of Caesar than we are warned that Antony intends to address the Roman people, that he intends to wreak vengeance on the conspirators, and that Octavius is biding his time on the outskirts of the city. We therefore wait with curiosity to hear Antony's oration, to see what form his bloody revenge will take, and to see the arrival of the future Augustus Caesar in the political arena. It must, no doubt, have been a problem for Shakespeare to prevent the play from losing its dramatic momentum once Caesar had been killed. He had devoted over two acts to preparing for it and, now that it had occurred, he had to sustain the audience's attention. He did so by allowing the hitherto silent Antony to assume the center of the stage and to confide in us his revolutionary intentions. But Shakespeare seldom satisfies our expectations immediately. He promises us extraordinary things and then makes us wait for them. In one case he makes us wait the length of two whole plays. Near the beginning of *Henry IV Part I*, Prince Hal confides in us his determination to sweep aside the "base contagious clouds" which now obscure him, but does not actually do so until he banishes Falstaff near the end of *Part II*. Only at that point are our expectations finally satisfied. Hence Shakespeare ensures that our appetite grows by what it feeds on, and that each of his plays is not a series of disjointed episodes but a single, uninterrupted, continuous experience during which he makes us always eager for more.

Teaching *A Midsummer Night's Dream*

JOHN WILDERS

Workshop

We shall be looking today at the first scene of Shakespeare's *Midsummer Night's Dream* and the plan is that I shall first spend about twenty minutes giving you some information, then some of the students will perform the scene up here on the platform, and then I shall ask you a number of questions about the scene they have performed. So the first part of the class is for me, the second part is for the actors, and the third part is for you. [For the text of *A Midsummer Night's Dream* 1.1.1–251, see pp. 163–65.]

I want to begin by telling you something about the way in which *A Midsummer Night's Dream* was first printed. There were three significant early editions, quarto editions. One was published in 1600, and another in 1619, and then the play was printed for a third time in the big volume of Shakespeare's collected plays, the First Folio, published in 1623. Now if you were to glance briefly at a copy of one of the quarto editions and compared it with the kind of modern edition you use for your classes—a paperback or, as I see some of you have with you, *The Riverside Shakespeare* —you would easily notice a difference between them. Whereas all modern editions of *A Midsummer Night's Dream* are divided into acts and scenes, there is no indication in the quartos of the point at which one act or one scene ends and the next one begins. The acts and scenes are not numbered. In the Folio edition of 1623, someone has added the act numbers, but the individual scenes are still not numbered. And since the First Folio was published seven years after Shakespeare's death, it is likely that the act numbers were added not by Shakespeare but by someone else, someone we might call an editor.

The division into acts and scenes in the plays of the First Folio is extremely inconsistent. Some of the plays, such as *The Tempest,* are split up into the acts and scenes with which we are now familiar; others, such as *A Midsummer Night's Dream,* are divided into five acts, but the acts are not divided into scenes; at the top of the first page of *Antony and Cleopatra* we see the words "Act One, Scene One" *(Actus Primus, Scoena Prima),* but after that neither acts nor scenes appear again, and many of the other plays are similarly undivided.

I mention this because it tells us something about the way Shakespeare wrote and the way in which he visualized his plays in performance. The absence of act and scene numbers suggests that he thought about each play not as a series of independent units connected like links in a chain, but as one, single, continuous, unbroken whole, which was designed to be played without any breaks or intermissions. If you have ever directed a Shakespearean play, you'll know that it is very difficult to decide where to put the intermission. Wherever you decide to put it, it is always wrong because it interrupts the continuous flow of the action. When I was a student we had no theater departments in British universities, but there was at Cambridge a very helpful professor who gave us a hand in the productions we arranged in our spare time. During rehearsals for one of our productions, he never came to see us because he was too busy, but he finally showed up for the dress rehearsal, and arrived in time for the intermission. "Where have you put the interval?" he asked. I told him and he said, "It's in the wrong place," and left. At any point in the play it would be wrong.

This idea is also supported by what we know of the design of the Elizabethan stage. As far as we know, it consisted of a large, bare platform which projected into the middle of the audience. At the back of it there was a wall with two doors leading from the tiring house (or dressing room) onto the stage itself. It was through these two doors that the actors made their entrances and exits, so that as one group of actors was leaving the stage through one door, another group could enter through the other. There were no scene changes because there was no scenery and no lighting changes because the plays were performed by daylight and there was no artificial lighting. Hence the performances could be absolutely continuous, a seamless garment. Insofar as Shakespeare thought of scenes, he didn't see them necessarily as changes in location—hence all those needless stage directions in recent editions which simply say, "Another part of the forest"—but as points at which, for a brief moment, the stage is empty and one group of characters is replaced by another.

Nevertheless, each one of Shakespeare's plays is constructed out of hundreds of small units or sections which are to an entire play as bricks are to a house, and the first thing I want to do with the first scene of *A Midsummer Night's Dream* is to split it up into sections. It is an ideal play for my purpose because the divisions are very clear. There are five sections. The first one finishes at the end of line 19 with the words of Duke Theseus, "With pomp, with triumph, and with revelling," and if you don't mind messing up your copy, you could draw a pencil mark under that line. The second unit begins with the entry of Egeus and continues through line 127, where Egeus says, "With duty and desire we follow you," and you could mess up your edition even more by drawing a line after the exit direction which follows it to indicate the end of section 3. Section 4 begins with Lysander's words, "How now, my love? Why is your cheek so pale?" and finishes at line 179, "Keep promise, love. Look, here comes Helen," and that is the end of section 3. Section 4 begins with the stage direction "Enter Helena." Then that section finishes at line 225 with the stage direction "Exit Lysander" and the fifth and final section begins with Helena's line, "How happy some o'er other some can be!" and continues to the end of the scene.

Now, the actors will perform the scene in a moment and, when it has been performed, I shall ask you what indicates the beginning of any one section and the ending of another. Having discovered that, we come to something more interesting, namely, the dramatic effects that Shakespeare creates by constructing the scene out of these five sections. To be more precise, what effects does the division into five sections actually have on the audience? And the audience, of course, is all of you. We might also consider how many plots Shakespeare sets in motion. How many plots are started in this one single scene? Then we can consider in what way Shakespeare prepares the audience for what is to follow later in the play. Finally, we shall consider the style in which the scene is written because, although clearly it is written in the English language, it doesn't sound like the kind of style in which we talk to one another every day. It is not at all naturalistic, and we shall consider what the features are of this particular style and what effects Shakespeare creates by using it.

[The students perform the scene.]

Now let us return to our first question. How do you recognize that one section has come to an end and another has begun?

Aud. The characters come on or go off.

Wilders: Right. The sections are divided by the entrances and exits of the characters. Now the entrance of a new character creates a variety of effects. For one thing it changes the relationship between people on the stage. Up until the entrance of Egeus, Theseus and Hippolyta are entirely preoccupied with each other and with their forthcoming marriage. When Egeus appears, all attention shifts onto him and the primary relationship is between Egeus and the other characters. What other effects are created by his entrance?

Aud.: He tells us about the plot.

Wilders: Correct. Whereas so far we have heard about the forthcoming marriage of Theseus and Hippolyta, we are now told about Hermia's love for Lysander and Egeus's opposition to it. In other words, we have probably assumed that the play was going to be about the duke's wedding, but we now discover that it's going to be about something different. Hence Egeus is cast in the role of interloper or obstruction. He wishes to prevent his daughter's marriage to the man she loves and he prevents Theseus and Hippolyta from contemplating their marriage. He's the obstacle who has to be overcome if the couples are to get what they want. What do you notice about the visual impression when everyone on the stage (with the exception of Lysander and Hermia) goes off at line 127?

Aud. They are on their own.

Wilders: And what message does this convey to us?

Aud.: They are lovers. They are friends.

Wilders: Fine. The fact that they are alone, speaking only to each other, is something that we notice, and you might also notice that this is the first point in the play at which they have actually spoken to each other. What does that tell us?

Aud.: They are confiding.

Wilders: Yes. It is only when they are on their own and the duke and the angry father have left, that they can speak to each other. And this suggests that they have something to say which they don t want anyone else to hear. It suggests secrecy and, of course, what they discuss is something intimate: their love for each other and the obstacles which stand in their way. But, quite apart from what they say, the simple visual effect of seeing them alone together tells us something about their relationship, both to each other and to the characters who have left the stage.

As you can see from this simple example, Shakespeare creates visual as well as verbal impressions on an audience. If the actors simply mimed those first three sections without speaking, we should get a rough idea of what was happening. It's a kind of sign language and Shakespeare's use of visual signs as well as of words is one thing which makes him a specially dramatic writer, a writer for the theater. His plays are full of eloquent visual effects, but I'll mention only two of them. One of them, with which you are probably familiar, occurs near the end of *King Lear* when the king enters carrying the body of his most loved and only remaining daughter. When he comes on and stands there, there is scarcely any need for Lear or anyone else to say anything. It is all conveyed in that one very simple, very moving visual image. The dialogue which follows his entrance does little more than expand what the image has already conveyed to us. The other example occurs in *Richard II* when the crown passes from the rightful king, Richard, to the usurper, Henry Bolingbroke. Richard removes the crown from his head and holds it between the two of them until finally Bolingbroke takes it from him. That demonstrates clearly and visually the transfer of power from the one to the other. And, again, words are scarcely necessary. When he shows us Hermia and Lysander alone in section 3 of our scene, Shakespeare is transmitting to us one of the visual messages of which his plays are full.

Let's look at another example. At the end of the fourth section, Hermia and Lysander make an exit and leave Helena to talk to us on her own. What is Shakespeare telling us by leaving Helena by herself?

Aud.: She's isolated. She's complaining about something.

Wilders: Excellent. And what she is complaining about in her soliloquy is that she's left on the shelf. Both Lysander and Demetrius love Hermia, but nobody loves her. And Helena's isolation is emphasized by the fact that the two characters who have just left are in love and are about to elope from Athens together that very night. Shakespeare makes impressions on our eyes as well as our ears.

Now there are other effects which Shakespeare creates in this scene and they are easier to recognize when you have divided it into sections. In the first section, as you saw when the scene was acted, Theseus and Hippolyta are on the stage, possibly with a few attendants. Then at the start of section 2, the stage fills up with the arrival of Egeus and the rest of them. In section 3 only a pair of characters is left, but they are joined by Helena, making a trio, and in the final section, Helena is left on her own. So, in each section, Shakespeare creates a new, different visual effect: lots of people, two people, three people, one person. Moreover, the effect is aural as well as visual, and what the audience hears, as one section follows another, is a series of different combinations of voices. Mozart does something similar in his operas. If you listen to the music from *The Magic Flute,* you will notice that he alternates between choruses, arias for solo voices (both men's and women's), duets, trios and so on. In that way, both in *A Midsummer Night's Dream* and in *The Magic Flute,* the audience's visual and aural impressions are constantly changing. Their senses are aroused and refreshed by the continual changes taking place on the stage, and this goes on until we reach the last line of the play.

Of course, Shakespeare does much more in this scene than create a series of sensations. What else does he do?

Aud.: He tells us a story.

Wilders: Yes. He gives us information about the feelings the characters have for one another and the way these feelings develop. In other words, he sets up and develops a plot. Which is the first of the plots we learn about?

Aud.: The marriage of Theseus.

Wilders: The forthcoming marriage of Theseus and Hippolyta. He can't wait to get married and she says, "Be patient, darling, we don't have to wait long." Then what is plot number two?

Aud.: The love story.

Wilders: So the second plot involves the love of Lysander and Hermia, and Egeus's opposition to their marriage. And what is plot number three?

Aud.: The lovers' triangle.

Wilders: Yes. Helena loves Demetrius, but Demetrius loves Hermia and not Helena. And there is also a hint of a fourth plot when Theseus asks Philostrate to go off and stir the Athenian youth to merriment and provide some entertainment. We don't, of course, see that entertainment until Bottom and his friends perform *Pyramus and Thisbe* right at the end of the play. So here, ten lines after the beginning of the first scene, Shakespeare is preparing us for what will happen in the middle of the last scene.

In all his plays, Shakespeare takes care to whet the appetite of the audience for what is going to happen next. Where do you find him preparing us in this scene for what is shortly to follow?

Aud: When they decide to escape to the woods.

Wilders: Exactly. Hermia and Lysander, prevented by Hermia's father from marrying in the city, decide to overcome his opposition by going out of Athens and marrying there. That makes us want to know if they will, in fact, escape and if they will actually marry. And our curiosity is aroused even further when Helena tells us that she will betray their plans to Demetrius who, she believes, will then follow them to the wood, and we want to know if he will follow them and what will happen then. The effect of all this preparation is to make us eager for the plot to develop (so that, at the very least, we shan't feel like walking out of the theater) and to bind the various scenes together so that the play—as I mentioned earlier—forms a continuous whole.

Incidentally, when the escape to the woods is mentioned for the first time, Shakespeare does something interesting with the dialogue. It suddenly becomes descriptive, and we get some idea of what the landscape of the wood is going to be like. Lysander describes the wood by moonlight—

> When Phoebe doth behold
> Her silver visage in the watery glass,
> Decking with liquid pearl the bladed grass

—and Hermia talks about the "faint primrose beds" on which she and Helena used to lie and confide in each other. This sudden appearance of descriptive writing would not be remarkable in itself were it not for the fact that, until that point, there have been no descriptive passages at all. During the central scenes of the play, we are constantly told about the features of the wood—the trees, the wild flowers, the insects and animals that inhabit it. There's probably more landscape poetry in *A Midsummer Night's Dream* than in any other play of Shakespeare. But of the city of Athens—its houses, streets and temples—he tells us absolutely nothing. Athens in this play is distinguished not by its topography, its architecture, but by its authoritarian social structure in which those who have power—the duke, the father— have absolute authority. By contrast, the wood is characterized by its organic, spontaneous, natural life. And in those brief references to the moonlight and the flowers, Shakespeare gives a hint of what is to come. That, too, is a kind of preparation—a preparation for the place we shall go to as well as a preparation for what may happen there.

So, having aroused our curiosity, does Shakespeare take us straight away in the next scene to the arrival of the lovers in the wood?

Aud.: No.

Wilders: No, he makes a complete shift and introduces us to Bottom and Quince and their friends and their plans for the rehearsal of their play. He hints at what he will show us next, but then keeps us waiting. That is a very deliberate effect and he uses it all the time. It's what you might call "The *Dallas* effect" and the scriptwriter of *Dallas* must have learned it— directly or otherwise—from him. And they use it for the same purpose—to keep the audience captive and anxious to see more.

But let us return to our three plots. What do all those rather different plots have in common?

Aud.: Resistance.

Wilders: Right. Each plot presents an obstacle to the fulfillment of he desires of the characters. Theseus and Hippolyta long to be married, but they must wait; Hermia and Lysander want to marry, but Egeus forbids it; Helena loves Demetrius, but he thinks only of Hermia. So they are all obstacles to what? To marriage, to the fulfillment of love. What really unites these three plots is the feeling of frustrated love. When we realize that, we discover something about the whole play. What sends the two lovers flying off into the forest is their frustrated love for each other; what makes Helena wring her hands and complain at the end of the scene is that she is crazy about Demetrius but Demetrius has no interest in her. Frustrated love is a very powerful, dominating, energetic kind of feeling and, as the play develops and the relationships become more and more complicated, so the feelings of the characters become more animated and passionate until they reach the greatest scene in the whole play, act 3, scene 2, where all four lovers chase each other in the darkness, each one dying to grab hold of his or her mate until finally they all collapse in exhaustion and fall asleep. It is the thwarting of their love, their sexual drive, which creates this energy, and you can feel some of it in this first scene.

In connection with this sexual energy, what happens at the end of the play? You'll remember that, after the couples have gone to bed, the fairies come in for the last time, and what do they do? Do they say, "Have a good night"?

Aud.: They sing and dance.

Wilders: They do that, yes, but they also bless the children who will be born from these marriages. They say,

> Never mole, harelip, nor scar,
> Nor mark prodigious, such as are
> Despised in nativity,
> Shall upon their children be.

The fairies cast a kind of spell, the effect of which will be that the couples will have beautiful children. The emphasis with which the play concludes is not so much on marriage as on the birth of children. The irresistible driving force which makes the lovers so passionate and energetic during the course of the play is not so much love as the desire to procreate. As Benedick says, "The world must be peopled!" It is that which fuels the action of *A Midsummer Night's Dream,* and we are made aware of it in act 1, scene 1, in Hermia's unaccustomed defiance of the father, in the resolution of the lovers to escape from authority, in Helena's unhappy awareness that her love is not reciprocated.

Now let us turn our attention to the style in which Shakespeare has written the dialogue in this scene. Perhaps you can identify it if we compare it with the style of the scene which follows, the one involving Bottom and his friends. Look at the way it opens:

> Here is the scroll of every man's name which is thought fit through all Athens to play in our interlude before the Duke and the Duchess on his wedding day at night.

This seems to me an entirely naturalistic, colloquial style, a style which reproduces the effect of people talking in an easy, relaxed way. The effect is created partly by the language which is mostly functional and factual, but also by the construction of the sentences, which hang together loosely and untidily. Now let me call your attention to one of the most uncolloquial passages in act 1, scene 1, the conversation between Hermia and Lysander in section 3:

> *Lys.* Aye me! For aught that I could ever read,
> Could ever hear by tale or history,
> The course of true love never did run smooth;
> But either it was different in blood—
> > *Her:* O cross!—too high to be enthrall'd to low.
> > *Lys.:* Or else misgraffed in respect of years—
> > *Her.:* O spite!—too old to be engaged to young.
> > *Lys.:* Or else it stood upon the choice of friends—
> > *Her.:* O hell, to choose love by another's eyes!
> > *Lys.:* Or if there were a sympathy in choice,
> War, death, or sickness did lay siege to it,
> Making it momentany as a sound,
> Swift as a shadow, short as any dream,
> Brief as the lightning in the collied night.

What makes that passage of dialogue seem not like people having a chat? What distinguishes it from the style in which Bottom talks to Quince?

Aud.: The lines are very short and very repetitive, but even though they are short, they're very formal.

Wilders: I think your word "formal" is right, and their formality consists in their being repetitive. The distinguishing features of this dialogue are the sentence structure and the way in which the structure is repeated.

Notice the way in which Hermia's three interjections begin: "O cross," "O spite," "O hell," and the way in which they continue: "Too high to be enthralled," "too old to be engaged," and the way in which they are balanced: "high . . . low," "old . . . young." Lysander's sentences also have this repeated pattern: "But either," "Or else," "Or else," and each of his sentences ends with a noun. This repeated pattern in the structure of the sentences is most obvious here, but you can find it throughout the scene, as in Hippolyta's first (and only) speech:

> Four days will quickly steep themselves in night;
> Four nights will quickly dream away the time;

and in Theseus's admonition to Hermia:

> question your desires,
> Know of your youth, examine well your blood.

There's a sequence of three imperative verbs followed by the word "you" followed by a noun. What is the word for these repeated patterns? They are figures of speech. And, nowadays, speaking for myself and, I imagine, speaking for you, we don't know much about figures of speech—not nearly as much as Shakespeare did. If I ask you to name some figures of speech, I suspect you could come up with "metaphor" and "antithesis," and perhaps "zeugma" and even "synecdoche," and after that you would stop. But when they went to school, Shakespeare and his contemporaries learned about hundreds of figures of speech. There were handbooks on the subject and they learned their Greek and Latin names, they learned examples of them, and then they practiced using them themselves. One such handbook gave examples of figures of speech taken exclusively from one work, Sir Philip Sidney's *Arcadia. The Arcadian Rhetoric* it was called.[1] It was something Shakespeare learned at a very early age and which became part of the way he thought. He used figures of speech all the way through his professional career, but in this fairly early play, the figures of speech are more noticeable than they are in his later plays. So the style of the scene is an artificial style, constructed very formally, and it consists to some extent in the repeated structure of the sentences—and also in the profusion of metaphors. Lysander uses a whole series of metaphors—"momentany as a sound," "swift as a shadow," "short as any dream." Which brings us to our final question: as you sit and listen to this dialogue, what effect does it have on you? What are you aware of?

Aud.: The characters may not be saying entirely what's in their minds. They are not being up-front.

Wilders: You may be right, but these characters are not very complex characters. They don't have inner feelings which they fail to express. What they say is all there is to know about them. Any other suggestions?

Aud.: It's a very deliberate sort of sentence structure, so that I get the feeling that he's trying to convey some important information that is very well thought out. In the prose, it's more familiar and easier to listen to, but you don't need to pay quite so much attention to it.

Wilders: Good. The very patterned organization actually makes the meaning more lucid. For example, the repeated structure of the lines which Hermia and Lysander speak to each other makes the important words more emphatic. And the fact that one line chimes exactly with another indicates something about the two characters. It shows that they, too, are similar. They are made for each other. I also suggest that, as we listen to this dialogue, we are almost as aware of the author who is organizing it as of what the characters are saying. Bottom and his friends are more like us. The artifice of the dialogue makes us feel that these are artificial characters, not people we might overhear in the street but characters who have been created by the author and placed in situations which he has devised. In other words we are conscious that we are watching a play. As a result of that we don't take them or their problems very seriously, as we might those, for example, in *Othello.* We are aware of the playwright and are intrigued by the intricate way in which he develops, interweaves, and finally resolves the plot. It's the kind of effect created by one of Bach's fugues. They can be very exciting, but one part of our minds notices the artfulness and ingenuity with which he handles the musical material. When it was first performed, *A Midsummer Night's Dream* was the most brilliant comedy that had yet been written. Shakespeare seems to have known this, and as we watch and listen even to the first scene, we can sense the pleasure and satisfaction he felt in exercising his creative powers.

Notes

1. Abraham Fraunce, *The Arcadian Rhetorike; or, The praecepts of rhetoric made plain by examples, Greeke, Latin, English, Italian, French, Spanich* . . . (London: Printed by Thomas Orwin, 1588). See Patricia Parker's essays in this volume on *The Merry Wives of Windsor* and *A Midsummer Night's Dream* for a more extensive use of sixteenth-century figures of speech. [Editors' note.]

A Midsummer Night's Dream, 1.1.1–251

(With permission from Houghton Mifflin, *The Riverside Shakespeare,* ed. G. Blakemore Evans, 1974.)

[ACT 1, SCENE 1]

Enter THESEUS, HIPPOLYTA, [PHILOSTRATE,] *with others.*

The. Now, fair Hippolyta, our nuptial hour
Draws on apace. Four happy days bring in
Another moon; but O, methinks, how slow
This old moon [wanes]! She lingers my desires,
Like to a step-dame, or a dowager,   5
Long withering out a young man's revenue.
    Hip. Four days will quickly steep themselves in
    night;
Four nights will quickly dream away the time;
And then the moon, like to a silver bow
[New] bent in heaven, shall behold the night   10
Of our solemnities.
    The.   Go Philostrate,
Stir up the Athenian youth to merriments,
Awake the pert and nimble spirit of mirth,
Turn melancholy forth to funerals:
The pale companion is not for our pomp.   15
                  [Exit Philostrate.]
Hippolyta, I woo'd thee with my sword,
And won thy love doing thee injuries;
But I will wed thee in another key,
With pomp, with triumph, and with revelling.

Enter EGEUS *and his daughter* HERMIA *and* LYSANDER *and* DEMETRIUS.

    Ege. Happy be Theseus, our renowned Duke! 20
    The. Thanks, good Egeus. What's the news with
thee?
    Ege. Full of vexation come I, with complaint
Against my child, my daughter Hermia.
Stand forth, Demetrius. My noble lord,
This man hath my consent to marry her.   25

Stand forth, Lysander. And, my gracious Duke,
This man hath bewitch'd the bosom of my child.
Thou, thou, Lysander, thou hast given her rhymes,
And interchang'd love-tokens with my child;
Thou hast by moonlight at her window sung   30
With faining voice verses of faining love,
And stol'n the impression of her fantasy
With bracelets of thy hair, rings, gawds, conceits,
Knacks, trifles, nosegays, sweetmeats—messengers
Of strong prevailment in unhardened youth.   35
With cunning hast thou filch'd my daughter's heart,
Turn'd her obedience (which is due to me)
To stubborn harshness. And, my gracious Duke,
Be it so she will not here before your Grace
Consent to marry with Demetrius,   40
I beg the ancient privilege of Athens:
As she is mine, I may dispose of her;
Which shall be either to this gentleman,
Or to her death, according to our law
Immediately provided in that case.   45
    The. What say you, Hermia? Be advis'd, fair maid.
To you your father should be as a god;
One that compos'd your beauties; yea, and one
To whom you are but as a form in wax,
By him imprinted, and within his power,   50
To leave the figure, or disfigure it.
Demetrius is a worthy gentleman.
    Her. So is Lysander.
    The.   In himself he is;
But in this kind, wanting your father's voice,
The other must be held the worthier.   55
    Her. I would my father look'd but with my eyes.
    The. Rather your eyes must with his judgment
look.
    Her. I do entreat your Grace to pardon me.
I know not by what power I am made bold,
Nor how it may concern my modesty,   60

In such a presence here to plead my thoughts;
But I beseech your Grace that I may know
The worst that may befall me in this case,
If I refuse to wed Demetrius.
    The. Either to die the death, or to abjure   65
For ever the society of men.
Therefore, fair Hermia, question your desires,
Know of your youth, examine well your blood,
Whether (if you yield not to your father's choice)
You can endure the livery of a nun,   70
For aye to be in shady cloister mew'd,
To live a barren sister all your life,
Chaunting fair hymns to the cold fruitless moon.
Thrice blessed they that master so their blood
To undergo such maiden pilgrimage;   75
But earthlier happy is the rose distill'd,
Than that which withering on the virgin thorn
Grows, lives, and dies in single blessedness.
    Her. So will I grow, so live, so die, my lord,
Ere I will yield my virgin patent up   80
Unto his lordship, whose unwished yoke
My soul consents not to give sovereignty.
    The. Take time to pause, and by the next new
        moon—
The sealing-day betwixt my love and me
For everlasting bond of fellowship—   85
Upon that day either prepare to die
For disobedience to your father's will,
Or else to wed Demetrius, as he would,
Or on Diana's altar to protest
For aye austerity and single life.   90
    Dem. Relent, sweet Hermia, and Lysander, yield
Thy crazed title to my certain right.
    Lys. You have her father's love, Demetrius,
Let me have Hermia's; do you marry him.
    Ege. Scornful Lysander, true, he hath my love; 95
And what is mine, my love shall render him.
And she is mine, and all my right of her
I do estate unto Demetrius.
    Lys. I am, my lord, as well deriv'd as he,
As well possess'd; my love is more than his;   100
My fortunes every way as fairly rank'd
(If not with vantage) as Demetrius';
And (which is more than all these boasts can be)
I am belov'd of beauteous Hermia.
Why should not I then prosecute my right?   105
Demetrius, I'll avouch it to his head,
Made love to Nedar's daughter, Helena,
And won her soul; and she, sweet lady, dotes,
Devoutly dotes, dotes in idolatry,
Upon this spotted and inconstant man.   110
    The. I must confess that I have heard so much,

And with Demetrius thought to have spoke thereof;
But, being over-full of self-affairs,
My mind did lose it. But, Demetrius, come,
And come, Egeus, you shall go with me;   115
I have some private schooling for you both.
For you, fair Hermia, look you arm yourself
To fit your fancies to your father's will;
Or else the law of Athens yields you up
(Which by no means we may extenuate)   120
To death, or to a vow of single life.
Come, my Hippolyta; what cheer, my love?
Demetrius and Egeus, go along;
I must employ you in some business
Against our nuptial, and confer with you   125
Of something nearly that concerns yourselves.
    Ege. With duty and desire we follow you.
            Exeunt. [*Maneant Lysander and Hermia.*]
    Lys. How now, my love? why is your cheek so
        pale?
How chance the roses there do fade so fast?
    Her. Belike for want of rain; which I could well
Beteem them from the tempest of my eyes.   131
    Lys. Ay me! for aught that I could ever read,
Could ever hear by tale or history,
The course of true love never did run smooth;
But either it was different in blood—   135
    Her. O cross! too high to be enthrall'd to [low].
    Lys. Or else misgraffed in respect of years—
    Her. O spite! too old to be engag'd to young.
    Lys. Or else it stood upon the choice of friends—
    Her. O hell, to choose love by another's eyes! 140
    Lys. Or if there were a sympathy in choice,
War, death, or sickness did lay siege to it,
Making it momentany as a sound,
Swift as a shadow, short as any dream,
Brief as the lightning in the collied night,   145
That, in a spleen, unfolds both heaven and earth;
And ere a man hath power to say "Behold!"
The jaws of darkness do devour it up:
So quick bright things come to confusion.
    Her. If then true lovers have been ever cross'd,
It stands as an edict in destiny.   151
Then let us teach our trial patience,
Because it is a customary cross,
As due to love as thoughts and dreams and sighs,
Wishes and tears, poor fancy's followers.   155
    Lys. A good persuasion; therefore hear me,
        Hermia:
I have a widow aunt, a dowager,
Of great revenue, and she hath no child.
From Athens is her house remote seven leagues;
And she respects me as her only son.   160

There, gentle Hermia, may I marry thee;
And to that place the sharp Athenian law
Cannot pursue us. If thou lovest me, then
Steal forth thy father's house to-morrow night;
And in the wood, a league without the town   165
(Where I did meet thee once with Helena
To do observance to a morn of May),
There will I stay for thee.
    Her. My good Lysander,
I swear to thee, by Cupid's strongest bow,
By his best arrow with the golden head,   170
By the simplicity of Venus' doves,
By that which knitteth souls and prospers loves,
And by that fire which burn'd the Carthage queen
When the false Troyan under sail was seen,
By all the vows that ever men have broke   175
(In number more than ever women spoke),
In that same place thou hast appointed me
To-morrow truly will I meet with thee.
    Lys. Keep promise, love. Look, here comes Helena.

Enter HELENA.

    Her. God speed fair Helena! whither away?   180
    Hel. Call you me fair? That fair again unsay.
Demetrius loves your fair, O happy fair!
Your eyes are lodestars, and your tongue's sweet air
More tuneable than lark to shepherd's ear
When wheat is green, when hawthorn buds appear.
Sickness is catching; O, were favor so,   186
[Yours would] I catch, fair Hermia, ere I go;
My ear should catch your voice, my eye your eye,
My tongue should catch your tongue's sweet melody.
Were the world mine, Demetrius being bated,   190
The rest I'll give to be to you translated.
O, teach me how you look, and with what art
You sway the motion of Demetrius' heart.
    Her. I frown upon him; yet he loves me still.
    Hel. O that your frowns would teach my smiles
        such skill!   195
    Her. I give him curses; yet he gives me love.
    Hel. O that my prayers could such affection move!
    Her. The more I hate, the more he follows me.
    Hel. The more I love, the more he hateth me.
    Her. His folly, Helena, is no fault of mine.   200
    Hel. None but your beauty; would that fault
        were mine!
    Her. Take comfort; he no more shall see my face;
Lysander and myself will fly this place.
Before the time I did Lysander see,

Seem'd Athens as a paradise to me;   205
O then, what graces in my love do dwell,
That he hath turn'd a heaven unto a hell!
    Lys. Helen, to you our minds we will unfold:
To-morrow night, when Phoebe doth behold
Her silver visage in the wat'ry glass,   210
Decking with liquid pearl the bladed grass
(A time that lovers' flight doth still conceal),
Through Athens gates have we devis'd to steal.
    Her. And in the wood, where often you and I
Upon faint primrose beds were wont to lie,   215
Emptying our bosoms of their counsel [sweet],
There my Lysander and myself shall meet;
And thence from Athens turn away our eyes,
To seek new friends and [stranger companies].
Farewell, sweet playfellow, pray thou for us;   220
And good luck grant thee thy Demetrius!
Keep word, Lysander, we must starve our sight
From lovers' food till morrow deep midnight.
    Lys. I will, my Hermia.   *Exit Hermia.*
        Helena, adieu:
As you on him, Demetrius dote on you!   225
        Exit Lysander.
    Hel. How happy some o'er other some can be!
Through Athens I am thought as fair as she.
But what of that? Demetrius thinks not so;
He will not know what all but he do know;
And as he errs, doting on Hermia's eyes,   230
So I, admiring of his qualities.
Things base and vile, holding no quantity,
Love can transpose to form and dignity.
Love looks not with the eyes but with the mind;
And therefore is wing'd Cupid painted blind.   235
Nor hath Love's mind of any judgment taste;
Wings, and no eyes, figure unheedy haste;
And therefore is Love said to be a child,
Because in choice he is so oft beguil'd.
As waggish boys in game themselves forswear,   240
So the boy Love is perjur'd every where;
For ere Demetrius look'd on Hermia's eyne,
He hail'd down oaths that he was only mine;
And when this hail some heat from Hermia felt,
So he dissolv'd, and show'rs of oaths did melt.   245
I will go tell him of fair Hermia's flight;
Then to the wood will he to-morrow night
Pursue her; and for this intelligence
If I have thanks, it is a dear expense.
But herein mean I to enrich my pain,   250
To have his sight thither and back again.   *Exit.*

Interpreting Through Wordplay:
The Merry Wives of Windsor

PATRICIA PARKER

Translation Lessons

For over a decade I have been interested in "translation" in Shakespeare, an interest which began simultaneously with an early inquiry into metaphor, the figure of *translatio* or "transport," and a problem in teaching Shakespeare's *Merry Wives*. The pedagogical problem involved how to interpret the grammar lesson of act 4, where Mistress Page asks the Welsh schoolmaster Parson Evans to run her son "Will" through his lessons.[1] It is not that the scene is difficult to teach; on the contrary, its veritable cornucopia of obscene double entendres, issuing from Will's imperfect learning and the malapropping female tongue of Mistress Quickly, makes it one of the most attractive of Shakespearean scenes to present to students, including those who have never before encountered Shakespeare.[For the text of *Merry Wives of Windsor* 4.1.1–85, see pp. 215–16.]

The problem, instead, is how to view this scene of instruction—with its translation out of Latin into double-meaning Englishings—in relation to the rest of *Merry Wives,* especially when a critic as influential as Northrop Frye once dismissed it as an irrelevancy, "dragged in merely to fill up time."[2] The problem, both critical and pedagogical, is exacerbated by the bulk of criticism and editing of the play which, often noting the scene's absence from the Quarto text, similarly dismisses it. Dr. Johnson pronounces it "a very trifling scene, of no use to the plot, and I should think of no great delight to the audience."[3] G. R. Hibbard's New Penguin edition (one likely to be encountered by students because of its relatively low price) flatly pronounces that the scene does not appear in the quartos because it is "a self-contained episode, totally unrelated to the rest of the action." Many of those who don't condemn it approve it for perfunctory or less-than-compelling reasons. Arden editor H. J. Oliver comments that the scene, "probably intended for an educated audience," has the virtue that it "avoids two successive Falstaff scenes," a sentiment echoed in the recent Oxford edition of T. W. Craik, who comments that it is "useful" since it "prevents two Falstaff scenes from occurring consecutively and with nothing but Ford's soliloquy to separate Falstaff's exit from his re-entry."[4]

My own experience with *Merry Wives,* however, diverges strikingly from views that would isolate from the rest of this play this scene of ever more vagrant translation. It is this different experience—beginning from this critically marginalized scene in a play which has also been treated more marginally within the canon as a whole—that I would like to record more fully here.[5] And I propose to start from networks of wordplay which link this controversial "grammar" scene to other parts of this "English" comedy, and then, through *Merry Wives,* to a consideration, however necessarily brief and telescopic, of the importance of translation and the "translative" throughout Shakespeare.[6]

Let us look, then, first at this grammar scene and its outrageous Englishings. The scene—coming just after the first of the tricks played on Falstaff, his conveyance out in the buck-basket and his dumping into the "ford" (3.5.35–36)—is in fact staged as a kind of interlude. Mistress Page, promising to come to Mistress Ford "by and by" (4.1.7), proceeds first to take her "young man" to "school" (4.1.8). When she discovers that there is "no school" but rather a "playing-day" (9–10), she asks the schoolmaster, Welsh parson Evans, to run her son through his Latin grammar, since it seems her husband has complained that young Will "profits nothing" at his book (4.1.15).[7] What follows is a mock grammar lesson, based on the humanist *Grammar* of Colet and Lily intended for "the bryngynge up of all those that entende to atteyne the knowlege of the Latine tongue" and commanded by Edward VI for use in all English schools—a text, in other words, familiar to Shakespeare as another schoolboy "Will."[8] The method of the lesson is the "double translation" developed in this official *Grammar,* as in Ascham's *Schoolmaster* and other humanist texts—a system of translating out of Latin into English and back into Latin again without loss or alienating difference.

Far from proceeding according to this prescribed schema of translation and its controlled pedagogical discipline, however, the lesson that proceeds in this grammar scene soon gets out of hand, mangled by the mispronunciations of the local schoolmaster, the lateral slidings into English of the truant "Will" and the unschooled vernacular of Mistress Quickly. Quickly's gloss on "Two" as the "numbers" in "nouns"—"Truly I thought there had been one number more, because they say, 'Ods's nouns" (21–

24), or "God's wounds"—leads rapidly to a series of slippages from Latin, the *sermo patrius* or "father" tongue, into a more vagrant mother tongue, as *pulcher* becomes "polecats" or "prostitutes" (25–29) and *lapis* slides into the "pebble" (Folio, "peeble") or "stone" which links it with "testicle" (31–34). The lesson quickly declines into cases which nowhere appear in the *Grammar* of Colet and Lily—the "focative" (for "vocative") and the "genitive" or "Jinny's case" (50–62), and the double-meaning "hick, hack, horum" and the English "case," "cods," and "keys" lurking beneath Latin *quaes*, *quods*, and *quis* (77–79).[9] Translation—which means in the literal sense a carrying or transporting away—is here carried well beyond both "father" tongue and the boundaries of Lily and Colet's prescribed system of control. Latin returns not to Latin, in a faithful and homogeneous rendering,[10] but rather escapes into meanings that betray their original, wandering too far afield to be firmly called back or reined in.

Translation, Construction, Property

This scene of translation out of Latin into English in act 4, moreover—far from being an isolated irrelevance to the rest of the play—forges links with other parts of *Merry Wives* which invoke the multiple and different senses of "translation" more generally, quite apart from the scene's direct verbal echoes of Falstaff's boast that he can make Mistress Ford the "key" (2.2.274) to her husband's "coffer" or of her own warning of "knights" who "will *hack*" (2.1.52), in lines which display a similar conflation of sexual and grammatical terms. The most striking invocation of "translation" in ways that anticipate 4.1 comes early in the play, when Falstaff announces what will become its central plot, his assault on the "honesty" of the two Windsor wives:

> *Falstaff.* I do mean to make love to Ford's wife. I spy entertainment in her. She discourses, she carves, she gives the leer of invitation. I can construe the action of her familiar style, and the hardest voice of her behavior (to be English'd rightly) is, "I am Sir John Falstaff's."
> *Pistol.* He hath studied her well [F "will"], and translated her will, out of honesty into English.
>
> (1.3.43–50)[11]

As in Mistress Ford's "hack" and the scene of grammatical instruction in act 4, this play on "translation" in *Merry Wives* combines the grammatical sense with its obscener double.[12] Falstaff's claim to "construe" the "familiar style" of a woman he intends to draw into profitable adultery depends on the contemporary meaning of "construe" as "translate," on precisely, that is, the exercise of construing or "construction" on which the grammar scene itself depends.[13] But the double meanings here give us translation this time not out of Latin into English as we might expect (or as a proper Latin "will" would need to be) but rather out of "*honesty*" into "English," as if "honesty" itself were also something that could be "translated."[14] Falstaff implies of Mistress Ford (as Shakespeare's Ulysses does of Cressida) that there is "language in her eye," and that he is the one who knows how to "translate" it.[15]

"Construing" or "construction," both in the grammar scene of act 4 and in this earlier one, appears, then, in the sense of interpreting or "translating"—out of Latin, or out of "honesty," into "English." "Construction" also appears, however, in a different context in *Merry Wives,* in a way that begins to compound and extend the implications of that sense. In a passage in the scene in which Ford (disguised as "Brook") approaches Falstaff to win the love of Mistress Ford, "construction" retains the sense of "translation" while it also conveys its other meaning of "property" or "edifice":

> *Falstaff.* Of what quality was your love then?
> *Ford.* Like a fair house built on another man's ground, so that I have lost my edifice by mistaking the place where I erected it. . . . Some say that, though she appear *honest* to me, yet in other places she enlargeth her mirth so far that there is shrewd *construction* made of her.
> (2.2.214–24)

"Construction" here—presented once again as something opposed to "honesty"—picks up the sense of "translation" still lingering from the scene in act 1 where Falstaff had spoken of this same Ford's wife ("I can *construe* the action of her familiar style," 1.1.46–50) and has similarly to do with what others "construe" or translate from the outward signs of a "merry" wife.[16] But it is also strengthened in its sense of "property" by the lines just before, where Ford-Brook complains that "Like a fair house built on another man's ground," he has lost his "edifice" by "mistaking" the "place" where he "erected" it.[17] The double meaning of "erection" here, as edifice and as a sexual form of "standing"—in the context of adultery as building on another man's ground—joins the double meaning of "building" in the exchange between Falstaff and Mistress Quickly after the would-be adulterer has been literally transported, in the buck-basket through which he is carried out and dumped into the "ford":

Quickly. Alas the day! good heart, that was not her fault. She does so take on with her men; they mistook their erection.
Falstaff. So did I mine, to build upon a foolish woman's promise.

(3.5.38–42)

Taken together with the elaborate wordplay on names which extends in the line just before this to the name of "Ford" ("Mistress Ford? I have had ford enough. I was thrown into the ford; I have my belly full of ford"), the "ford" Falstaff is thrown into is here proclaimed by Quickly not to be the (sexually double-meaning) "fault" of Mistress Ford.[18] His transporters simply "mistook their erection." If the adulterous "Brook" complains in the earlier scene that his love is "like a fair house built on another man's ground," then we have to deal in both scenes with the problem of mistaking an "erection."

The link between translation and edifice, as between language and property through the various senses of "construction," should not, of course, come as a surprise in a play from a period when education itself was so closely tied to the etymological resonances of "edification" as "building." In the complex wordplay of this bourgeois play—filled not only with a mock-humanist grammar scene but with multiple references to language, to grammar, and to property—terms like "erection" link several semantic fields at once. But it is important as well to note that the image of mistaking an erection by building on another man's ground is also here an image of adultery in the sense that it was understood in this period as a form of theft.[19] In a context in which wives were a form of property, and their chastity the guarantor of the legitimate line linked with the proper foundation of a "house," adultery had literally to do with usurping, thieving, and building on another man's ground.

The notion of adultery as thievery sounds throughout the period. One later example of this linkage describes adultery as a sin

> very heinous in respect of our Neighbour, whose hedge we break down, and whose enclosure we lay wast; while we do not only purloyn and defile and dishonour that which is his most proper possession . . . but we invade and incroach upon his inheritance also by making our Bastard his Heir.[20]

Stealing a wife, as such descriptions make clear, has to do with "purloining" a man's "most *proper* possession," as it also does with leaving, like the cuckoo, one's offspring in another's "house."[21] Concern with women as "movable" property—as crossing boundaries from a father's to a husband's "house" and hence as dangerously open to the "translation" of adultery[22]—invokes anxieties about property not only as the threat that a "private" place might become a "common" place or that a rival might usurp or "build" on the husband's proper "ground," but that such translation could destroy the integrity of a "house."[23]

"Translation," then, both in *Merry Wives* and in its social context, links two spheres in a single term—the translating of words and a theft or "purloining" of property. Words, like wives in this patriarchal view, can be transported, borne off or carried away. They have difficulty being "proper" for long, especially when subject to the vernacular and its vagrancy. Adultery is understood as a form of "translation," just as translations adulterate, carry or bear away the integrity of an original. The wife transported into adultery has a counterpart in the translation or transport into other words which turn, or vary, an original text.[24] Both proper meanings and property, including wives, can be "translated" into something else, with no guarantee of unaltered, or unadulterated, return. "Translation" is compatible with "edification" only if kept within bounds, in something like the carefully structured humanist discipline of "construction" parodied in act 4 of *Merry Wives* and carried quickly beyond bounds by the lateral slidings of Mistress Quickly's malapropping "female" tongue, unschooled by the edifying discipline that was part, in Shakespeare's day, of a pedagogical economy of men and boys.[25]

Conveyance and Theft

To draw attention to the relation this wordplay sets up between terms of language and terms of property—including wives—is in one sense to draw attention to the linguistic counterparts of the bourgeois context of *Merry Wives*. Ford, the jealous husband of the play, thinks expressly in these terms:

> See the hell of having a false woman! My bed shall be abus'd, my coffers ransack'd, my reputation gnawn at, and I shall not only receive this villainous wrong, but stand under the adoption of abominable terms. . . . I will rather trust a Fleming with my butter, Parson Hugh the Welshman with my cheese, an Irishman with my aqua-vitae bottle, or a thief to walk my ambling gelding, than my wife with herself. (2.2.291–305)[26]

The play's concern with property and hence with theft, with what was also referred to as its "translation" or alienation, sounds throughout, and may even inform the puzzling "An-heires" of act 2, since Anne and what she stands to inherit are such an important part of the play as a whole.[27] Perhaps because of the emphasis on bourgeois property in *Merry Wives*, there is a corresponding emphasis on "trade" and on "conveyance" as a form of bearing or carrying, as well as on "translation" both as linguistic transport and as theft. Cozening, cheating, and pilfering accompany the characters the play shares with the history plays—not just Falstaff but Pistol and Nym. Cozening as well as thievery runs throughout the multiple plots of this comedy, from the references at its beginning to Falstaff's poaching on Shallow's ground and deer, to Ford's anxieties about his "coffers" and his wife, and the puzzling German thieves who suddenly appear out of nowhere in act 4. The form of "translation" or "conveyance" that is theft is so insistent even at the verbal level that the stage directions for the final scene read, "Dr. Caius comes one way, and *steals away* a boy in green; and Slender another way; he takes a boy in white: and Fenton *steals* Mistress Anne Page" (5.5).

The prohibitions of the Decalogue against adultery and covetise are linked in *Merry Wives*, as in the tradition of commentary, with the general prohibition "Thou shalt not steal." Theft and adultery in the play are introduced together when Pistol warns Ford to beware of the "horn" ("Take heed, have open eye, for thieves do foot by night. / Take heed, ere summer comes or cuckoo-birds do sing," 2.1.122–23). And the lines from the commandment on covetousness ("Thou shalt not covet thy neighbour's wife . . . nor his oxe nor his ass, neither any thing that is thy neighbour's [Geneva Bible, Exod. 20:17]) are echoed in the play (as in the bourgeois context of *The Taming of the Shrew*) in the exchange which accompanies the final exposure of Falstaff, the would-be adulterer/thief ("*Falstaff.* I do begin to perceive that I am made an ass. / *Ford.* Ay, and an ox too; both the proofs are extant," 5.5.119–20).[28]

Merry Wives' emphasis on property—and on its "translation"—is also joined by its emphasis on a plot which involves crossings in both directions of the boundaries of class, as well as repeated reminders of mercantile forms of "trade." Though much of early criticism of the play focusses on its rural and ritual aspects (undeniably important in the punishment of Falstaff and the Herne the Hunter of the Windsor Forest scene), the England the play evokes is also the newer one of social mobility and monetary fluidity, of the pursuit of burgher purses by impoverished gentlemen and

its inverse, the phenomenon of "gentlemen made cheap" and titles deval-
ued through the selling of honors and lineages, part of a new context in
which "all ways do lie open" if *"money* go before" (2.2.168–69).[29] The
sense of the fluidity of "coinage" in the monetary as well as the linguistic
sense is as much a part of *Merry Wives* as its reminiscences of ancient
rituals or its incorporated homage to Windsor Castle and the Order of the
Garter, in a plot where the aristocratic motto of "Honi soit qui mal y pense"
is more applicable to the jealous suspicions of burgher husbands of "honest" wives.[30]

The play begins with references to Shallow's rise to the status of "gentleman born" and proceeds with a plot in which higher-born figures like
Fenton and Falstaff pursue women who appear to promise access to a
burgher purse. It suggests a verbal link between upward translation as
social mobility and the scene of grammatical and linguistic translation in
act 4 when, in response to the impecunious Falstaff's offer to make her
"gentle," Mistress Page warns Mistress Ford, "These knights will hack and
so thou shouldst not alter the article of thy gentry" (2.1.52–53). Falstaff's
pursuit of the wives, and of this burgher "purse," is explicitly termed a
form of "trade" in a passage in which punning on "exchequers" and "cheat-
ers" links his assault on them with other contemporary forms of pillaging:

> She bears the purse too; she is a region in Guiana, all gold and bounty. I
> will be *cheaters* to them both, and they shall be *exchequers* to me. They
> shall be my East and West Indies, and I will *trade* to them both.
>
> (1.3.68–72)

To "trade" in this series of images, is to be a "cheater." The term carries
with it the sense of "betray" as well as the form of translation Falstaff seeks
to engage their "honesty" in.[31]

Carrying, Conveying, and Bearing Away

"Translation," then, in the period of *Merry Wives,* links the transporting or
translating of words with the transfer, conveying or stealing of property. To
follow the workings of this network of wordplay within this play is to
introduce students to the importance of language not just in an older "New
Critical" sense but as a way into the historically contemporary resonances
of the language on which such wordplay depends. "Translation"—the bur-
den of the scene of instruction in act 4—carries with it in the whole of

Merry Wives all of the various resonances so far traced, from translation between tongues and the form of metaphorical conveyance Puttenham termed the "Figure of Transport" to adultery and the "conveyance" or transporting of goods and property.[32] Far from being a self-contained episode, unrelated to the rest of *Merry Wives,* the scene of grammatical instruction in act 4 is thus implicated in a larger discursive network which has to do not only with translation out of Latin—or "honesty"—into English, but with all the other senses of translation or transport, including theft.

Merry Wives, it has often been noted, is full of references both to language in general and to English in particular, appropriately enough for the canon's only "English" comedy. These range from the linguistic manglings of the French Dr. Caius who, as it is put by the malapropping Quickly, abuses both "God's patience and the King's English" (1.4.5–6), to Nym, described as "a fellow [who] frights English out of his wits" (2.1.138–39), and Ford's promise to the Welsh schoolmaster at its end ("I will never mistrust my wife again, till thou art able to woo her in good English," 5.5.133–34). The play is also full of translations and mock-translations. The Host of the Garter provides a jesting *mis*translation to the French doctor who is vulnerable to such cozening because of his less than perfect command of English ("*Caius.* Mock-vater? vat is dat? / *Host.* Mock-vater, in our English tongue, is valor, bully," 2.2.59–61). When the Welsh parson Evans translates *Pauca verba* as "good worts," Falstaff further translates these "worts" into "good cabbage" (1.1.120–21). Beyond mere "worts" or words, Falstaff's ducking in the Thames involves another form of mis-translation, as an immersion suggestive of mock-baptism. Mistress Ford says of the unregenerate knight to be unceremoniously dumped in that river, "I am half afraid he will have need of washing, so throwing him into the water will do him a benefit" (3.3.182–84). The lines pick up a sense of "washing" which here, as in the histories, might be the kind of "translation" the unregenerate knight is so often claimed to need[33]—mock-water, perhaps, in a somewhat different form.

Beyond "translation" in linguistic contexts, the play is filled with translating in a more literal sense—as conveying, transporting, or carrying. It contains not just thieves but a multiplicity of conveyers or "carriers"; and its language goes out of its way to iterate the notion of bearing, carrying, or "conveying." Mistress Quickly, the outrageous transporter of meanings from their proper sense in the scene of grammatical instruction in act 4, is identified as one of Cupid's many "carriers" (2.2.135), in a play filled with carriers or go-betweens.[34] As a conveyer of messages she is in a class by herself, acting as go-between for the wives and Falstaff but also as a representative and message-bearer for three different suitors to Anne Page. In a play filled with "Pages," as with references to letters, books, and print, the little "page" who conveys messages back and forth between Falstaff and the wives is described as being as apt to "carry a letter twenty mile, as easy as a cannon will shoot point blank twelve score" (3.2.32–34). (His "carrying" is, in one intriguing passage, also ambiguously linked with "honesty.")[35] Ford asks Falstaff to help him "carry" his "money": "If you will help to *bear* it, Sir John, take all, or half, for easing me of the *carriage,*" (2.2.171–73), an offer to which Falstaff replies, "Sir, I know not how I may deserve to be your *porter*" (2.2.174–75). The Host, in one of the play's many instances of verbal iteration or doubling, declares of Fenton's suit for Anne, "he will carry't, he will carry't" (3.2.69). Evans's questioning of Slender's desire for this same Anne ("can you *carry* your good will to the maid?" 1.1.230–31) similarly iterates the notion of "carrying" ("if you can carry her your desires towards her," 1.1.236) in another passage suggesting an uncertain "erection." The wives themselves are connected with conveying from a "house" (an act of conveyance which links a literal form of transport to adultery as "bearing away") when, in resisting Ford's inquiry as to where the buck-basket is being "conveyed" in act 3, they respond by reminding him that he has nothing to do with what is "borne" (or "born") out of it ("Why, what have you to do whither they bear it?" 3.3.154–56).[36] And in Quickly's instructions to Falstaff ("she desires you once more to come to her, between eight and nine. I must carry her word quickly," 3.4.45–47), a go-between or "carrier" is described as "carrying" a word, as if words, like "letters," were items to be transported.

A similar verbal harping sounds throughout the play on the multiple senses of "conveyance." When news comes of Ford's imminent arrival in the scene of Falstaff's first visit to Ford's wife, Mistress Page warns her friend, "If you have a friend here, convey, convey him out" (3.3.117), and then urges her to "bethink [herself] of some conveyance" (3.3.127)—a word which means both stratagem and means of transport—before he is literally conveyed or "carried" (3.3.147) out of the house in the buck-basket of foul linen. "Convey" is also, however, as Pistol reminds us, a polite word for "steal" ("'Convey,' the wise call it. 'Steal'? foh! a fico for the phrase!" 1.3.29–30); and the "conveyance" so much harped on as the means of carrying Falstaff out is also the stratagem by which he, like the suitors at the comedy's end, "steals" away.[37]

Behind these scenes of translating, conveying, stealing, or going between in *Merry Wives* lurks, as so often in Shakespeare, the figure of Mercury. Mercury is explicitly invoked when Mistress Quickly, the mistranslator of 4.1 and the play's principal go-between, is called a "she-Mercury" (2.2.80), a phrase which links this translative female to the figure who is at once a translator/interpreter and a notorious conveyer, patron both of language and of thieves. That a reference to Mercury should appear in a play as concerned with bourgeois matters as it is with property, language, convey-ing and stealing should come as no surprise, given that the links between Mercury and all of these, as with the mercantile world of "trade," are so long-standing.[38] (To take just one of many possible classical examples, Ovid underlines the link between the mercurial *interpres*—interpreter or go-between—and the merchant or *mercator*, including their common in-volvement with "glozing," with "cheating" and with cozening.)[39] To call Mistress Quickly a "she-Mercury" is therefore to summon as background for this burghers' play all the contemporary associations of the mercurial—with messengers, including "pages" (one Elizabethan text calls Mercury Jove's "Prety Page"),[40] with merchants' trading, with language, with writ-ing, and with cozening and theft. Mercury was in early modern England a "translator" and "traytor" in the realm of language and rhetoric as well as of thievery.[41] John Eliot's *Ortho-epia Gallica: Eliots Fruits for the French* (1593), a manual of translation directly pertinent to Shakespeare since it is echoed in *Romeo and Juliet*,[42] invokes "Mercurie the God of cunning" in an introductory letter which identifies the god both with language-learning and with "translating." Nashe in *Summers Last Will and Testament* (a text closely contemporary with *Merry Wives*) calls "Hermes" the inventor of "letters to write lies withall,"[43] a description we need to keep in mind besides the letters, print, and multiple "pages" of Shakespeare's play.

Cozening Germans

So far we have traced in *Merry Wives* the network of wordplay—on trans-lation, conveying, construing and construction—which links terms of lan-guage with terms of property, including the bearing or transporting of words away from a "proper" sense. This intersection of language and prop-erty, involving "translation" as a form of "conveyance" in every sense, brings us now to the need to consider this play's mysterious "cozen Germans" or German thieves. These thieving "Germans" appear out of nowhere in act 4 of *Merry Wives*, the act which begins with the controversial translation scene (4.1) and then goes on to remind us of Falstaff's having been "convey'd" out of the "house" to which he comes as would-be adulterer or thief (4.2.146):

> *Bardolph.* Sir, the Germans desire to have three of your horses. The Duke himself will be to-morrow at court, and they are going to meet him.
> *Host.* What duke should that be comes so secretly? I hear not of him in the court. Let me speak with the gentlemen; they speak English?
> *Bardolph.* Ay, sir; I'll call them to you.
> *Host.* They shall have my horses, but I'll make them pay; I'll sauce them. They have had my house a week at command. I have turn'd away my other guests; they must come off. I'll sauce them, come.
>
> (4.3)

The scene in which these apparently "honest" Germans are revealed instead to be "thieves" is full of play on "cousining" and "cozening," on "germans" as "honest" but these "cozen Germans" as duplicitous instead.[44] The play's next reference to them comes in scene 5, when the Host discovers that his horses have been stolen, just after another reference to cozening (Falstaff's "the very same man that beguil'd Master Slender of his chain cozen'd him of it," 4.5.36–38):

> *Bardolph.* Out alas, sir, cozenage! mere cozenage.
> *Host.* Where be my horses? Speak well of them, varletto.
> *Bardolph.* Run away with the cozeners; for so soon as I came beyond Eton, they threw me off from behind one of them, in a slough of mire; and set spurs and away, like three German devils, three Doctor Faustuses.
> *Host.* They are gone but to meet the Duke, villain, do not say they be fled. Germans are honest men.
>
> [Enter] Evans
>
> *Evans.* Where is mine host?
> *Host.* What is the matter, sir?
> *Evans.* Have a care of your entertainments. There is a friend of mine come to town, tells me there is three cozen-germans that has cozen'd all the hosts of Readins, of Maidenhead, of Colebrook, of horses and money. I tell you for good will, look you. You are wise and full of gibes, and vlouting-stocks, and 'tis not convenient you should be cozen'd. Fare you well.
>
> [Enter] Caius
>
> *Caius.* Vere is mine host de Jarteer?
> *Host.* Here, Master Doctor, in perplexity and doubtful dilemma.

Caius. I cannot tell vat is dat, but it is tell-a me dat you make grand preparation for a duke de Jamany.

(4.5.63–87)

The usual way of glossing this scene and these honest-seeming but duplicitous, thieving, or "translating" Germans is by recourse to a possible topical reference to Count Mömpelgard, the duke of Württemberg, whose name may be reflected in the "three sorts of cosen garmombles" of the Quarto text and "Dear be a Garmaine Duke come to court" and whose application to membership in the Order of the Garter would link him to the Windsor Garter ceremony.[45] Whether or not, however, the Quarto's "cosen garmombles" and its reference to a "Garmaine Duke" link that version topically to Frederick, duke of Württemberg, as the "three Doctor Faustuses" which appear in all the texts of the play link this scene to Marlowe's *Doctor Faustus,* set in one of its versions specifically in Württemberg.[46] In any case, the Folio's play on "german" as both "honest" and as coming from Germany, and on "cozen" both as cousin and as cozener, bears relating to what we have already seen in *Merry Wives* as its elaborate network of wordplay on conveying and theft, and on translation (including out of "honesty") both as stealing and as conveying away.

Let us look, then, at "german" and at "cozening," and at these Shakespearean "cozen-germans" more particularly. The Host's incredulous "Germans are honest men" is a phrase which, along with "cozen-Iermans" and the translation scene of 4.1, appears only in the Folio text. "German" in English comes from *germanus,* which in Latin means simultaneously brother or close kind, faithful or "true," and geographically "German."[47] The Host's *"Germans* are *honest* men" thus plays on the fact that "german" is a synonym for "honest" as well as for "cousin" or kind, as in the "constant," "kind" and "true" of Shakespeare's Sonnet 105. "Cosingermans" are everywhere in Shakespeare, as is the play on "cousin" and "cozen" and the sense of "german" as both "honest" and kind or kin.[48] But the Shakespearean canon also plays repeatedly on the tension between "german" as "honest," "genuine," or "true" and the doubled sense of "cozen" both as relative or kindred and as cheating and cozening. Shakespearean playing on "germane" and "german" in context which sometimes evoke its closeness in sound to "gemmen" (twin) conveys just such an awareness of the potentially duplicitous, treacherous or cozening "german." In *The Winter's Tale,* the shepherd and his son are faced with the conflicting demand to be both "german" in the sense of "honest" and "true" and yet not "germane" in the sense of "kin" to Perdita, from whom they need to alienate themselves (4.4.773ff.) when Autolycus reports the king's wrath at his son's dalliance with a "shepherd's daughter." Hamlet remarks of Osric's extravagant, metaphorically transported terms, "The phrase would be more german [or, as the First Quarto has it, "more cosin-german"] to the matter if we could carry a cannon by our sides" (5.2.158–59). Other Shakespearean instances exploit the potential cozenage or cheating of the "cozen-german" as cozening accompaniment or duplicitous duplicate.

This scene of honest-seeming thieves or cozening "germans" from *Merry Wives* combines concentrated play on "Germans" who speak a language other than English, who are thieves or translators though they appear to be "honest," and who, "cousins" or kin, are something less than "kind." We have again to do with "translation," with something that conveys or translates, as with "cozen Germans" who cannot be "faithful, kind, and true" because, though "german," they are also "cozening." The inclusion of these "cozen-Germans" or duplicitous thieves within the play also allies them with its other forms of cozenage, including the conveyance or stratagem of Falstaff the "porter" between "Brook" and Ford's wife (2.2.175), described as one who has also "cozen'd" him (5.5.166–67).

The scene of translation or grammatical instruction with which we began introduces into the play a parody of contemporary humanism through its echoing of the official *Grammar* of Colet and Lily, and its system of closed translation from Latin into English and back again, in a rendering meant to be "constant," faithful and "true." As a comic version of the ideals of humanism functioning less than perfectly in practice, it takes, as we have seen, the form of a Welsh schoolmaster (who has neither competent Latin nor the King's English) catechizing the scion of an upwardly mobile bourgeois family whose name ("Will Page") recalls Shakespeare's own much-punned-on name of "Will," as well as the "page" associated elsewhere in the play with message-bearing, "carrying" or conveying (and with the new world of books and print).[49]

The already summoned context of humanism in the translation or grammar lesson of 4.1 forges thus another link between Germans and "translation" both within and beyond the bounds of *Merry Wives*. The reference to "three Doctor Faustuses" in the scene of translating or duplicitous "Germans" already focusses attention on Germany and (whether or not there is a topical reference to the duke of Württemburg) on Wittenberg as the other site of the Doctor Faustus of Marlowe's play. Even without this tantalizing reference, "Germans" might put us in mind of the contemporary associations of Germans more generally, famous as translators as well as fellow traders in a mercantile link with England that was one of the likely motives behind the possibility of accepting a "duke de Jamany" or Germany to the quintessentially English Order of the Garter in 1597.[50] Nashe's "To the Gentlemen Students of both Universities" praises the "laudable kinde of Translation" begun by "that aged Father Erasmus" and continued by "manie other reverent Germaines." His *Unfortunate Traveller* (1594)—a text whose "induction to the Pages" puns like *Merry Wives* on the "page" who is a conveyer of messages and the "page" of a book which carries words—includes the famous episode of the humanists at Wittenberg and of the "servile Ciceronianism" of the Wittenberg orator who, as a translator-copier of Cicero, "stealeth not whole phrases but whole pages out of Tully," a form of "absurd imitation," servile iteration or copying it attributes, along with translation more generally, to "leaden headed Germanes."[51]

There is, however, an even more suggestive link between the contemporary reputation of "Germanes" as translators and the wordplay in *Merry Wives* on the faithful or "germane." The writing of Erasmus (invoked elsewhere in Shakespeare, both directly and obliquely) is central in the passages from Nashe on "Germaines" both as humanist translators and as servile imitators, iterators, or copyists.[52] This particular "German" humanist and translator was also the *sensus germanus,* or "German sense," the possibility of a faithful translational rendering that would not betray or alienate its original. Erasmus developed this "german" sense as model of the "genuine, faithful, and true" paraphrase or duplicate in connection with his paraphrases of Scripture.[53] The method was put forward as an alternative to more extravagant allegorical commentary which deviated far from—and hence betrayed—a sacred original.

The *sensus germanus* was to be a mode of authenticity, paraphrased as a faithful "speaking alongside," though in *other* words. It was thus opposed to the *sensus alienus,* a rendering which deviates from or alienates and betrays the meaning it translates. As Terence Cave describes it, the "German sense" is a figure of authenticity by means of which Erasmus attempted "to close the fissure between the text and what it signifies, or—more problematically—between the discourse of Scripture and a new discourse seeking to reproduce its sense." The "German sense," as both "faithful" and "true," offered the ideal of transparent translation, reproduction without distortion in which the duplicating text would be both "german" and "germane," genuine or true and kindred or kin. Yet, as Cave's treatment reminds us, wherever there is twoness rather than singularity, there is the possibility of duplicity and deviance. Even paraphrase, as commentary which goes faithfully "alongside," involves a gap or separation from an original, an alienation into "other" words. It may be finally not a faithful "cozen-german" but itself involved in "cozenage," the alienating, conveying, or transporting such translation seeks to avoid.

Erasmus's much-punned-upon *sensus germanus* or "German sense" represented the attempt by a figure who was both humanist and interpreter of sacred text to claim the possibility of a glossing or translation without error or duplicitous, alienating gap. In Shakespeare's *Merry Wives,* a figure called the "Host" similarly attempts to reconcile what he terms "the terrestrial" and "the celestial"—in the figures of the warring Doctor and Parson of the play. And their revenge on *him* is to send those Germans whom he takes to be "honest men" (4.5.72) but who cheat him and literally translate or alienate, in the sense of "steal," his property—"cozen germans" who finally "cozen" him.

Germany, Jamany, Gemini: Mechanical Reproduction

There is one other fascinating link between translating or conveying in *Merry Wives* and its scene of thieving "cozen-Germans," a link that leads us first into the sound slide this scene effects between "Germans" and *gemini* (duplicates or twins) and then into the problem of the reconciling of "terrestrial" with "celestial," in a play which raises repeatedly the problem of "atonement" or making "one." Immediately after the lines on the duplicitous "cozen-Germans" who steal the horses of the Host, the French doctor of the play pronounces Germany as "Jamany," a slip in sound that links these cozening "Germans" with the "geminy" (2.2.8) Nym and Pistol, who may indeed be these thieving Germans in disguise and who have already planned their revenge on Falstaff in a scene which ends with one of them saying, "I *second* thee" (1.3.104–5). The emphasis on duplication or "twos" in this play is already suggested by the two "wives" of its title. But like the history plays it resembles, it is also crammed with the form of verbal iteration known as "geminating" or "twinning" (in English called the "Doublet")—iteration or repetition without anything that comes *between.* The character of "Shallow" who appears both in the histories and in *Merry Wives* is consistently "iterative," as Cowden Clarke once remarked: "he repeats and repeats."[54] And such verbal iteration or reproduction without intervening difference is literally everywhere in *Merry Wives,* from Shallow's own "'Tis your fault, 'tis your fault" (93–94), "Come, coz, come, coz" (1.1.206) and "conceive me, conceive me" (1.1.242) to Slender's "You'll not confess, you'll not confess" (1.1.92), the Host's "he will carry't, he will carry't" (3.2.69) and Falstaff's "Let me see't, let me see't" (3.3.136).

Such repetition or iteration is of even further importance in *Merry Wives* because of its link with reproduction of another kind, and because of its curious links with the iterative "cuckoo cuckoo" and duplicity of cuckoldry. *Geminatio verborum* or the "gemination" of words was rendered in Puttenham by the homely "Cuckoospell" as the English name for such mechanical reproduction at the verbal level. The link was based on the iterative call of the bird which, as cozener and adulterer, is also an outsider taken in by a host, leaving offspring which might be mistaken for the true heir, a simultaneously cozening and adulterous instance of "building on another man's ground." The figure of the iterative cuckoo's song is also an image in Erasmus's *De copia* for what there is called *homoiologia,* the mechanical iteration of the same idea, contrasted with *copia* as a more fruitful form of "varying."[55]

I mention this related network of wordplay on twinning, duplicating, and iterative copying not only because it affects the verbal forms of iteration so frequent in *Merry Wives,* but because iteration, copying and twinning also appear in the "letters" sent by Falstaff, identical duplicates, "letter for letter," linked to the forms of mechanical reproduction made possible by the power of print:

> *Mistress Ford:* . . . Did you ever hear the like?
> *Mistress Page.* Letter for letter; but that the name of Page and Ford differs! To thy great comfort in this mystery of ill opinions, here's the twin-brother of thy letter; but let thine inherit first, for I protest mine never shall. I warrant he hath a thousand of these letters, writ with blank space for different names (sure, more!); and these are of the second edition. He will print them, out of doubt; for he cares not what he puts into the press, when he would put us two.
>
> (2.1.68–79)

The buried reference to Jacob and Esau ("let thine inherit first") evokes the story of twins in which the question of priority is uppermost, a story echoed in the reference to a "mess of porridge" in act 3 (3.1.63). But it does so in a context in which it is impossible to distinguish first from second, copy from original ("this is the very same: the very hand; the very words," 2.1.82–83). Duplication or iteration here is a form of mechanical reproduction, part of the endlessly reduplicating power of print. But duplicates or doubles in Shakespeare connote not just twos and twins, but duplicity and treachery—as *Henry VIII* makes clear in its "Say untruths, and be ever double / Both in his words and meaning" (4.2.38–39), as *The Comedy of Errors* suggests in its references to double-dealing in a plot of twins (3.2.17, 20), or as the doubled senses of the witches in *Macbeth* only too late reveal. Jacob and Esau are both "germans" or brothers and "geminy" or twins, as one English translation of the story makes clear in calling one the other's "germane brother."[56] As with the *germanus* or "kindred, faithful" sense, the *geminus* or twin appears to promise the faithful duplication of an original, like the second "letter" described in *Merry Wives* as the "twin-brother" of the first. But where there is twoness rather than singularity, there is also the potential for duplicity. The duplicate "cousins" but it also "cozens." And Jacob himself, the identical twin summoned in the allusion to Falstaff's identical letters, is also a famously "cozening" brother.

Atonement, Simples, Hosts

To note the frequency in *Merry Wives* of conveyers, of cozening "germans," and of duplicitous duplicates is to note also, finally, how frequently the play raises the question of "atonement" and hence the problem of how in the midst of all this translating, conveying, and cozening to be "at one." The notion of "atonement" in the sense of "making one" is introduced early on in *Merry Wives* by Parson Evans, who volunteers to act as go-between or reconciler for the quarreling Shallow-Slender and Falstaff: "I am of the church, and will be glad to do my benevolence to make atonements and compromises between you" (1.1.32–34). His offer is almost immediately seconded by Page ("I would I could do a good office between you," 1.1.99–100). And the mediators or go-betweens who are to make all "one" in this dispute soon multiply into three:

> *Evans.* Peace, I pray you. Now let us understand. There is three umpires in this matter, as I understand: that is, Master Page (*fidelicet* Master Page) and there is myself (*fidelicet* myself) and the three party is (lastly and finally) mine host of the Garter.
> *Page.* We three to hear it and end it between them.
>
> (1.1.136–43)

In the same shift of letters that transforms "vocative" into "focative" in the grammar scene, the Welsh schoolmaster here turns "videlicet" into "fidelicet, a mock-Latin term evocative of "fidelity." But his enumeration of those who are to make the warring parties "one" quickly becomes something more than simple or singular, at the beginning of a play which will play repeatedly on the proliferation of ones, twos, and threes.

The singular as synonymous with the "simple" in this play—as in the related Shakespearean histories—is suggested in the *sotto voce* implications of the name of "Simple," the figure who appears as another of its carriers or go-betweens. In one scene of *Merry Wives,* the French doctor Caius, searching for "simples" (1.4.63), finds instead a different "Simple," come as messenger for his rival Slender and conveyed into the closet by Mistress Quick-lie in order to hide her duplicitous (or triplicitous) promises as conveyer of messages for more than one suitor at once. The line of communication, in a play filled with misunderstandings between speakers of different languages, is also anything but "simple." The French doctor's frustrated "Do intend vat I speak?" in this same scene, just lines before he finds the double-dealing "Simple," reflects not only the comic difficulty of understanding in this play (the French *entendre* which editors remind us lies behind his anglicized "intend") but the fact that speech itself may wander away from and hence frustrate any simplicity of "intent."[57]

A sense of the problem of making "one" also attends the offices of this play's "Host" and his attempts at "atonement." The aim of the Garter Host in *Merry Wives* as mediator in the quarrel between Dr. Caius and Parson Evans is stated, as we have seen, to be the reconciling of "celestial" and "terrestrial," "curer of bodies" and "curer of souls" (2.3.39):

> *Host.* Peace, I say, Gallia and Gaul, French and Welsh, soul-curer and
> body-curer! . . . hear mine host of the Garter. . . . Shall I lose my doctor?
> No, he gives me the potions and the motions. Shall I lose my parson? My
> priest? my Sir Hugh? No, he gives me the proverbs and the no-verbs.
> Give me thy hand, terrestrial; so. Give me thy hand, celestial; so . . .
>
>   (3.1.97–106)

The Host's aim here is an at-one-ment of "body" and "soul," "terrestrial" and "celestial." But for his efforts he is termed a "mad host" (3.1.112) and the "body-curer" and "soul-curer" he attempts to bring to "peace" conspire to get their "revenge" on him (3.2.119), a revenge which may be to send those "cozening Germans" who seem to be "honest" but who cozen all the "hosts."[58]

The "Host" of the "Garter" who seeks to atone, or make "one" both "body" and "soul," cannot fail to summon echoes of the "Host" of the other

"Garter" whose office is also to "atone"—the Host traditionally presented as the true mercurial *interpres* or go-between, mediator and reconciler of "celestial" and "terrestrial." But just as the "Garter" in this bourgeois play— even with the elaborate set-piece on Windsor Castle in act 5—remains principally the name not of an aristocratic order but of a tavern or inn, so its "Host" is anything but successful at making "at one." If the other "Host" is the true bearer of a Word made flesh, an atoning "host" taken in through the mouth, what we encounter in *Merry Wives* are instead very different versions of bodies or words turned into food—the "worts" or words Falstaff pronounces "good cabbage" in act 1, the Welsh parson who "makes fritters of English" (5.1.143), Slender described as having "drunk himself out of his five sentences" (1.1.175), and Falstaff's "Heavens defend me from that Welsh fairy, lest he transform me to a piece of cheese!" (5.1.80–82). Harmony or at-one-ment seems as difficult to achieve as the at-one-ing of Falstaff's "disposition" and the "truth of his word," which "do no more adhere and keep place together than the hundred Psalms to the tune of 'Green-sleeves'" (2.1.60–63). "God's wounds," the means of atonement in a theological sense, are transformed by the malapropping tongue of Mistress Quickly in the Grammar Scene into "Od's nouns," a conveying or translation of the at-one-ment of a "Host" into a new character called "Ods," not one but three, in a play which emphasizes repeatedly the "odd" as opposed to the harmoniously paired, or even.

The question of whether there can be "atonement" in the midst of so much cozening and duplicity also affects the question of the harmony which may be achieved at this play's end. Apart from the generic expectation linking consummation to the end of comedy, *Merry Wives* underscores this expectation in Falstaff's "after we had embrac'd, kiss'd, protested, and, as it were, spoke the prologue of our comedy" (3.5.73–75). But the *frustration* of consummation is instead largely what this comedy leads to— for at least three who thought by the end to be "at one." Early in act 1, Mistress Quickly's "You shall have Anne—fool's-head of your own" (1.4.126–27) suggests in its linking of "Anne" and "fool's-head" not just an insult deferred until Dr. Caius is safely out of hearing, but also the link with the fool or "ass" which in the language of the French doctor would be a homophonic *âne*.[59] In the play's final scene, in which Falstaff's tranformation recalls the transformation of Bottom (or the one in Marlowe's *Faustus*) to precisely such an ass or *âne*, two suitors mis-take (or "steal away") with a counterfeit or false "Anne" rather than the genuine or "true" one. Not only is Falstaff baffled in the amorous poaching of more "deer"

(5.5); Slender, far from "dispatch'd" (5.5.179)—contemporary slang for "scoring"—is stuck with a "great lubberly boy" (184) he is unable to "have" ("If I had been married to him," he complains, "for all he was in woman's apparal" he would not have "had" him, 191–93), while Dr. Caius, like the Host cozened by "cozen-Germans," is "cozen'd" (205, 207) by the substitution of "oon garsoon, a boy" (205) for the genuine "Anne." Everyone except Fenton in this anticipated comic close ends up frustrated by a cozening counterfeit. But even Fenton—the suitor who apparently gets "the right Anne" (211)—is mated to a transvestite boy, who for all he is in "woman's apparel" is also neither genuine nor true.[60]

It has often been argued that things are harmonized or "at one" by this comedy's end.[61] Fenton, the rejected suitor, is accepted by both of Anne's parents when their elopement is announced. "Brook" is to get the consummation he so devoutly wished and as the double or duplicate for himself is finally pronounced to be at "one" with Ford. The play ends with this "at-one-ment" of identities that had for much of *Merry Wives* been divided into two: "To Master Brooke you yet shall *hold your word*, / For he to-night shall lie with Mistress Ford" (5.5.244–45). But "terrestrial" and "celestial" are never convincingly reconciled and it is not clear even at this end that "brook" and "ford"—synonymies though they may be—can ever truly be made identical, that the "word" is really "held," or that "lie" even in this final line does not palter with us in a double sense.

Translating Property, Translating Plots

> What doe the best, then, but gleane after others harvest? borrow their colours, inherite their possessions? What doe they but translate? perhaps, usurpe? . . .
>
> —John Florio, translator of Montaigne

> conveyers are you all.
>
> —Shakespeare, *Richard II*

In the Grammar Scene with which we began, a woman "translates" meaning, obscenely or "dis-honestly," from a father tongue, and something is translated "out of honesty into English." In the larger plot of the "merry wives," two burgher wives whose "honesty" Falstaff and the counterfeit "Brook" conspire to "translate" or traduce prove that, contrary to the stereotypes of unfaithful women, wives may be "merry" and yet "honest" too

(4.2.105).[62] To this doubled link between translation and women in particular we will return. First we need to look beyond the play on "translation" in *Merry Wives* to what I referred to at the beginning as the ubiquity of the "translative" more generally in Shakespeare.

To do this we need to return to the literal resonance of "translation" in early modern usage—as transporting, carrying, or conveying—and to the sense of "translate" as well as "convey" as synonyms for "theft," as in Richard's "conveyers are you all" at the beginning of the histories so intimately related to *Merry Wives*. "Translate," as we have seen, bears in its early English uses its double Latin sense, both as linguistic transfer and as "a carrying or removing from one place to another" (so Cicero, for example, could speak of money as "translated" just as other classical authors treat of *translatio* as a term not just for metaphor but for transfers of property). A "translator" is "he that doth transporte, translate, or convey from one place to another," according to one English-Latin dictionary of 1587.[63] Hence the availability of "translate," with "convey," as what *Merry Wives* reminds us is simply a politer form of "steal."

This is the reason why "translating" in the specifically literary sense could so easily slide into a synonym for stealing lines or plots (as in Ben Jonson's "I could tell you, he were a translater, / I know the authors from whence he ha's stole").[64] Accusations of this kind of "translation" or pilfering were frequent in the sixteenth century and increased along with the articulation of notions of authorship, authority, and intellectual property in a century which witnessed the movement from early humanist doctrines of faithful copying or *imitatio* to the development of the more modern sense of "plagiarism" (Latin *plagiarus,* "kidnapper") as a result of the progressive sharpening of such boundary lines.[65] (We might remember in this regard that in a passage with striking resonances for the thieving Germans of *Merry Wives,* Montaigne compares literary thievery not just to other forms of pilfering but specifically to *horse* theft, in an essay also preoccupied with questions of imitation, or influence, and of copying.)

The English were notorious for "translation" in this sense. Texts such as Puttenham's *Arte of English Poesie* traced the history of "English" poetry as a history of the translation of foreign texts; and the uncertain boundary between imitation, translation and thievery is a running motif of English literary history from the beginning. Early English articulations of property in literature often appeared under the cover of explications of the Decalogue command "Thou shalt not steal," as in John Hooper's *Declaration of the Ten Holy Commandments* (1549), which includes literary theft in its discussion. And a lively debate raged in sixteenth-century England on the subject of such "translation" and its relation to what Puttenham called "petty larceny."[66] John Harington's Epigram 27 dismisses those who claim that the "English have small, or no invention . . . and all our works are barren, / But for the stuffe, we get from Authors forren," wittily asking that he himself be numbered in the company of Wyatt and Surrey as "honorable thieves."[67] Ironically, *The Merry Wives of Windsor*, Shakespeare's only "English" comedy and the one in which the "translating" both of language and of property gets so much emphasis, is, as far as we know, one of the very small number of Shakespeare plays *not* translated or pilfered from other (including foreign) texts and plots. This indeed may be part of the joke. Shakespeare in this bourgeois play, according to the familiar anecdote about the circumstances of its writing, translates the "will" of the queen into the commissioned plot of his only "English" comedy, a plot where in this respect the usually "translating" Shakespeare, famous for his pilferings, is instead as "honest" as his English wives.

Translation in the sense of theft, however, *is* linked to the name of William Shakespeare, as well as appearing in the other anecdote which associates this "Will" with a specific incident of thievery at the beginning of *Merry Wives*. Probably the earliest published reference to Shakespeare as an actor and playwright is the accusation of translation or literary theft leveled notoriously by Robert Greene, who represented the player from Warwickshire not only as a "rude groom" but as an "upstart Crow" parading in "borrowed plumes," the most common of contemporary images for literary theft.[68] *Merry Wives* begins with Falstaff's thievery or poaching on another man's ground, a beginning which since the eighteenth century has been linked with the tradition that Shakespeare was forced to leave Stratford to make his way as a player upon the London stage because he had stolen deer from the aristocratic Lucys of nearby Charlecote.[69] As a figure from the burgherly world of merchants rather than the university or aristocracy, this other translated Will had his own links with the realm of property transfers and conveyances, with trafficking and "trade."[70]

To link Shakespeare with translation in the sense of theft, however bogus at the level of pseudobiographical anecdotes, is to begin to glimpse the importance of the "translative" in the plays in ways that make *Merry Wives,* a marginalized text whose Falstaff has been disparaged as a lesser copy of the histories' robust original, one place to begin a rereading of the canon as a whole in this regard.[71] The sense of "translation" as a bearing or carrying away from a unitary original, betrayed by a copy or cozening duplicate, is something we need, therefore, to explore briefly, if telescopically, before leaving the dizzying wordplay on "translation" in *Merry Wives* itself.

"Translation" in the senses we have traced is everywhere in Shakespeare and not just in the canon's series of imitated, stolen or (linguistically) translated plots. It informs the scenes of translation between languages which link the Grammar Scene of *Merry Wives* to the scene from *The Taming of the Shrew* in which a supposedly submissive Bianca refuses to be a "breeching scholar" to the prescribed pedagogical disciplines of Ascham, Colet, and Lily, and to the scene from *Henry V* where Katherine's language lesson anticipates *her* translation or conveyance, with that of her French territory, to English rule. In the Lancastrian series of Shakespearean histories—the plays which begin with Richard's "conveyers are you all"— "translation" in the senses we have traced through *Merry Wives* takes the form of Bolingbroke's theft or usurpation of the crown (and its "conveyance" upon another line), a founding event echoed in the petty thieveries of the tavern world in *Henry IV Part 1* and *Part 2,* and continued in the translation of the literal transporting from England to France that this usurper counsels his son to pursue as a distraction from the taint of theft. It becomes at the climax of *Henry V,* the questionable though elaborately justified claim to that foreign soil, a claim to property realized only after another "translation" scene involving the wooing of the daughter of the king of France by an English monarch described in an earlier appropriating context as a master of "tongues."[72]

Translation and Women

all translations are reputed femalls, delivered at second hand . . .
—John Florio

There is much more that needs to be said of the "translative" in Shakespeare, including in these same histories or in *Hamlet,* a play which sounds its own multiple variations on "interpret" and "translate." There is also much more to be said of the relation of such translation in Shakespeare to the problem of iteration, of copying and of print, which in such Shakespearean contexts is bound up with reproduction and hence with the problem of women who "come between" fathers and sons. In the more limited space available here, however, I want simply to focus on the link between translation and women already suggested in the sideways slidings of Mistress Quickly in *Merry Wives*.

Florio's notorious statement that "translations are reputed femalls" in the "Epistle Dedicatorie" to his translation of Montaigne makes clear that part of this link comes from the sense of both translation and women as secondary or "second hand," following a prior model or original. The longer version of the passage from Florio describes translations, in this analogy with "females," as a "defective edition" or falling off, recalling the centuries-long combination of Aristotle and Galen with the story of Eve's creation from Genesis through which the female is viewed as an inferior or "defective" version of a male original.[73]

As R. Howard Bloch has argued in relation to one part of this longstanding tradition, the model of Adam or man as primary (participating in "an original unity of being") and of Eve or the female as "secondary" or "derivative," the "offshoot of division and difference" whose creation logically prefigures decline and fall, was a powerfully established paradigm by the beginning of the early modern period. Commentary on the creation of Eve—as the figure of woman taken from Adam's side and leading to the fall into all of history—associated her with the lateral and hence with *translatio*, translation, and metaphor, as well as more generally with the secondary and accessory.[74] "Translation" and the female—both seen as secondary, accessory or "defective"—are thus already linked before the period of *Merry Wives*, even without recourse to reminders that the activity of translating in the Renaissance was often the only sphere of writing open to women (and hence, perhaps, characterized as a "feminine" activity even when male writers like Florio engaged in it).[75]

The other link between women and translation might be illustrated most succinctly through a different figure from the prefaces to Florio's translation of Montaigne. The passage affixed to book 1 which begins by playing on "translation" (and its synonym "turning") as a "turning of Bookes" which threatens the overturning of Libraries," ends with an exploitation of "turning" in the sexual sense. A link is thus forged between "Learning" made "common" (since translation involves "turning" from Latin to the "vulgar," and making what should be "close" or concealed to be "knowne of all")[76] and the specific figure of the harlot or "common" woman ("Why but who is not jealous, his Mistresse should be so prostitute?"). Even without reference to the figure of the prostituted or "common" woman, the hierarchical relation of women to a learned Latin tradition associates "femalls" with translation and with the commonness and accessibility of the "vulgar," "mother" tongue.[77]

Translation as decline from an original—figured, like the "defective" Eve, as both secondary and female—is joined by the powerfully grammatical tradition of "cases" as a declining or declension, a falling away from the nominative as the *casus erectus* most often illustrated by the Latin *homo* and understood as the standard from which the subsequent cases fall or "decline." This, indeed, is the tradition *Merry Wives* pointedly recalls in the Grammar Scene and the translation there of Latin case into "Jinny's case," the generative/generative "case" of the generic female, in a scene whose double entendres clearly invoke the sexual "cases" of women.[78] We might recall Shakespeare's other exploitation of this wordplay in the name of the rebel "Cade"—from *cadere, casus,* "fall"—in the early *de casibus* histories which involve a sense of decline ascribed in part to the influence of foreign wives or the reminders in *Troilus and Cressida* of the grammatical as well as other senses of "decline" (in a context which has to do with the declining, or falling, of faithless women).[79]

Immediately after the Grammar Scene of *Merry Wives,* and Mistress Quickly's translative slidings from Latin or the *sermo patrius* into the vernaculars of "Jinny's case," we encounter the familiar description of women as "Eve's daughters" (4.2.24) and hence reference to Eve as the emblem of the female open to being "conveyed" or translated "out of honesty," as well as of feminine wiles and "conveyances." The second time Falstaff the builder on another man's ground is transported or "conveyed" away, it is in women's clothing as the transvestite "witch" of Brainford (4.2.98) whose description as a "cozening quean" (4.2.172) who works by "daub'ry" or imposture (4.2.176–78) links her/him to those imposter Germans who turn out to be not "honest" but "cozening." The sense of mistaking an "erection" already introduced into the play by the malapropping Mistress Quickly as by the "falling" of "Fal-staff" in a phallic sense links both with the declining or "falling away" from the *casus erectus* that is punningly involved in an effeminate as well as female "case," including the sense of impotence that surrounds the play's final images of witchcraft or the evocation of this earlier "witch" in *Merry Wives*.[80] Even the role of the go-between as a bearer or conveyer of messages seems in one otherwise gratuitous passage to be linked with the effeminating, as Pistol refuses the imputation that might attach to becoming a messenger in the "trade" between Falstaff and the two wives ("Shall I Sir Pandarus of Troy become, / And by my side wear steel?" 1.3.75–76).

Exploitation of the links between women and translation as decline are frequent in Shakespeare, in contexts that suggest, however, not just the familiar logocentric structure of the female as defective or inferior second

but the production of that very paradigm as a structure of secondariness—
not to be confused with the "view" of Shakespeare any more than we now
conflate "Shakespeare" with the speech of Ulysses on degree.[81] Women
are linked with "translation" in *Troilus and Cressida*—with the "common"
Helen (whose adulterous theft is the beginning not only of the war in Troy
but all of subsequent history seen as *translatio* and decline), with the "faithless" Cressida (whose infidelity is linked to the sense of "truth tired with
iteration," mechanical iteration of well-worn and even tawdry literary
themes),[82] and with the rhetoric of adulteration and duplicity that in Troilus's
speech on "bifold authority" seeks to put male, "simple," and "true" in
opposition to female, "duplicitous," and "false," as if, again, there were a
link between the female and a translation or conveyance from "honesty."
The play does so, however, in ways that make this phallogocentric logic
the reasoning of a particular character and the projection of a particular
gendered frame.[83] Shakespeare's Viola in *Twelfth Night* repeats the familiar image of woman's frailty and falsity—"How easy is it for the proper-
false / In women's waxen hearts to set their forms! / Alas, our frailty is the
cause, not we, / For such as we are made of, such we be" (2.2.29–32). But
the question of what would constitute the oxymoron "*proper*-false" in the
context of a character named "Viola" who is not a "femall" but a transvestite boy, complicates, again, the model of simple male "truth" from which
a female "falsity" translatively or duplicitously declines.

Players, like women, finally, were also frequently described in texts
contemporary with Shakespeare as "translators"—as betrayers or conveyers who made "greatness familiar" on the public stage and hence threatened (as Hamlet the aristocrat complained in another link with the stereotypes of untrustworthy women) to make vulgar or "common" what should
be "close" or concealed.[84] We might, then, make provisional close to a
much longer subject by setting beside the Grammar Scene of *Merry Wives*
and the irrepressible tongue of its "she-Mercury" Quickly the translation
involved when Shakespeare the "player" and "rude groom" of Greene's
contemptuous (and undoubtedly envious) description—the figure linked
there not only with the thieveries of Aesop's "crow" but with the most
memorable of foreign women from the histories—returns in *The Winter's
Tale,* near the end of a canon in which "translation" appears so pervasively,
to steal this time a plot from Greene himself, his early accuser and university man, and then to add to *this* stolen or translated plot two distinctly
Shakespearean figures: Paulina, with her "female" tongue, and Autolycus,
the notorious thief, "littered under Mercury."[85]

Closing Speculations: Going Between (Texts)

The argument I have been making about "translation" from *Merry Wives* is an argument about wordplay, about the multiple breaches in the integrity of a word made by the ease of association and transportability. The text I have been using in this argument is neither an exclusively Folio nor an exclusively Quarto version of the play—although more the former (and longer) than the latter. The Riverside edition is a modern conflated text, a composite assembled through its own transports and transfers of material. But recent scholarship has begun to question not only the integrity (and priority) of any single Shakespeare text but the validity of such conflations; and *Merry Wives* itself (with its dramatically different Quarto and Folio versions) may soon, like *Lear* and *Hamlet,* be presented to students in these differing versions rather than the present composite editions.

What is remarkable about this recent scholarship—what Leah Marcus has called its "growing discomfort with the time-honored editorial practice by which variant early texts are ranked hierarchically on the basis of their fidelity to a presumed Shakespeare 'original'"—is that it calls into question the very terms (including "fidelity") we have encountered as part of this same wordplay on the "translative" in *Merry Wives.*[86] Earlier forms of textual editing often employ a charged language of "debased copy" or "debased derivative" (in relation to the so-called "bad" quartos linked to players rather than authorial authority), a language that also renders such "defective" texts feminized as both secondary and derivative, lacking the integrity as well as the authority of an authorial (and hence "authoritative") original, and linked with all of the language of imperfection, lapse, or breaches of "fidelity" that we have seen associated with the translative as the adulterated or less faithful feminine. *Merry Wives,* then, along with this broader network of wordplay on the translative, curiously provides a set of terms for what undoes such assumptions, even as it complicates (with all of its play on duplicates and copies) the priority of an "original."

Marcus, indeed, notes that there is strong evidence that neither the 1623 Folio (the one where Brooke becomes "Brookme," and there is so much more of Windsor and the Court) nor the shorter 1602 Quarto can be successfully established as an "original"—that there is something about this play that subverts the hierarchization which such assumptions seek to institute.[87] And so we need to ask: What might such an undoing of the authority of a single text imply for wordplay or networks of wordplay that seem so often to occupy the space *between* texts, to breach in their own way the integrity of any single text by their very mobility and transportability? What do we do, for example, with the fact that the "terrestrial/celestial" play of the Quarto does not exist in the Folio (which does, however, begin with "attonements"), or that the Folio's punning reference to "Cozen-Iermans" does not appear with the Quarto's "cosen garmombles," though the latter does speak of a "Garmaine Duke" and of the cozening of Hosts? And what about the fact that the Grammar Scene and its linguistic translations appear in the Quarto not at all? Is it necessary to assume that one or the other text is in this regard the greater authority—especially when composite texts like the Riverside (or the Oxford) engage in their own forms of smuggling and transport across such boundaries? Does an emphasis on wordplay in particular necessarily presume the kind of textual integrity or wholeness that lay behind New Critical interpretive assumptions? Or are there more flexible and less bounded ways of considering homophonic and other kinds of verbal play that do not depend on or imply such forms of enclosure or authorial control? Does an attentiveness to wordplay, in other words, require the assumptions of individuality, authenticity, and authorial mastery on which so much Shakespeare criticism has relied?

All of these questions—as questions for teaching, for interpreting, and for editing—are opened up not just by the existence of different versions for plays like *Merry Wives* but by such verbal transports across the boundaries of different versions and separate texts, in ways that often summon the possibility that such networks are part of an independent homophonic or metaphorical logic. Perhaps, then, in this sense as well, *The Merry Wives of Windsor*—marginalized by New Critical and other assumptions about wholeness and integrity and long derided as secondary, defective copy or derivative—may offer in the multiple implications of its plot of going-between, of fidelity, and of mechanical reproduction a place to begin to think about the "translative" or translational in this sense too, and to conceive of Shakespearean wordplay, differently.

Notes

1. For the original work on metaphor, reprinted in shortened form in my *Literary Fat Ladies: Rhetoric, Gender, Property* (London and New York: Methuen, 1987), pp. 36–53, see "The Metaphorical Plot" in David S. Miall, ed., *Metaphor: Problems and Perspectives* (Brighton, 1982). Parts of this inquiry in relation to "cases," translation, and "iteration" as a form of "mechanical reproduction" in *Merry Wives* and Shakespeare's *Henriad*, also appeared in *Literary Fat Ladies,* esp. pp. 27–31 and 69–77. The edition of Shakespeare used

throughout is *The Riverside Shakespeare*, ed. G. Blakemore Evans (Boston: Houghton Mifflin, 1974).

2. See Northrop Frye, *A Natural Perspective* (New York: Columbia University Press, 1965), p. 36.

3. Dr. Samuel Johnson, *The Plays of William Shakespeare* (London, 1813), p. 156. Act 4, scene 1 appears in the Folio (1623) but not in the Quarto (1602), the only two texts of the play with independent authority, since the other quartos are virtual reprints of these two texts.

4. See the New Penguin *Merry Wives,* ed. G. R. Hibbard (Harmondsworth: Penguin Books, 1973); the Arden edition of H. J. Oliver (London: Methuen, 1971), pp. 102, xxix–xxx; and the Oxford edition of T. W. Craik (Oxford: Oxford University Press, 1990), esp. p. 5. H. J. Oliver writes that the scene was likely omitted from the Quarto ("whether by the reporters or in an intermediate version they were reporting") because "it would lose all its fun for an audience that did not know Latin, and most of it for an audience that had not been brought up on William Lily's Latin grammar text" (xxix; see also p. 102). Craik (p. 152) contests the argument from an alternative version of the play, put forward recently in Gerald D. Jonson's *"The Merry Wives of Windsor,* Q1: Provincial Touring and Adapted Texts," *Shakespeare Quarterly* 38, no. 2 (1987): 154–65, 152. Notable exceptions to the more negative view of the scene may be found in the treatments of linguistic slippage in William Carroll's "A Received Belief: Imagination in *The Merry Wives of Windsor, " Studies in Philology* 74 (1977): 186–215; in Godshalk, "An Apology for *The Merry Wives of Windsor, " Renaissance Papers 1973,* ed. Dennis G. Donovan and A. Leigh Deneef (Durham, N.C.: Southeastern Renaissance Conference, 1974), pp. 97–106; and in Russ McDonald, *Shakespeare and Jonson, Jonson and Shakespeare* (Lincoln: University of Nebraska Press, 1988), p. 41.

5. As indicated above, brief excerpts from this larger work on *Merry Wives* have already appeared in *Literary Fat Ladies,* including partial treatment of 4.1.

6. The relative slighting of *Merry Wives* in the criticism of Shakespeare may also be one of the results of the view of the play as a command performance. It was presumed therefore to be less an "original" production than a response to the command of a queen who desired to see Falstaff in love, and a hurriedly composed one at that.

7. The scene of the Welsh schoolmaster is one of the most suggestive Shakespearean instances to place beside the argument concerning humanism at a local level made in Antony Grafton and Lisa Jardine, *From Humanism to the Humanities* (Cambridge: Harvard University Press, 1986).

8. On the influence of Lily and Colet's *A Shorte Introduction of Grammar,* see, for example, T. W. Baldwin, *William Shakespere's Small Latine & Lesse Greeke,* 2 vols. (Urbana: University of Illinois Press, 1944), 1:557–68.

9. See especially the Arden editor's comments on the double meanings here, pp. 104–5.

10. On the relation of the prescribed system of "double translation"—out of Latin into English and faithfully back again—to the pedagogical economy of men and boys which for the most part excluded women, see Walter J. Ong, S.J., "Latin Language Study as a Renaissance Puberty Rite," in his *Rhetoric, Romance, and Technology* (Ithaca, N.Y.: Cornell University Press, 1971), pp. 113–41.

11. The Arden edition (p. 24) gives the variants here: the Folio's "studied her will, and translated her will," the Quarto's "studied her well," Pope's "study'd her well, and translated her well," Collier's "studied her will, and translated her well," Grant White's "studied

her well and translated her will," and conj. Camb. "studied her well and translated her ill." The Arden editor notes, "Emendation seems unnecessary although Whiter (p. 83) and Farmer noted that 'well'—'deep' (as in 1.48) was a Shakespearean image-link. Pistol surely means 'will,' her intention or desire, possibly with a quibble on 'will' meaning 'carnal desire' and certainly with a pun on the legal will that has to be 'translated' into ordinary English to be understood." "Honesty" here means "chastity," as in other contexts in Shakespeare and Elizabethan usage. See also William Carroll on the link between the Grammar Scene in 4.1 and this earlier reference to translating into "English."

12. See, on the meanings of "voice" and "action," for example, T. W. Baldwin, *Small Latine,* 1:569.

13. For "construing" or "construction" as the term used for the exercise of translating out of Latin into English and back again, see ibid., 1:581–90 and *The Taming of the Shrew,* 3.1.

14. For the Shakespearean mixing of sexual double entendres in the context of a "Will" and terms from language and discourse such as "common place," see, for example, Shakespeare's Sonnets 135–37. "English" here may also carry with it here a sound-link with "ingle" or "ningle," or in other words with what Falstaff desires to translate this wife's "honesty" into. See Helge Kökeritz, *Shakespeare's Pronunciation* (New Haven: Yale University Press, 1953), pp. 104–5. Particularly interesting in relation to *Merry Wives* is the pairing of "coz" and "ningle" Kökeritz cites. See the section on "cousin Germans," below. The link between "English" and its spelling as "Inglish" or "Ingles" (as in the Spanish tongue evoked in tatters in this play in its *paucas* and *labras)* is suggested by the note in Sir Arthur Quiller-Couch and John Dover Wilson's Cambridge edition (Cambridge: Cambridge University Press, 1954), p. 107: "into English. Pistol seems to be quibbling upon 'ingle' = to cuddle. 'Inglis' or 'Ingles' was a common sp. of 'English' at this period." The link between "English" and "ingle" (or "corner") is also made possible through the fact that the English are "Angles" (as in Polydore Virgil's *Anglia historia,* to take just one instance from a period which moved between English and Latin more frequently than modern readers do). Both "angle" and "corner" have sexual double meanings elsewhere in Shakespeare—in Bertram's "she did *angle* for me" in *All's Well* (5.3.212) or in Othello's jealous "keep a *corner* in the thing I love" (3.3.272). The relation of such "angles" or "corners" to female sexuality (as to the context of the "ingle" or boy appropriate as a resonance in a transvestite theatrical context) is commonplace; but the link between English/ingles/angles may be further suggested in this passage of *Merry Wives.* Just three lines later it mentions Ford's "legend of angels," another double-meaning term (coins but also "angels") which was often involved in wordplay with "angles" (as in the Venerable Bede).

15. The fact that it is Ulysses who says this of Cressida makes this comment, and its ascription of such "language" to a "faithless" female, doubly ironic in the light of his own links with the arts of language and discourse.

16. See Anne Parten, "Falstaff's Horns: Masculine Inadequacy and Feminine Mirth in *The Merry Wives of Windsor,* " *Studies in Philology* 82, no. 2 (Spring 1985): 184–99.

17. For a reading of "building on another man's ground" in relation to the theater itself, see the intriguing argument of Andrew Gurr in "Intertextuality at Windsor," *Shakespeare Quarterly* 38, no. 2 (Summer 1987): 189–200.

18. This kind of wordplay on "fault" as crevice or female cleft also turns up near the end of the play when Falstaff refers to this same Mistress Ford as "my doe with the black scut" just after another reference to a "fault" (5.5.8, 18).

19. For a linking of adultery and property (and hence of theft) in studies of this play, see, for example, Marilyn French in *Shakespeare's Division of Experience* (New York: Summit, 1981), pp. 106–10, and Coppélia Kahn, *Man's Estate: Masculine Identity in Shakespeare* (Berkeley and Los Angeles: University of California Press, 1981), esp. pp. 128–29, 146–50. See also Carol Thomas Neely, "Constructing Female Sexuality in the Renaissance: Stratford, London, Windsor, Vienna," in *Feminism and Psychoanalysis,* ed. Richard Feldstein and Judith Roof (Ithaca, N.Y.: Cornell University Press, 1989), pp. 209–29.

20. Mordecai Moxon, *The Character, Praise, and Commendation of a Chaste and Virtuous Woman in a Learned and Pious Discourse Against Adultery* (London, 1708), p. 4. For more extended commentary on texts such as this one, and the threat of the "wandering" or wayward wife, see my *Literary Fat Ladies,* chap. 6, esp. pp. 103–13.

21. On the threat to property that straying wives represent, see, for example, Benedetto Varchi, *The Blazon of Jealousie,* trans. R. Toste (London, 1615), p. 20: "when this our high-pric'd Commoditie chanceth to light into some other merchants hands, and that our private Inclosure proveth to be a Common for others, we care no more for it." For a now-classic treatment of these and other such passages in relation to wives understood as a "territory" or "ground," see Peter Stallybrass, "Patriarchal Territories: The Body Enclosed," in *Rewriting the Renaissance,* ed. Margaret W. Ferguson et al. (Chicago and London: The University of Chicago Press, 1986), pp. 127–29. The language of such passages is also reflected in Shakespeare's Sonnet 137 on the woman who should be an enclosure or "private" place become the "wide world's common place"—a sexualized language of possession, of "private" and "common" property, which pervades *Othello* as well.

22. For an illuminating perspective on the pedigree of this paradigm, see Anne Carson, "Putting Her in Her Place: Woman, Dirt, and Desire," in *Before Sexuality: The Construction of Erotic Experience in the Ancient Greek World,* ed. David M. Halperin, John J. Winkler, and Froma I. Zeitlin (Princeton: Princeton University Press, 1990), 135–69.

23. In Marlowe's *Massacre at Paris* (4.5.4–9), the "tenant" who threatens his landlord's exclusive control of his own wife is accused of having "set up [his] standing where [he] should not" and of "tilling" the "ground" which only her "master" should "occupie." This sense of "occupation" (simultaneously sexual and evocative of property) also sounds in the farewell to Othello's "occupation" and in the complaint against what has happened to the term "occupy" in *2H 4,* another play in which Falstaff appears. See *Christopher Marlowe: The Complete Plays,* ed. J. B. Steane (Harmondsworth: Penguin, 1969), 568–69; Peter Stallybrass, "Patriarchal Territories"; and *Literary Fat Ladies,* pp. 109, 131–32 on *occupatio* and "occupy."

24. This link between "variable" woman and linguistic "varying" or "turning" (an early modern synonym for "translating") is also suggested early in Shakespeare in *Love's Labour's Lost* 1.1.284–99. On the link between linguistic translation and adultery, see also Juliet Fleming, "The French Garden: An Introduction to Women's French," *English Literary History* 56 (1989): 49 n. 20.

25. See Ong, "Latin Language Study" (note 10). It should be clear, both in the context of a transvestite theater where the women's parts were played by male actors and in the undercutting of Parson Evans in 4.1 in relation to any humanist "standard," that to speak of Mistress Quickly's "female" tongue is not in any way to essentialize any opposition here between "male" and "female." Humanist texts in the sixteenth century themselves repeatedly undercut this very opposition, or unwittingly reveal its instability even as they seek to set it up, when, for example, tongues coded as "female" turn out to be tongues possessed by

men, including the writer himself. See my "On the Tongue: Cross-Dressing, Effeminacy, and the Art of Words," *Style* 23 (1989): 445–65, which begins with Erasmus's *Lingua* and its discussion of the "female" tongues of men.

26. In addition to the studies of French, Kahn and others cited above, see George K. Hunter, "Bourgeois Comedy: Shakespeare and Dekker," in *Shakespeare and His Contemporaries,* ed. E. A. J. Honigmann (Dover, N.H.: Manchester University Press, 1986), pp. 1–15.

27. See, for example, the comments in the Arden edition, p. 48.

28. In *The Taming of the Shrew* (a translation—or theft—of Gascoigne's *Supposes,* which in turn translates or carries over into English Ariosto's *Suppositi),* the Decalogue is echoed in the covetise of "ox" and "ass" which also extends to the property of wives (3.2.230–32).

29. For the complaints against "gentlemen made cheape" or the buying and selling of lineages, see Sir Thomas Smith, *De republica anglorum,* ed. Mary Dewar (Cambridge: Cambridge University Press, 1982), bk. 1, chap. 20, pp. 71–72.

30. See Godshalk.

31. When Pistol and Nym refuse to be messengers/conveyers in this trade, Falstaff sends his "little page" (Robin) to "Sail like my pinnace to these golden shores" (1.3.80).

32. See George Puttenham's *Arte of English Poesie,* along with Patricia Parker, "The Metaphorical Plot" (note 1).

33. Jeanne Addison comments on this sense of mock-baptism in Falstaff's ducking, though not on its links with other kinds of mistaken translations or "transports" in the play. See her *Shakespeare's English Comedy: "The Merry Wives of Windsor" in Context* (Lincoln and London: University of Nebraska Press, 1979).

34. Letters are frequently carried between its characters. Evans sends a letter to Mistress Quickly "to desire and require her to solicit [Slender's] desires to Mistress Anne Page" (1.2.9–11); Falstaff sends an identical letter to the two wives; and Anne, finally, sends one that Fenton refers to in the final act.

35. Mistress Page requests him from Falstaff (2.2.113–16): "Mistress Page would desire you to send her your little page, of all loves. Her husband has a marvellous infection to the little page: and truly Master Page is an honest man." The combination of "infection" with "honest" here, whatever it suggests of Page's relationship with this "little page" (especially in a play where "ingles" have already been lurking in the "inglish" of "translated her will, out of honesty into English") once again links the conveying of messages to a possible translation out of "honesty." See also 2.2.124: "he may come and go between you both; and . . . never need to understand any thing; for 'tis not good that children should know any wickedness."

36. A study of conveyance as "bearing" and of the "bearing" away from a "house" involved in adultery would have to consider the extended network of Shakespearean plays on "bear" and "born(e)." See Stephen Booth's "Exit, Pursued by a Gentleman Born," in *Shakespeare's Art from a Comparative Perspective,* ed. Wendell M. Aycock (Lubbock: Texas Tech Press, 1981), pp. 51–66; and Margreta de Grazia's discussion of "bearing/borne(e)" in "Homonyms Before and After Lexical Standardization," *Deutsche Shakespeare-Gesellschaft West Jahrbuch,* 1990.

37. What I am suggesting here is that "conveyance" in the sense of being both "conveyed" and "stolen" away is still present in this final scene.

38. Mercury was worshipped by merchants at Rome, just as Hermes was the patron of

Greek commerce. See the Loeb editor's comment on Ovid, *Fasti* (6.663–72) and, for a recent book-length study linking Shakespeare with the figure of Mercury, which draws on these and other examples, Joseph Porter's *Shakespeare's Mercutio* (Chapel Hill and London: University of North Carolina Press), with Norman O. Brown, *Hermes the Thief* (Madison: University of Wisconsin Press, 1947), esp. p. 43 on Mercury as the "friend of merchants."

39. *Ovid's Fasti,* trans. James George Frazer (London: Heinemann, 1931), 5.663–92; Porter, *Shakespeare's Mercutio,* p. 28.

40. Abraham Fraunce, *The Third Part of the Countess of Pembroke Yuychurch* (1592), sig. K_3.

41. Porter, *Shakespeare's Mercutio,* p. 90, cites Gascoigne's *Kenelworth* (1587), which treats of that "taling traytor Mercuri / who hopes to get the gole, / By curious filed speech, / abusing you by arte," since "in his tongue / consistes his cheefest might" (sig. Civ.).

42. See J. W. Lever, "Shakespeare's French Fruits," *Shakespeare Survey* 6 (1953): 79–90, with Porter, *Shakespeare's Mercutio,* p. 79.

43. Thomas Nashe, *A Pleasant Comedy, Called Summers Last Will and Testament* (London, 1600), sig. F_4; see Porter, *Shakespeare's Mercutio,* p. 86.

44. On the puns on "cousin" and "cozen," and on "germane," see Kökeritz, *Shakespeare's Pronunciation,* pp. 92, 101.

45. See ibid., p. 72; Craik, Oxford ed., p. 199: "Q's reading 'cosen garmombles' seems to play upon the name Mömpelgard . . . but whether it was in the original text is debatable. It would be unlike Shakespeare's usual practice to use a word that made no sense except as an anagram. . . . " But in his introduction Craik argues that Mömpelgard's election *in absentia* as Knight of the Garter in 1597 (a reflection of England's mercantile interests) suggests that "there is every reason to connect his election *in absentia* with the references, in the episode involving the stealing of the Host's horses, to three Germans and to a German duke who is alleged to be coming to the English court" (Oxford intro., see pp. 5–6).

46. On the link between Marlowe's play in its different versions and this reference in *Merry Wives,* see Leah Marcus's recent essay, "Textual Indeterminacy and Ideological Difference: The Case of Doctor Faustus," in *Renaissance Drama,* n.s. 20, ed. Mary Beth Rose (Evanston: Northwestern University Press, 1989).

47. C. T. Lewis and C. Short, *A Latin Dictionary,* 1st ed. (1879; rpt. Oxford, 1962), s.v. "germanus."

48. Kökeritz, *Shakespeare's Pronunciation,* p. 101, notes that "cousin-cozen" is found in *1 H 4* 1.3.254–55; *R 3* 4.4.223; *TNK* 3.1.43–44.

49. On this aspect of the play, discussed in Parker, *Literary Fat Ladies,* esp. pp. 73–76, see also Elizabeth Pittenger, "Dispatch Quickly: The Mechanical Reproduction of Pages," *Shakespeare Quarterly* 42 (1991): 389–409.

50. T. W. Craik notes in his introduction to the Oxford *Merry Wives,* p. 5, that the deterioration of England's trading relations with German lands made it very much "in England's interest to secure the friendship of as many German princes as possible" by 1597, and hence strengthened Mömpelgard's chances of election as Knight of the Garter in that year.

51. *The Works of Thomas Nashe,* ed. Ronald B. McKerrow (London: Sidgwick and Jackson, 1910), 2:251. This whole section of *The Unfortunate Traveller* may be a satire on English humanists of the strict Ciceronian kind, especially Gabriel Harvey. Nashe acknowledges the fact that "Wittenberg" here was read as the "Cambridge" of Harvey and the other

Ciceronians, noting in "To the Reader" (p. 182) that "there be certaine busie wits abrode, that seeke in my Iacke Wilton to anagramatize the name of Wittenberge to one of the Universities of England." Harold Ogden White, *Plagiarism and Imitation During the English Renaissance* (Cambridge: Harvard University Press, 1935), p. 89, notes: "Now although Nashe subsequently denied that he was criticizing Cambridge orators, as he was at once accused of doing, the final sentence quoted makes doubtful the sincerity of his protest. As Harvey had for three years been lecturer on rhetoric at Cambridge, and had represented the university in public debates before the queen similar to those inflicted on the duke of Saxony by the Wittenberg scholars in *The Unfortunate Traveller*, it seems highly probable that Nashe had him in mind when he dragged such a critical digression into his narrative." A more recent commentator agrees, commenting that *The Unfortunate Traveller* "contains a brief passage about the 'verie solemne scholasticall entertainment of the Duke of Saxonie' at the University of Wittenberg. The scene is somewhat reminiscent of Queen Elizabeth's visit to Audley End in 1578. A speech is delivered by the University Orator, who seems to me intended as a parody of Harvey." See Virginia F. Stern, *Gabriel Harvey: His Life, Marginalia and Library* (Oxford: Clarendon Press, 1979), p. 121.

52. Erasmus himself, of course, wrote in the *Ciceronianus* against the excesses of the strictest of the Ciceronians. In *The Unfortunate Traveller*, just before the encounter with the orators of Wittenberg the travelers meet in Rotterdam with "aged learnings chiefe orna-ment, that abundant and superingenious clarke, Erasmus, as also with merrie Sir Thomas Moore, our Countriman, who was come purposelie over a little before us, to visite the said grave father Erasmus"—the one at work on *The Praise of Folly*, the other on *Utopia*. The oration at Wittenberg is for the duke of Saxony, before whom "because hee was the chiefe Patrone of their Universitie, and had tooke Luthers parte in banishing the Masse and all like papal iurisdiction out of their towne, they croucht unto extreamely."

53. For Erasmus's *sensus germanus,* see Terence Cave, *The Cornucopian Text* (Oxford: Clarendon Press, 1979), pp. 88–89, 78ff., 107–10, and the discussion in my *Literary Fat Ladies,* 76–77. Of Erasmian texts, see the *Convivium religiosum,* am. 1–3, p. 251 (*Opera omnia,* vol. 1, Amsterdam, 1969); *Preface to St. John Paraphrase,* P. S. Allen, ed., *Opus epistolarum,* 12 vols.; *Ecclesiastes* (Basel: Froben, 1540), fr. 5, pp. 849, 854, 861, 868, 873 (LB 1019, 1026, 1033, 1041, 1048, in the facsimile of the edition by J. Le Clerc [Leyden, 1703–6]).

54. See Cowden Clarke, *Shakespeare's Characters* (London: Smith and Elder, 1863), 8:204.

55. See Puttenham's translation, in the *Arte of English Poesie,* of Greek *Epizeuxis* and Latin *Geminatio verborum* as the "Cuckoospell"; and Erasmus's definition of *homoiologia* (Greek, "identical repetition") as "singing out the same old phrase like a cuckoo." Shakespeare uses "cuckoo" in this sense of mechanical iteration in *I Henry IV* (2.4.353). The OED also cites the "never changed notes" of the "Cuckolds' chorister" from Greene's *Upstart Court-ier* (1592): "cuckow for the one Tune, No King, no King" from *The Cuckows Nest* in *Harl. Misc.* (1745) (v. 552); and, much later (1832), G. Downes's "He had two English words, 'very good! very good!' which, cuckoo-like, he was constantly reiterating."

56. See the *Towneley Mysteries* (1460), 5.29: "Iacob, that is thyne owne germane brother." In relation to the possibility that a "cousin" or "brother" might be a "cousine germane" who proves to be "cozening," we might note that in the 1587 edition of Holinshed, the account of the kingship of Bolingbroke, the usurper of the crown from Richard II, is entitled "Henrie

the Fourth, Cousine Germane to Richard the Second, latelie deprived." See *Holinshed's Chronicles of England, Scotland, and Ireland,* 6 vols. (London, 1808), 3:1.

57. For a discussion of the "simple" in a Shakespearean corpus which routinely undermines it, see Geoffrey Hartman, "Shakespeare's Poetical Character in *Twelfth Night,"* in Patricia Parker and Geoffrey Hartman, eds., *Shakespeare and the Question of Theory* (London: Methuen, 1985), pp. 37–53.

58. See Godshalk, "An Apology," p. 106.

59. In this speech in act 1 (1.4.126–27), the Folio spells "Anne" as "An." On the "Anne/ âne" homophone, see Frankie Rubinstein, *A Dictionary of Shakespeare's Sexual Puns and Their Significance* (London: Macmillan, 1984), p. 10.

60. William Carroll, "A Received Belief" (see note 4), p. 213 emphasizes this reminder of artifice and theatricality in which the audience, like the characters, is also "cozened." See also Godshalk, "An Apology," p. 106 and 3.3.7–72.

61. See, for example, Ann Barton in the Riverside introduction (p. 288), who emphasizes the oneness of the community in spite of its linguistic and other differences. See also Craik, Oxford ed., pp. 46–47.

62. See, among other treatments of the "merry" wives, Anne Parten's "Falstaff's Horns" (see note 16), pp. 184–99, and Sandra Clarke, "'Wives May Be Merry and Yet Honest Women Too': Women and Wit in *The Merry Wives of Windsor* and Some Other Plays," in *Fanned and Winnowed Opinions: Shakespearean Essays Presented to Harold Jenkins,* ed. J. W. Mahon and Thomas A. Pendleton (London: Methuen, 1987), pp. 249–67.

63. See Charlton T. Lewis and Charles Short, *A Latin Dictionary* (Oxford: Clarendon Press, 1975), s.v. *translatio,* which cites among others Cicero's *pecuniarum translatio a justis dominis ad alienos,* a transfer or "alienation" of money which uses parallel terminology to Cicero's definition of metaphor or *translatio* as transferring a word to an "alien" (*alienus*) place, and hence bequeathes to early modern English the sense of "alienate" and "translate" as synonyms for theft as well as terms related to the definition of metaphor. On the Ciceronian tradition in relation to property, see my essay "The Metaphorical Plot" (note 1). For the definition of "translator" cited in the text, see Thomas Thomas, *Dictionarium Linguae Latinae et Anglicanae* (1587). The doubleness of the Latin sense of "translate" also occurs in other Romance languages. Randle Cotgrave's *Dictionarie of the French and English Tongues* (1611; rpt. Menston, England: Scolar Press, 1968) gives for the French "translater" the English equivalents both of "to turne out of one language into another" and to "remove from one place unto another."

64. See Jonson, *Poetaster,* 5.3, in *Ben Jonson,* ed. C. H. Herford and Percy Simpson (Oxford: Clarendon Press, 1932), 4:307.

65. Latin *plagiarus* is rendered as "Stealer of bokes" in Richard Huloet's *Abecedarium anglico-Latinum* (1552; Menton, England: Scolar Press, 1970).

66. For Puttenham's denunciation of all translations that do not acknowledge themselves as such as "petty larceny," see *Arte,* 3.22, with White, *Plagiarism and Imitation.* Hooper's inclusion of literary theft under "Thou shalt not steal" may be found in *Early Writings of John Hooper,* ed. Samuel Carr (Cambridge: Cambridge University Press, 1843).

67. See White, *Plagiarism and Imitation,* pp. 75–78, and *The Epigrams of Sir John Harington,* ed. Norman Egbert McClure (Philadelphia, 1926).

68. On Greene's accusation and the figure from Horace of Aesop's crow, repeated in the charge against the upstart player Shakespeare at any early stage in his career, see White,

Plagiarism and Imitation, and more recently, Joseph Porter, *Shakespeare's Mercutio,* esp. p. 124. Porter emphasizes more the "charge of literary theft" than the charge against Shakespeare as upstart arriviste, but both are important.

69. For this anecdote and its debunking, see, inter alia, T. W. Craik's introduction to the Oxford edition, pp. 6–8.

70. See Joseph Porter, *Shakespeare's Mercutio,* esp. p. 120, which outlines the resulting Shakespearean affinity with the figure of Mercury related to merchants and to trade as well as to literature and language.

71. See Jeanne Addison Roberts, *Shakespeare's English Comedy,* chap. 5 for a summary of these charges against *Merry Wives* and specifically the sense of its Falstaff as a decline from, or disappointing secondary version of, the more robust Falstaff of the histories.

72. On Hal's mastery of "tongues" in relation to political governance and control of the divergent languages and peoples of the realm, see, inter alia, Steven Mullaney, *The Place of the Stage* (Chicago: University of Chicago Press, 1988), pp. 79–87.

73. See the "Epistle Dedicatorie" of book 1 of Florio's translation of the *Essayes* of Montaigne. The relation of women to translation in both of these senses is frequently part of this sense of translation as a "fall," declining or falling away from the integrity of the original. One of the prefatory proems to book 1 of Florio's translation of the *Essayes* speaks of "th' original / Of this, whose grace must by translation fall," a sense of translation as a falling or declining which appears routinely in early modern texts. See, for example, Thomas Rainolde, translator from Latin of a text called in English *The Byrth of Mankynde* (1560), who, in hastening to claim that his translation has "varied or declined nothyng at all from the steppes of his Latine auctor," simultaneously evokes the assumption that a translation might be expected both to "vary" and to "decline." On the "secondariness" of women as a "defective" version of a male original, derived from the overlaying of Aristotle with the story of the secondary creation of Eve in Genesis 2, see my "Coming Second: Women's Place," in *Literary Fat Ladies.* For an extended description and critique of the Aristotelian and Galenic views of this female "detour" and "imperfection," see Helkiah Crooke's *Description of the Body of Man* (1615), bk. 5, quest. 1, p. 271. This might be seen as the "translational" counterpart to the sense of the female as "leaky" and "incontinent" in contrast to a model of the male as a whole and integral body. See Gail Kern Paster's "Leaky Vessels: The Incontinent Women of City Comedy," in *Renaissance Drama,* n.s. 18 (1987), ed. Mary Beth Rose (Evanston, Ill.: Northwestern University Press), pp. 43–65.

74. See R. Howard Bloch, "Medieval Misogyny," *Representations* 20 (Fall 1987): 1–24, esp. 10–11. Bloch traces the patristic tradition of Eve to the link between women and ornament, and the "adulteration" of the accessory more generally. Something of this sense of translation as "femall" in relation to a manly original hovers around Chapman's translation of Homer, for example, and his presentation of Virgil as secondary to Homer's epic original. See White, *Plagiarism and Imitation,* p. 157.

75. On the role and accomplishments of women as translators, see, among other recent work, *Silent But for the Word: Tudor Women as Patrons, Translators, and Writers of Religious Works,* ed. Margaret Patterson Hannay (Kent, Ohio: Kent State University Press, 1985).

76. See Florio's "To the curteous Reader" in book 1 of his translation of the *Essayes* of Montaigne.

77. For a contemporary review of this tradition, see Allon White, "The Dismal Sacred

Word: Academic Language and the Social Reproduction of Seriousness," *JTP: Journal of literature, teaching, politics* 2 (1983): 4–15.

78. See my discussion of grammatical "case" and female "case" in the title essay of *Literary Fat Ladies*. There is also a rich series of linkages between the notion of Eve's "fault" and initiation of the original *lapsus* or "Fall," and the "fault," "laps," and sexual "cases" of women generally. See Janet Adelman, *Suffocating Mothers* (New York and London: Routledge, 1992), pp. 23ff. and my "Dilation, Spying and the Secret Place of Woman," forthcoming.

79. William Camden links the breaches in England's self-enclosed integrity through marriages with foreign wives to the adulterating of the purity of the English language that had obtained prior to the Norman invasion and other incursions. See his *Remains Concerning Britain,* ed. R. D. Duncan (Toronto: University of Toronto Press, 1984), p. 32.

80. For the thematics of impotence in the play, see once again Nancy Cotton, "Castrating (W)itches: Impotence and Magic in *The Merry Wives of Windsor,*" *Shakespeare Quarterly* 38, no. 3 (Autumn 1987): 320–26. The fact that Falstaff is called a "cuckold" at the play's end (5.5.109) may be not simply that he literally has "huge horns on his head" (4.4.43) but that he, like Ford, has been betrayed or tricked by women. There is certainly phallic imagery in the glowworms of the final scene and a sense of impotence in Mistress Page's "The truth being known, / We'll all present ourselves; dis-horn the spirit, / And mock him home to Windsor" (4.4.63–65). There is also a sense of detumescence or falling from the "erect" not only in "mistook their erection" but in the time "'twixt twelve and one" mentioned by Fenton in act 4 (4.5.48–49), a time reference related to a phallic "falling" traced in other Shakespearean contexts by Frankie Rubinstein, p. 160. One of the detumescence references in *Merry Wives* links the effeminated Fal-staff dressed in women's clothes directly with the "witch" of Brainford associated with spells that cause impotence: "I went to her, Master Brook, as you see, like a poor old man, but I came from her, Master Brook, like a poor old woman" (5.1.15–17).

81. This would be my criticism of Jonathan Goldberg's "Rebel Letters: Postal Effects from *Richard II* to *Henry IV,*" *Renaissance Drama* 19 (1988): 3–28, which elides the question of gender and which at least appears to see Shakespeare's Lancastrian tetralogy as embodying a logocentric structure I would argue they simultaneously illustrate and critique.

82. On this aspect of the play, see Elizabeth Freund, "'Ariachne's Broken Woof': The Rhetoric of Citation in *Troilus and Cressida,*" in Hartmann and Parker, eds., *Shakespeare and the Question of Theory,* pp. 19–36. Chaucer's version of the story in *Troilus and Criseyde* not only focusses on the translational thematics of historical and cultural *translatio* but links it with a story of an "unfaithful" woman.

83. See the study of these oppositions in Mihoko Suzuki, *Metamorphoses of Helen: Authority, Difference, and the Epic* (Ithaca and London: Cornell University Press, 1989), chap. 5, incorporating the argument of her "'Truth tired with iteration': Myth and Fiction in Shakespeare's *Troilus and Cressida,*" *Philological Quarterly* 66, no. 2 (Spring 1987): 153–74.

84. See my "Dilation, Spying and the Secret Place of Woman," and Hamlet's concern that the players will "tell all" in lines which treat as well of a sexualized female "show" and "tell." The link between women as "showing" or telling "secrets," and the players who will "tell all" is part, in the Play Scene in *Hamlet*, of the wordplay on "show" and "tell" which makes both women and players double-meaning "translators" and "interpreters." Florio

treats of players as translators in this sense in the same frontal material to book 1 of his translation of Montaigne's *Essayes* in which he writes that "translations are reputed femalls."

85.   Autolycus in Golding's Ovid is "such a fellow as in theft and filching had no peere." See Arthur Golding, trans. *Ovid's Metamorphoses* (London, 1567), sig. T$_4$, with Porter, *Shakespeare's Mercutio*, pp. 27, 129–30.

86.   See Leah S. Marcus, "Levelling Shakespeare: Local Customs and Local Texts," *Shakespeare Quarterly* 42, no. 2 (Summer 1991), pp. 168–78. My discussion here is indebted to this essay and to communications and conversations with Professor Marcus and Margreta de Grazia, whose *Shakespeare Verbatim: The Reproduction of Authenticity and the 1790 Apparatus* (Oxford: Clarendon Press, 1991) demonstrates the post-Shakespearean historical production of the very assumptions about originality, authenticity, and authorship on which so much of subsequent Shakespeare scholarship and editing has relied.

87.   Marcus, "Levelling Shakespeare," p. 175.

Teaching and Wordplay: The "Wall" of *A Midsummer Night's Dream*

PATRICIA PARKER

Workshop

"Now is the morall downe . . . "

—Folio *MND* 5.1.210

What I want to outline here is a particular pedagogical experience, one that turned out to connect a problem in pedagogy to a problem in editing, of determining, in the production of Shakespeare's texts, which lines or variants students actually get to read.

The example I am going to use is an experience from exploring some lines from act 5 of *A Midsummer Night's Dream* with students. [For the text of 5.1.28–370, see pp. 217–21.] These are the lines that stage the wonderful series of double meanings in the play of Pyramus and Thisbe put on by the so-called "rude mechanicals" for their aristocratic audience. Within the mechanicals' play is a character called "Wall"—"that vile Wall, which did these lovers sunder" (5 .1.132)—from the story of these lovers in Ovid's *Metamorphoses*. The Wall first presents its "crannied hole or chink" (158). There then follows an extended series of double entendres, which, beginning with Pyramus's insistent "O" ("O wall! O sweet, O lovely wall"), start to give an obscene sense to the "hole or chink" between the lovers, in a passage that harps repeatedly on "stones" and ends with the following exchange:

> *Pyramus.* O, kiss me through the hole of this vild wall!
> *Thisby.* I kiss the wall's hole, not your lips at all.
> *Pyramus.* Wilt thou at Ninny's tomb meet me straight-
> way?
> *Thisby.* 'Tide life, 'tide death, I come without delay.
> [*Exeunt* Pyramus and Thisby.]

> *Wall.* Thus have I, Wall, my part discharged so;
> And being done, thus Wall away doth go. [*Exit.*]
>   *Theseus.* Now is the *moon used* between the two neighbors.
>   *Demetrius.* No remedy, my lord, when walls are so wilful to hear without warning.
>
>   (5.1.200–209)

I'm quoting here, as some of you will recognize, from the Riverside edition of the plays of Shakespeare. But as is well known to teachers of the play, there is also another version for the comment of Theseus I have italicized. The Riverside editor has chosen to use the Quartos' "Now is the moon used between the two neighbors." But the Folio text of *A Midsummer Night's Dream* gives instead "Now is the *morall downe* between the two neighbors," a line which most editors emend (following Pope) to "Now is the mural down," as a phrase befitting the departure of a "Wall."[1]

The Quartos' "moon used" is a perfectly sensible line, as the editors and critics who argue for it hasten to point out: once the Wall has departed, the Moon or "Moonshine" comes in instead, to usher in the final part of the mechanicals' play. In its context, however, "Now is the moon used between the two neighbors" does not work as well as does the Folio's "morall" (at least with Pope's sense of "mural") when followed by Demetrius's immediate response: "No remedy, my lord, when walls are so wilful to hear without warning." This discrepancy in texts is the editorial crux I decided to begin with as an introduction for a group of senior students to the considerations that might go into exploring these lines from the Folio, both in their immediate context and in relation to the rest of *A Midsummer Night's Dream*. With these controversial lines began a pedagogical adventure that turned out, for all of us, to be an interpretive one as well.

What I asked the students to do, first, was to suspend initial judgment and simply to consider the possibilities of the Folio's "Now is the morall downe." Their first response was the one that had occurred to Pope: that "morall" here might well be punning on "mural," a pun generally defended by editors who adopt the Folio text by reference to Shakespeare's use of "mure" elsewhere instead of "wall." The second was the more mundane sense of "morall" which, however abstrusely it has been argued among editors, is almost immediately connected by students to the lines that speak of "willfull" walls or follow the obscene double entendres of the "chinks," the "O's," and Thisby's "I kiss the wall's hole not your lips at all." We are, after all, dealing with the playwright who earlier in his career had no difficulty transforming "enfranchise" into the name "Francis" or Ovidius Naso into "Ovid the Nose." And if a "Wall" is down between such eager lovers (especially when the passage keeps linking it to the hymeneal wall), the notion that the "morall" might follow is, in students' minds, in my experience, generally not far behind. In fact, within the *Dream* and the larger plot of lovers which the mechanicals' play parodically recaps, once these lovers (like Pyramus and Thisbe when the "wall" is "down") meet outside parental boundaries in the woods, the emphasis is there, too, on the impeaching of "modesty" and the threat to "virginity" (2.1.219; 2.2.57), in ways that recall the double-meaning "walls" of "maids" at the beginning of *Romeo and Juliet*, the other play whose source is this same story out of Ovid's *Metamorphoses*.

What I did at this point was to ask that initial group of students if they could go beyond the immediate context of these lines to consider the Folio's "morall downe" in relation to the play as a whole. This adventure began when a student in the class, who was taking it as a side-interest to a major in Classics, noted (after we had looked at editorial glosses that break "morall" or "mural" into "more-all/mure all") that *mora* in Latin means "delay" and that the wall's being down now meant, for the previously separated lovers, that there would be no more "delay." Thisby, this student pointed out, even says as this Wall departs, "'Tide life, 'tide death, I come without delay."

This is where our exploration started to get interesting. First we decided to examine the link with "delay," since delay (and especially erotic delay) is already such a central part of *A Midsummer Night's Dream*. The play begins, after all, with another impatient lover—Theseus—anxious (far more than Hippolyta) to see the end of the four-day interim before the consummation of his wedding night. The play-within-a-play of Pyramus and Thisbe, staged by the "rude mechanicals" in act 5, is another dramatic interlude whose "wall" must be down before this erotic waiting can come to an end, and Theseus and Hippolyta, along with the other pairs of lovers in this "marriage" play, can, finally, go to bed. Bottom's "No, I assure you, the wall is down that parted their fathers" (5.1.352) calls repeated attention, at the play's end, to the "wall" whose being "down" makes both consummations possible.

We began therefore to consider the possibility of an echoing of *mora* or "delay" in the Folio's "morall," on the encouragement of Thisby's "I come without delay" as this Wall departs. We decided to bring into the discussion not just the various editions of Shakespeare the students had already brought to class but also the text most pertinent to this part of *A Midsummer*

Night's Dream—the story of Pyramus and Thisbe told in Book 4 of Ovid's *Metamorphoses* and in Golding's translation. And here is where we began to make discoveries that led us from the Folio's "morall" and Thisby's "delay" to the rest of the *Dream*, and back again.

The text from Ovid, we found, is filled with a sense of delay, as it is of the forbidding "wall" that connects the impatient lovers but also stands between them as an obstacle. It also added another interlingual pun to our growing collection, at the point where Pyramus, acting suddenly (*nec mora*, without delay) kills himself and so changes the color of the berries (*mora*) of the mulberry tree (*morus*) at which the lovers were to meet. The story from Ovid goes out of its way to emphasize these links, choosing the plural (*mora*, mulberries) rather than the singular (*morum*) in the same lines that begin with the *nec mora* of Pyramus's rash act and then adding to it the further verbal link with *moriens* or "dying" (*nec mora, ferventi moriens . . . purpureo tinguit pendentia mora*). In Ovid's version of the lovers' story, the *mora* or berries of the mulberry tree are dyed purple by Pyramus's death, after he sees Thisbe's cloak and rushes to his death—without *mora* or delay.

Golding's translation, though it is deprived in English of this rich Latin punning on *mora* (delay) and *mora* (mulberries), still seems to pick up something of this link when it first mentions the mulberry tree where the lovers decide to meet. For it adds to Ovid's line "they were to meet at Ninus' tomb and hide in the shade of a tree" (*conveniant ad busta Nini lateantque sub umbra / arboris*) a further emphasis on tarrying or delay: "They did agree at Ninus Tumb to meete without the towne, / And *tarie* underneath a tree that by the same did grow / Which was a faire high Mulberrie"—a sense it gets perhaps more generally not just from Ovid's *mora / mora* play but from the sense of delay, slowness or tardiness Ovid adds just after the appearance of this mulberry, as the lovers long for the "tardy" sun to set (*lux, tarde discedere visa*).

We then decided as a group to go back to *A Midsummer Night's Dream* to see what Shakespeare's version made of this. And there they were, both passages conflated—Ovid's *mora / mora* lines on Pyramus's death and Golding's "tarrying" beneath the mulberry tree:

> Anon comes Pyramus, sweet youth and tall,
> And finds his trusty Thisby's mantle slain;
> Whereat, with blade, with bloody blameful blade,
> He bravely broach'd his boiling bloody breast;

> And Thisby, *tarrying in mulberry shade*,
> His dagger drew, and died. . . .

(*MND* 5.1.144–49)

At this point, a student who had studied Dante commented that the erotic passion of the Pyramus and Thisbe story appears in the tradition of "Ovid moralized" as an allegory of the passion of Christ, the passion that turned the mulberry from white to red, or black. When we consulted the version of the story in the *Ovide moralisé*, we found that it, too, draws attention to the verbal links that move from *mora* or delay to the *morus* or mulberry and *moriendi* or dying. This moralized tradition—in its articulation of an allegorization familiar not just to Dante but to Elizabethans—gave us even more to think about in relation to *A Midsummer Night's Dream*. And here is where, having started with the controversial "morall downe" of the lines from act 5, we were led into the rest of the play before we came back again to this famous editorial crux.

The tradition of Ovid "moralized," like so much of such allegorical commentary, overlays the story from the *Metamorphoses*—and particularly its "Wall"—with a rich network of biblical passages. In particular it conflates the "Wall" that separates the two lovers from one another with the similarly separating "walls" of biblical tradition. One of these is the "wall of partition" from Eph. 2 (already echoed in *The Comedy of Errors*, set in Ephesus), actually recalled when Demetrius uses the term "partition" for the character of "Wall" (5.1.166), a dividing "wall" that will be "down" anagogically only in the Apocalypse. Another, in an explicitly erotic context, is the wall that separates the lovers in Canticles or the Song of Songs, a wall that will be finally "down" in the apocalyptic marriage of Bridegroom and Spouse. This wall is the wall the beloved stands behind in Canticles 2:9 and that the tradition of "Ovid moralized" easily associated with the frustratingly separating "wall" of Ovid's story of Pyramus and Thisbe .

To bring these biblical "walls" (and their final, anagogic removal in the Apocalypse) to bear on interpretation of the "Wall" of the mechanicals' play of Pyramus and Thisbe—the play within Shakespeare's larger "marriage" play—was, we discovered, not only appropriate to the parodically erotic context of the lines that include the Folio's "morall downe" but to the strikingly biblical and apocalyptic echoes that pervade *A Midsummer Night's Dream* more generally. This is the play, after all, that contains the scrambling of the text from Cor. 2:9 when Bottom awakens from his dream

(4.1.210–12) and that already assimilates one element of Ovid "moral-ized"—the association of the lion frightening Thisbe with the "roaring lion" of 2 Pet. 5, from the period before Apocalypse—into the "hungry lion roars" of Puck's final speech.

Once we moved from the Folio's "morall downe" to the conflations of biblical and Ovidian "walls" in the *Ovide moralisé* tradition and to the "wall" that separates Bridegroom and Spouse in the erotic or "marriage" contexts of Apocalypse and the Song of Songs, we began to see other elements in the *Dream* differently as well, particularly the scene in act 3 where these same "mechanicals" rehearse the play whose "wall" is finally "down" in act 5. The erotic imagery of the Song of Songs—with its lily and rose, its "fair" or "lovely" beloved, its odorous "smells," and even its "let me see thy countenance, let me hear thy voice"—is explicitly burlesqued within this "marriage" play, not just in the staging of the mechanicals' play in act 5 (in its "fair" Pyramus, "I see a voice" and "I can hear my Thisby's face") but in their rehearsal in act 3, with its comic echoing of this imagery of white and red in its "red rose" and "lily-white of hue," and in its malapropping "odious savors sweet."

Let us look, as we did, more carefully at this earlier rehearsal scene, and consider it in relation to the "wall" or (Folio) "morall" of act 5. In the "moralized" Ovid tradition that conflates the Ovidian and the biblical, Pyramus becomes the "lovely" Bridegroom of the Apocalypse and the Song of Songs, while Thisbe is the Spouse separated from her beloved by a "wall" in the period of absence before he "comes again." "Thisbe," in this "moral," is also the figure for the Spouse as the Church, who, in the period of this Bridegroom's absence, wanders in search of her beloved. (As the students who had read Book 1 of *The Faerie Queene* were quick to recog-nize, this was an imagery and allegory widely current in Elizabethan Eng-land.) In the rehearsal scene in act 3 of the *Dream*, we encounter the fol-lowing, as Bottom/Pyramus departs only "a while" from his Thisbe and promises to return:

> *Bottom.* . . . Stay thou but here a while,
> And by and by I will to thee appear.
> [*Puck.*] A stranger Pyramus than e'er played here.
> > [*Exit .*]
> *Flute* [*Thisby*]. Must I speak now?
> *Quince.* Ay, marry, must you; for you must understand
> he goes but to see a noise that he heard, and is to come
> again.

> *Flute.* Most radiant Pyramus, most lily-white of hue,
> Of color like the red rose on triumphant brier,
> Most brisky juvenal, and eke most lovely Jew. . . .

The Pyramus here described (in the familiar "lily-white" and "red" of the Canticles) as "most lovely Jew" is the player Pyramus who will later provide a (mock) resurrection on stage when he rises from the dead in act 5 to assure the gentles that the "wall" is "down" (5.1.351). Here he promises to "come again," after an interim in which it is Thisby's turn to "speak." As one student pointed out, the possibility that the mechanicals' "Thisby" is linked by these resonances to this "moralized" Spouse, left to seek a Bridegroom who has not yet returned, may retrospectively illuminate Flute's otherwise curious "What is Thisby? a wand'ring knight?" (1.2.45) when we recall the links between the wandering and "seeking" of this Spouse and the romance motif of questing knights, also exploited in Book 1 of Spenser's epic. Certainly the cross-gendering that makes the moralized Thisbe into a figure for the (female) Church would in this Shakespearean "marriage" play be only too appropriate in scenes where Flute's objection to this female part ("I have a beard coming," 1.2.47–48) calls comic attention to the context of a transvestite theater where women's parts were played by boys.

Thisbe/Flute, in the rehearsal scene, delivers prematurely the line "I'll meet thee, Pyramus, at Ninny's tomb" (transforming "Ninus" to "ninny" in an interlingual joke at the point in the story where the lovers meet *ad busta Nini*). And when Pyramus/Bottom returns or "comes again," it is in the "translated" form of a body with an ass's head, both a literalization of this "Bottom's" name and an actual metamorphosis into the sign of the "ninny" or fool. As the play proceeds, the lowly "Bottom," who will become the mummers' play actor or parody Christ who rises from the dead in act 5, is associated with the resonances of the "low" made "high" and with the paradoxical wisdom of the fool, the bottomless "bottom of Goddes secretes" (Geneva Bible, 1557), contrasted in the passage from Cor. 2 with the wisdom of the rulers of this world, including presumably Athenian Theseus.

From the complex our exploration had led us to—Ovid, delay, and mulberries, the Bridegroom and Spouse of Canticles, Apocalypse, and Ovid moralized—our seminar group then returned to the Folio lines on the "morall downe" with which we had begun:

> *Thisbie.* 'Tide life, 'tide death, I come without delay.
> *Wall.* Thus have I Wall, my part discharged so;

And being done, thus Wall away doth go.

[Exit Clowns.]

Duke. Now is the morall downe between the two
Neighbors. . . .

From the perspective of all the contexts we had traced, Thisby's "I come
without delay," with the Folio's "Now is the morall downe," now summoned echoes of that apocalyptic marriage—of the other "consummation"
made possible through a "passion" (a word used several times in this scene),
the one through which the "moral" was to give way to the apocalyptic or
anagogical. Lysander, we noted, makes earlier reference to a "moral" in
this scene (5.1.120). And, as with Thisby's "I come without delay" (at the
point where this "wall," along with the hymeneal one, is about to be "down"),
the final Marriage celebrated in the Apocalypse—conflated by the "moralized" tradition with the "passion" of Ovid's Pyramus and Thisbe—ends
with a repeated "come" and "come quickly," before the final consummation in which there is to be no more *mora* or delay. (We also glanced at the
Vulgate version of Matt. 24–25, the other New Testament text that treats of
this apocalyptic *consummatio*, and found there, once again, much made of
this Bridegroom's coming only after a period of *mora* or delay.)

Echoes of this apocalyptic marriage, when a "wall" is to be "down"
and the "moral" to be superseded by the anagogical, would, we concluded,
not be inappropriate to the marriage plot and context of *A Midsummer
Night's Dream*, especially since the Ceremony of Matrimony itself (echoed several times within the play) explicitly links the marriage ceremony
with this final union of Bridegroom and Bride. But the play's own ending,
once the mechanicals' "wall" is down and Theseus's long-awaited consummation comes, is also far from this kind of apocalyptic consummation
outside history. Puck's concluding speech, with its "hungry lion roars,"
places its more uncertain or open-ended ending still within the time before
Apocalypse. And its Theseus is still very much a ruler of this world, with a
limited "wisdom" and his own unfinished and highly ambiguous ongoing
history.

There were other intriguing sidelines to our exploration of the resonances within the play both of *mora* and of "morall downe." One was the
discovery that the *morus* or mulberry tree—in the moralized tradition a
figure for the passion of the "cross" that turns its fruit from white to red and
joins Bridegroom and Bride through the blood of Pyramus/Christ—was
also surrounded with this range of associations that permeate the play. John
Minsheu's dictionary of 1617 tantalizingly gives as one of its several names

the "Moral" tree.[2] It was also known in English by the name of "more" (Wyclif's translation of what the Geneva Bible would render as the "mulberry" of Luke 17:6, the counterpart to the Vulgate's *arbori moro*) and linked routinely with *mora* or delay, with the *morus* or foolish, and with the "black" or "moor." It is the dark color of its fruit or *mora nigra* that links this "more" or "moral" tree with the phallic-shaped "morel" or "night-shade" that Herbert Ellis suggests as yet another association for the Folio's "Now is the morall downe between the two Neighbors," coming as it does after lines whose double entendres so clearly link the departed "Wall" with the hymeneal one. (Ellis notes that this double-meaning "morel" also lurks within the "morall meaning" of another Shakespearean scene in *Much Ado About Nothing*. And the fact that Ovid's mulberry or *morus* had long been associated with the *morus* or "fool" as well as with the wisdom of the apparently foolish made us wonder whether these associations might some-how also be hovering around the figure of the wise fool in that passage where Bottom the "ass" scrambles the biblical verses from Corinthians on the wisdom that is folly to the wise, or to the rulers of this world. We resolved, therefore, before we were through, not just to think about the links between "more" and "moor" that might be relevant to a play that puts such emphasis on "fair" and "dark" (as when Hermia is called an "Ethiop") but about the implications of the fact that the mulberry associated with the Ovidian lovers (and, in the moralized tradition, with a different "passion") is transferred to an entirely different part of Shakespeare's *Dream*—the passage in act 2 that describes the deflecting of Cupid's shaft from a "fair vestal" who may recall England's Elizabeth and the creation of the "little western flower, / Before milk-white, now purple with love's wound" (2.1.166–167) that becomes part of the "cross" and crossing of the lovers in the woods, and causes another Queen or ruler of this world to fall, "prepost'rously" (3.2.134), for an "ass" or fool.

Before we were through with the Folio's controversial "morall downe," we had brought into our exploration a broad variety of interpretive tools—the sources for its play-within-a play, from Ovid and from Golding, the network of biblical allusion this had led us to, and, beyond these, both the resources of what Spitzer called "historical semantics" and, more serendipitously, the linguistic talents of the students themselves, in tracing the resonances of richly translingual wordplay from a period of far more permeable linguistic boundaries. Most important, perhaps, we had brought to bear on a long-standing editorial controversy the critical possibilities of starting interpretively from Shakespeare's language itself, and from that fatal Cleopatra, the Shakespearean pun.

Notes

1. Among recent editions, see for example Stanley Wells, ed., *A Midsummer Night's Dream* (Harmondsworth: Penguin Books, 1967), p. 114, which adopts Pope's "mural down"; and the adoption of Pope's emendation in R. A. Foakes's New Cambridge edition of *A Midsummer Night's Dream* (Cambridge: Cambridge University Press, 1984), p. 125, with his note on p. 140, which criticizes Harold Brooks's Arden edition of the play (London: Methuen, 1979) for unnecessarily revising the line entirely to the conjectural "mure rased," a revision also used in A. L. Rowse's edition of the *Dream* for the Contemporary Shakespeare series (Lanham, Md,: University Press of America, 1984).

2 See John Minsheu, *Ductor in Linguas* (London 1617), which gives under "Mulbery" both "Moral" tree and the following: "*Morum* the Mulbery, of *Mora*, lingring, or slow comming forth, because it doth not budde, nor come forth, till other trees have done, least it should be also nipped with cold, and therefore also it is stiled and called *Prudentissima arbor*, the most wise or advised tree. Alius a *Mauros*, . . eius enim fructi nigri fuit coloris priusquam sanguine Pyrami & Thisbe tingeretur nam sub hac arbore miseri amantes accubuere, unde vocatur Morus Pyramea." Alciati's and other moralized emblem books in the period also provide commentaries on the *Morus* or Mulberry that make the link between the (Greek) *mauros* (*nigra* or "black"), *mora* or delay and *morus* or foolish (Greek *Moria*, folly—as in the "More" exploited in Erasmus's *Encomium Moriae* or *Praise of Folly*, a text that has also been cited in relation to the "fools-head" and lowly "ass" of *A Midsummer Night's Dream*), adding that the association with the *morus* or foolish suggested by its Latin name is contradicted by the wisdom or *sapientia* of its delay (*mora*) in putting forth its fruit. (They often in this connection cite Erasmus's adage *Maturior moro* from the Adages.) See, for example, *Omnia Andreae Alciati Emblema cum commentarius . . . per Claudium Minoem* (Antwerp, 1577), p. 667.

3. See Herbert A. Ellis, *Shakespeare's Lusty Punning in "Love's Labour's Lost"* (The Hague: Mouton, 1973), pp. 1641–65, and *Much Ado* 3.4.73–80.

The Merry Wives of Windsor 4.1.1–85

(With permission from Houghton Mifflin, *The Riverside Shakespeare,* ed. G. Blakemore Evans, 1974.)

Enter Mistress Page, [Mistress] Quickly, William.

Mrs. Page. Is he at Master Ford's already, think'st thou?

Quick. Sure he is by this—or will be presently. But truly he is very courageous made about his throwing into the water. Mistress Ford desires you to come suddenly.   6

Mrs. Page. I'll be with her by and by; I'll but bring my young man here to school.

[*Enter*] Evans.

Look where his master comes; 'tis a playing-day, I see. How now, Sir Hugh, no school to-day?   10

Evans. No; Master Slender is let the boys leave to play.

Quick. Blessing of his heart!

Mrs. Page. Sir Hugh, my husband says my son profits nothing in the world at his book. I   15 pray you ask him some questions in his accidence.

Evans. Come hither, William; hold up your head; come.

Mrs. Page. Come on, sirrah; hold up your head. Answer your master, be not afraid.   20

Evans. William, how many numbers is in nouns?

William. Two.

Quick. Truly, I thought there had been one num-ber more, because they say, " 'Ods nouns."

Evans. Peace your tattlings! What is "fair," William?   26

Will. Pulcher.

Quick. Poulcats? There are fairer things than poulcats sure.

Evans. You are a very simplicity oman; I pray you peace. What is *lapis,* William?   31

Will. A stone.

Evans. And what is "a stone," William?

Will. A pebble.

Evans. No, it is *lapis.* I pray you remember in your prain.   36

Will. Lapis.

Evans. That is good William. What is he, William that does lend articles?   39

Will. Articles are borrow'd of the pronoun, and be thus declin'd, *Singulariter, nominativo, hic, haec, hoc.*

Evans. Nominativo, hig, hag, hog; pray you mark; *genitivo, hujus.* Well, what is your accusative case?

Will. Accusativo, hinc.   45

Evans. I pray you have your remembrance, child. *Accusativo,* [*hung*], *hang, hog.*

Quick. "Hang-hob" is Latin for bacon, I warrant you.   49

Evans. Leave your prabbles, oman. What is the focative case, William?

Will. O—*vocativo, O.*

Evans. Remember, William, focative is *caret.*

Quick. And that's a good root.

Evans. Oman, forbear.   55

Mrs. Page. Peace!

Evans. What is your genitive case plural, Wil-liam?

Will. Genitive case?

Evans. Ay.   60

Will. [*Genitivo,*] *horum, harum, horum.*

Quick. Vengeance of Jinny's case! Fie on her! never name her, child, if she be a whore.

Evans. For shame, oman.   64

Quick. You do ill to teach the child such words. He teaches him to "hic" and to "hac," which they'll do fast enough of themselves, and to call "horum," —fie upon you!   68

215

Evans. Oman, art thou [lunatics]? Hast thou no understandings for thy cases and the numbers of the genders? Thou art foolish Christian creatures as I would desires.

Mrs. Page. Prithee hold thy peace.

Evans. Show me now, William, some declensions of your pronouns.   75

Will. Forsooth, I have forgot.

Evans. It is *qui,* [*quae*], *quod:* if you forget your *qui*'s, your [*quiae*'s], and your *quod*'s, you must be preeches. Go your ways and play, go.

Mrs. Page. He is a better scholar than I thought he was.   81

Evans. He is a good sprag memory. Farewell, Mistress Page.

Mrs. Page. Adieu, good Sir Hugh. [*Exit Evans.*] Get you home, boy. Come, we stay too long.   85
                                          Exeunt.

A Midsummer Night's Dream 5.1.28–370

(With permission from Houghton Mifflin, *The Riverside Shakespeare*, ed. G. Blakemore Evans, 1974.)

Enter lovers, LYSANDER, DEMETRIUS, HERMIA, *and* HELENA.

The. Here come the lovers, full of joy and mirth.
Joy, gentle friends, joy and fresh days of love
Accompany your hearts!

    Lys.   More than to us   30
Wait in your royal walks, your board, your bed!

    The. Come now; what masques, what dances shall we have,
To war away this long age of three hours
Between [our] after-supper and bed-time?
Where is our usual manager of mirth?   35
What revels are in hand? Is there no play
To ease the anguish of a torturing hour?
Call Philostrate.

    Phil.   Here, mighty Theseus.

    The. Say, what abridgment have you for this evening?
What masque? what music? How shall we beguile   40
The lazy time, if not with some delight?

    Phil. There is a brief how many sports are ripe.
Make choice of which your Highness will see first.
                       [Giving a paper.]

    The. [*Reads.*] "The battle with the Centaurs, to be sung
By an Athenian eunuch to the harp."   45
We'll none of that: that have I told my love,
In glory of my kinsman Hercules.
"The riot of the tipsy Bacchanals,
Tearing the Thracian singer in their rage."
That is an old device; and it was play'd   50
When I from Thebes came last a conqueror.
"The thrice three Muses mourning for the death
Of Learning, late deceas'd in beggary."
That is some satire, keen and critical,
Not sorting with a nuptial ceremony.   55

"A tedious brief scene of young Pyramus
And his love Thisby; very tragical mirth."
Merry and tragical? Tedious and brief?
That is hot ice and wondrous strange snow.
How shall we find the concord of this discord? 60

    Phil. A play there is, my lord, some ten words long,
Which is as brief as I have known a play;
But by ten words, my lord, it is too long,
Which makes it tedious, for in all the play
There is not one word apt, one player fitted.   65
And tragical, my noble lord, it is;
For Pyramus therein doth kill himself;
Which when I saw rehears'd, I must confess,
Made mine eyes water; but more merry tears
The passion of loud laughter never shed.   70

    The. What are they that do play it?

    Phil. Hard-handed men that work in Athens here,
Which never labor'd in their minds till now;
And now have toiled their unbreathed memories
With this same play, against your nuptial.   75

    The. And we will hear it.

    Phil.   No, my noble lord,
It is not for you. I have heard it over,
And it is nothing, nothing in the world;
Unless you can find sport in their intents,
Extremely stretch'd, and conn'd with cruel pain, 80
To do you service.

    The.   I will hear that play;
For never any thing can be amiss,
When simpleness and duty tender it.
Go bring them in; and take your places, ladies.
                      [Exit Philostrate.]

    Hip. I love not to see wretchedness o'ercharged,
And duty in his service perishing.   86

    The. Why, gentle sweet, you shall see no such thing.

Hip. He says they can do nothing in this kind.
The. The kinder we, to give them thanks for
   nothing.
Our sport shall be to take what they mistake;   90
And what poor duty cannot do, noble respect
Takes it in might, not merit.
Where I have come, great clerks have purposed
To greet me with premeditated welcomes;
Where I have seen them shiver and look pale,   95
Make periods in the midst of sentences,
Throttle their practic'd accent in their fears,
And in conclusion dumbly have broke off,
Not paying me a welcome. Trust me, sweet,
Our of this silence yet I pick'd a welcome;   100
And in the modesty of fearful duty
I read as much as from the rattling tongue
Of saucy and audacious eloquence.
Love, therefore, and tongue-tied simplicity
In least speak most, to my capacity.   105

[*Enter Philostrate.*]

Phil. So please your Grace, the Prologue is
   address'd.
The. Let him approach.   [*Flourish trumpet.*]

Enter [QUINCE *for*] *the Prologue.*

Pro. If we offend, it is with our good will.
That you should think, we come not to offend,
But with good will. To show our simple skill,   110
That is the true beginning of our end.
Consider then, we come but in despite.
We do not come, as minding to content you,
Our true content is. All for your delight
We are not here. That you should here repent you,
The actors are at hand; and, by their show,   116
You shall know all, that you are like to know.
The. This fellow doth not stand upon points.
Lys. He hath rid his prologue like a rough colt;
he knows not the stop. A good moral, my lord: it is
not enough to speak, but to speak true.   121
Hip. Indeed he hath play'd on this prologue like
a child on a recorder—a sound, but not in govern-
ment.
The. His speech was like a tangled chain;   125
nothing impair'd, but all disorder'd. Who is next?

Enter [*with a Trumpet before them*] PYRAMUS *and*
THISBY *and* WALL *and* MOONSHINE *and* LION.

Pro. Gentles, perchance you wonder at this show;

But wonder on till truth make all things plain.
This man is Pyramus, if you would know;
This beauteous lady Thisby is certain.   130
This man, with lime and rough-cast, doth present
Wall, that vile Wall, which did these lovers sunder;
And through Wall's chink, pour souls, they are con-
   tent
To whisper. At the which let no man wonder.
This man, with lantern, dog, and bush of thorn,   135
Presenteth Moonshine; for if you will know,
By moonshine did these lovers think no scorn
To meet at Ninus' tomb, there, there to woo.
This grisly beast, which Lion hight by name,
The trusty Thisby, coming first by night,   140
Did scare away, or rather did affright;
And as she fled, her mantle she did fall,
Which Lion vile with bloody mouth did stain.
Anon comes Pyramus, sweet youth and tall,
And finds his trusty Thisby's mantle slain;   145
Whereat, with blade, with bloody blameful blade,
He bravely broach'd his boiling bloody breast;
And Thisby, tarrying in mulberry shade,
His dagger drew, and died. For all the rest,
Let Lion, Moonshine, Wall, and lovers twain 150
At large discourse, while here they do remain.

Exit [*with Pyramus,*] *Thisby, Lion,*
and Moonshine.

The. I wonder if the lion be to speak.
Dem. No wonder, my lord; one lion may, when
many asses do.
Wall. In this same enterlude it doth befall   155
That I, one [Snout] by name, present a wall;
And such a wall, as I would have you think,
That had in it a crannied hole or chink,
Through which the lovers, Pyramus and Thisby,
Did whisper often, very secretly.   160
This loam, this rough-cast, and this stone doth show
That I am that same wall; the truth is so;
And this the cranny is, right and sinister,
Through which the fearful lovers are to whisper. 164
The. Would you desire lime and hair to speak
better?
Dem. It is the wittiest partition that ever I heard
discourse, my lord.

[*Enter* PYRAMUS.]

The. Pyramus draws near the wall. Silence!
Pyr. O grim-look'd night! O night with hue so
   black!   170

O night, which ever art when day is not!
O night, O night! alack, alack, alack,
I fear my Thisby's promise is forgot!
And thou, O wall, O sweet, O lovely wall,   174
That stand'st between her father's ground and mine!
Thou wall, O wall, O sweet and lovely wall,
Show me thy chink, to blink through with mine eyne!
           [*Wall holds up his fingers.*]
Thanks, courteous wall; Jove shield thee well for this!
But what see I? No Thisby do I see.
O wicked wall, through whom I see no bliss!   180
Curs'd be thy stones for thus deceiving me!

The. The wall methinks, being sensible, should curse again.

Pyr. No, in truth, sir, he should not. "Deceiving me" is Thisby's cue. She is to enter now, and   185
I am to spy her through the wall. You shall see it will fall pat as I told you. Yonder she comes.

Enter THISBY

This. O wall, full often hast thou heard my moans,
For parting my fair Pyramus and me!
My cherry lips have often kiss'd thy stones,   190
Thy stones with lime and hair knit [up in thee].

Pyr. I see a voice! Now will I to the chink,
To spy and I can hear my Thisby's face.
Thisby!

This.   My love thou art, my love I think.   194

Pyr. Not Shafalus to Procrus was so true.

This. As Shafalus to Procrus, I to you.   199

Pyr. O, kiss me through the hole of this vild wall!

This. I kiss the wall's hole, not your lips at all.

Pyr. Wilt thou at Ninny's tomb meet me straightway?

This. 'Tide life, 'tide death, I come without delay.
           [*Exeunt Pyramus and Thisby.*]

Wall. Thus have I, Wall, my part discharged so;
And being done, thus Wall away doth go. [*Exit.*] 205

The. Now is the moon used between the two neighbors.

Dem. No remedy, my lord, when walls are so willful to hear without warning.

Hip. This is the silliest stuff that ever I heard. 210

The. The best in this kind are but shadows; and the worst are no worse, if imagination amend them.

Hip. It must be your imagination, then, and not theirs.   214

The. If we imagine no worse of them than they of themselves, they may pass for excellent men. Here come two noble beasts in, a man and a lion.   218

Enter LION *and* MOONSHINE.

Lion. You, ladies, you, whose gentle hearts do fear
The smallest monstrous mouse that creeps on floor,
May now, perchance, both quake and tremble here,
When lion rough in wildest rage doth roar.   222
Then know that I as Snug the joiner am
A lion fell, nor else no lion's dam,
For, if I should, as lion, come in strife   225
Into this place, 'twere pity on my life.

The. A very gentle beast, and of a good conscience.

Dem. The very best at a beast, my lord, that e'er I saw.   230

Lys. This lion is a very fox for his valor.

The. His discretion, I am sure, cannot carry his valor; for the goose carries not the fox. It is well; leave it to his discretion, and let us listen to the Moon.

Moon. This lanthorn doth the horned moon present—

Dem. He should have worn the horns on his head.   241

The. He is no crescent, and his horns are invisible within the circumference.

Moon. This lanthorn doth the horned moon present;
Myself the man i' th' moon do seem to be.   245

The. This is the greatest error of all the rest. The man should be put into the lanthorn. How is it else the man i' th' moon?

Dem. He dares not come there for the candle; for, you see, it is already in snuff.   250

Hip. I am a-weary of this moon. Would he would change!

The. It appears, by his small light of discretion, that he is in the wane; but yet in courtesy, in all reason, we must stay the time.   255

Lys. Proceed, Moon.

Moon. All that I have to say is to tell you that the lanthorn is the moon, I the man i' th' moon, this thorn-bush my thorn-bush, and this dog my dog. 259

Dem. Why, all these should be in the lanthorn; for all these are in the moon. But silence! here comes Thisby.

Enter THISBY.

This. This is old Ninny's tomb. Where is my love?

Lion. O!   [*The Lion roars. Thisby runs off.*]

Dem. Well roar'd, Lion.   265

The. Well run, Thisby.

Hip. Well shone, Moon. Truly, the moon shines with a good grace. [*The Lion shakes Thisby's mantle.*]

The. Well mous'd, Lion.

Enter PYRAMUS.

Dem. And then came Pyramus. [*Exit Lion.*] 270

Lys. And so the lion vanish'd.

Pyr. Sweet Moon, I thank thee for thy sunny beams;

I thank thee, Moon, for shining now so bright;

For by thy gracious, golden, glittering [gleams],

I trust to take of truest Thisby sight.   275

    But stay! O spite!

    But mark, poor knight,

    What dreadful dole is here!

    Eyes, do you see?

    How can it be?   280

    O dainty duck! O dear!

    Thy mantle good,

    What, stain'd with blood?

    Approach, ye Furies fell!

    O Fates, come, come,   285

    Cut thread and thrum,

    Quail, crush, conclude, and quell!

The. This passion, and the death of a dear friend, would go near to make a man look sad.

Hip. Beshrew my heart, but I pity the man, 290

Pyr. O, wherefore, Nature, didst thou lions frame?

Since lion vild hath here deflow'r'd my dear;

Which is—no, no—which was the fairest dame

That liv'd, that lov'd, that lik'd, that look'd with cheer.

    Come, tears, confound   295

    Out, sword, and wound

    The pap of Pyramus;

    Ay, that left pap,

    Where heart doth hop. [*Stabs himself.*]

    Thus die I, thus, thus, thus.   300

    Now am I dead,

    Now am I fled;

    My soul is in the sky.

    Tongue, lose thy light,   304

    Moon, take thy flight, [*Exit Moonshine.*]

    Now die, die, die, die.   [*Dies.*]

Dem. No die, but an ace, for him; for he is but one.

Lys. Less than an ace, man; for he is dead, he is nothing.

The. With the help of a surgeon he might yet recover, and yet prove an ass.   311

Hip. How chance Moonshine is gone before Thisby comes back and finds her lover?

[*Enter* THISBY.]

The. She will find him by starlight. Here she comes, and her passion ends the play.   315

Hip. Methinks she should not use a long one for such a Pyramus. I hope she will be brief.

Dem. A mote will turn the balance, which Pyramus, which Thisby, is the better: he for a man, God warr'nt us; she for a woman, God bless us.   320

Lys. She hath spied him already with those sweet eyes.

Dem. And thus she means, *videlicet*—

This.   Asleep, my love?

    What, dead, my dove?   325

    O Pyramus, arise!

    Speak, speak! Quite dumb?

    Dead, dead? A tomb

    Must cover thy sweet eyes.

    These lily lips,   330

    This cherry nose,

    These yellow cowslip cheeks,

    Are gone, are gone!

    Lovers, make moan;

    His eyes were green as leeks.   335

    O Sisters Three,

    Come, come to me,

    With hands as pale as milk;

    Lay them in gore,

    Since you have shore   340

    With shears his thread of silk.

    Tongue, not a word!

    Come, trusty sword,

    Come, blade, my breast imbrue!

                [*Stabs herself.*]

    And farewell, friends;   345

    Thus Thisby ends;

    Adieu, adieu, adieu.   [*Dies.*]

The. Moonshine and Lion are left to bury the dead.

Dem. Ay, and Wall too.   350

[*Bot.*] [*Starting up.*] No, I assure you, the wall is down that parted their fathers. Will it please you to see the epilogue, or to hear a Bergomask dance between two of our company?

The. No epilogue, I pray you; for your play needs no excuse. Never excuse; for when the players are all dead, there need none to be blam'd. Marry, if he that writ it had play'd Pyramus, and hang'd himself in Thisby's garter, it would have been a fine tragedy; and so it is, truly, and very notably 360 discharged. But come, your Bergomask; let your epilogue alone.   [*A dance.*]

The iron tongue of midnight hath told twelve.
Lovers, to bed, 'tis almost fairy time.
I fear we shall outsleep the coming morn   365
As much as we this night have overwatch'd.

This palpable-gross play hath well beguil'd
The heavy gait of night. Sweet friends, to bed.
A fortnight hold we this solemnity,
In nightly revels and new jollity.   *Exeunt.* 370

"A Political Thriller": The Life and Times of Henry V

In the *New York Times* for 1 March 1991, Anthony Lewis, a usually reliable liberal columnist, began his commentary for the day as follows:

> At the end of the battle of Agincourt in Shakespeare's "Henry the Fifth" King Henry says:
>
>> This note doth tell me of ten thousand French
>> That in the field lie slain.
>> Where is the number of our English dead?
>> Edward the Duke of York, the Earl of Suffolk,
>> Sir Richard Ketley, Davy Gam, esquire;
>> None else of name; and of all other men
>> But five and twenty. O God, thy arm was here.
>
> Victory in the war with Iraq leaves us with such feelings of awe. With half a million soldiers on each side, the United States and its coalition partners had only about 140 killed. . . . The casualties are as disproportionate as they were at Agincourt. Estimates of the number of Iraqi soldiers killed approach 50,000.

Why do we teach Shakespeare? This question means something different depending on which word one accentuates. "Why do we *teach* Shakespeare?" admits that the plays as "literature" have been detached from their native environment, the live theater, and transformed into cultural monuments, a process which, we now realize, developed in the late nineteenth century, and which had the effect, if not the intention, of neutralizing their extraordinary capacity to seem topical (again) with each new production. What A. A. Lipscomb saw in 1882 as a desirable transformation ahead— that the most popular playwright of his own time was "destined to become the Shakespeare of the college and university, and even more the Shakespeare of private and select culture,"[1] we may now, with a certain suspicious hindsight, have cause to regret.

To ask instead: "Why do *we* teach Shakespeare?" reminds us that these plays have a peculiar status indeed—even if we have no difficulty with their segregation from popular culture, their transfer (in Lipscomb's phrase) "to a new and higher sphere in the firmament of intellect"—in the modern *American* classroom. What do we say to students when they themselves raise the question of Shakespeare's relevance to themselves? Obviously, this line of inquiry has been central to the canonical debates of this past decade, which seem to be continuing with unabated fervor and increased malevolence into the 1990s. On one side stand supporters of a "Great Books" tradition in higher education in the liberal arts, declaring that it is vital to protect Shakespeare, and other authors of his stature, from the shift in educational priorities that results from a more diversified student and faculty population; on the other stand the proponents not just of "American" literature (already itself assured of canonical status) but also of African-American or Latin-American or Chinese-American writers, all of whom deserve space in the curriculum. Somewhere caught in the middle are people like myself, who also observe with dismay the possibility that major British writers from earlier periods might become an endangered species in the American academy, yet who do not share the values and motives of the more notorious "Great Books" advocates; on the contrary, we believe that teaching young Americans to understand Shakespeare is consistent with multicultural models of higher education, with the belief that historical and demographic change should be honored when defining the cultural record. For if change itself is to be rendered intelligible, we should not banish the founding texts of Anglo-American culture; rather we should place them under a strong light, to determine their influence in cultural formation.

As for the third possibility of emphasis: "Why do we teach *Shakespeare?*" this is actually to beg the central question of what "Shakespeare" has meant in Anglo-American culture hitherto, and whether that meaning is fixed or contingent, flexible to pedagogic strategy and individual conviction. The question would be clearer if reformulated as "*How* do we teach Shakespeare?" or "*What* Shakespeare do we teach?" Either implies that we have a choice of methods and foci, which might seem too obvious to mention, except that such is seldom admitted in the canonical disputes. For what can we make our students curious? Should we read the plays as poetry? Do we try to impress on linguistically impoverished minds (the television generation) how rich and innovative and metaphoric and daring and riddling is the language of plays whose plots alone are a challenge to disentangle? Or do we read the plays for the issues they raise, as cogently and as powerfully as the new works currently being brought in from the margins: the issues of gender written so large and so differently in *Macbeth* and *The Taming of the Shrew*, of class in *Henry VI, Part 2, A Midsummer Night's Dream* and *Coriolanus*, of race in *Othello, The Merchant of Venice* or *The Tempest*, of generational hostility in *Romeo and Juliet*, of economic difference in *King Lear*. And one might add to this list another, slightly less obvious set of issues that nevertheless can engage with concerns of local and immediate currency: the interrogation of the law in *Measure for Measure*, of militant patriotism in *Troilus and Cressida* and *Henry V*, and, most relevant of all to our academic squabbles, Shakespeare's investigation, in *Hamlet*, of the values or dangers of a university education.[2]

In my experience, readers at all levels are eager for opportunities to discuss these issues in the complex way that Shakespeare demands. And, it is inevitable, the "Shakespeare" that results from such discussions will by no means appear the reliable conveyor of conservative values—of political obedience, of male superiority, of a vertical hierarchy in all relations from divinity downwards—or of traditional dualisms: king/subject, male/female, the nation/its enemy, philosopher/thing of darkness. This is not to say, however, that we can clearly assign him the *opposite* values, or lean with any confidence on the space between dualisms—the half-Trojan, half-Greek entity that is Ajax, or the going-between personality of Pandarus, who can only bequeath us his diseases. The discovery that the Shakespearean playtext is, rather, a screen upon which the *difference* between value systems is rendered in particularly sharp focus is stimulating to readers of all persuasions precisely because it is contestatory, because its allegiances cannot easily be identified.

We might, then, decide on empirical grounds both that an issue-oriented pedagogy works for Shakespeare and that it justifies his continuing centrality in the contemporary American classroom. But to what extent will such a principle of selection determine the most-valued plays *within* the Shakespeare canon, as years of critical evaluation have formed it? Should we demote some of the most revered (usually, since Bradley, the tragedies) and move to the center others that have hitherto languished on the margins? Should *Coriolanus*, one of the least-taught plays, replace *Julius Caesar,* a pedagogic favorite, and what would be the consequences in terms of the political values available for inspection? Should *Troilus and Cressida*, one of the earliest sites of a deconstructive criticism,[3] and which takes apart every conceivable ground of security, including our capacity to categorize (is it comedy, tragedy, "history," satire, problem play), be properly at the center of a pedagogy which privileges contestation? How much cynicism do we really want in a state-of-the-art Shakespeareanism whose own justification is that it is no longer simply reverent before the name of greatness?

But if these questions promote unease, others, still more unsettling, stem from the last decade's discovery or claim that the entire program of Shakespearean editing in the twentieth century had been misconceived; that the search for the definitive text, the invention of the Hinman collator, the theory of the bad quartos, and the endless disputes about how textual variants occurred, were misguided. It would be better, the new bibliographers (Michael Warren, Gary Taylor, Steven Urkowitz) have asserted, to admit that Shakespeare's plays were never "texts" in the sense that New Criticism established textuality as the necessary object of our discipline; but rather that they existed in several states (with some of them, like the Second Quarto version of *Hamlet*, much too long to have been performed on the stage); and were subjected to revision and condensation by his own theatrical company, and perhaps by himself.[4] What version, then, of a Shakespeare play should we teach? In the case of *King Lear* and *Hamlet*, does the logic of the new bibliography imply that we should teach from facsimiles of the Quarto and Folio versions, side by side? And how much patience have students, at any level of sophistication, with the minutiae of textual differences? In my own experience, not very much. Yet it does not seem to me compatible with a responsible pedagogy simply to ignore the textual problematic, especially when an interpretation can hang on a contested passage, like the Fool's Prophecy in *King Lear;*[5] or when, as in the supposedly "bad" quarto of Hamlet, Hamlet's most famous soliloquy contains more direct social criticism than does the accepted version. In *Troilus and Cressida* the tone of the entire play can be altered by its beginning: in the 1609 Quarto, with a sardonic prose preface claiming the play as a comedy but insisting on the relation of that genre to the marketplace, to *commodity;* in the 1623 Folio, with a high-minded verse prologue that claims the play as a tragic classical epic.

In the second half of this essay, I shall try to ground some of these remarks, and leave some of those questions a little less open, by focusing on *Henry V.* [For the text of *Henry V* 4.6.1–38 and 4.7.1–65, see pp. 252–53.] It seems a fair guess that *Henry V* has been less frequently taught in the college classroom than *Henry IV, Part 1*, if only because the latter was selected by the Norton Anthology. Yet it is, I shall argue, a test case of whether and how Shakespeare should be taught in the American academy; and, because it also exists in two celebrated film versions, it has also been more influential at the level of popular culture—of cultural formation—than almost any other play.

The history, or legend, of Henry and the battle of Agincourt has always been at the center of British culture, and especially of popular culture. Immediately after Agincourt there were ballads written celebrating the English victory, which survive in many manuscripts. An early fifteenth-century chronicle interpolates one such ballad, whose refrain insists on the divine assistance received by the English:

> Stedes ther stumbelyd in that stownde,
> That stood stere stuffed under stele;
> With gronyng grete thei felle to frownde,
> Her sydes federid whan thei gone fele.
> Owre lord the kynge he foght ryght wele,
> Sharpliche on hem his spere he spent,
> Many on seke he made that sele,
> Thorow myght of god omnipotent.
> . . . .
> Lordes of name an hunderde an mo
> Bitterly that bargain bowght;
> Two thousand cot-armers also,
> After her sorow thedere thai sowght.
> Ten thowsand ffrensshemen to deth were browght,
> Off whom never none away went:
> All her names sothely know I nowght;
> Have mersy on hem cryst omnipotent.[6]

One can fully understand the epic impulse in the fifteenth-century chronicler (although even he uses the refrain to admit a moment of remorse for the huge French casualties); but it is harder to understand why modern historians have adopted the same uncritical, celebratory tone. The distinguished historian of fifteenth-century England, K. B. McFarlane, offered this as a summary of the reign. "Take [Henry] all round and he was, I think, the greatest man that ever ruled England."[7]

Significantly, the lecture from which this statement is taken was delivered to the Workers' Educational Association in London in November 1954, and it reflects the popular patriotism (or its promotion) necessary to survive the Second World War and its aftermath. Harold Hutchinson's biography of Henry, published in 1967, has no such excuse. In tone it lies somewhere between popular and academic history; but its unself-conscious jingoism is of pertinence here, since, for Hutchinson, the *meaning* of the reign and of the battle of Agincourt has been determined partly by Shakespeare's play:

> The battle of Agincourt is renowned as perhaps the most overwhelming victory won against fearsome odds that *our* history has ever known. Its fame has been glamourized by the magic of Shakespeare's muse, and even today it is an unquestioned part of an *English* myth which believes that our national genius is to snatch victory from the jaws of defeat.[8]

Such statements assume that the meaning of *Henry V* is itself unproblematic, that Shakespeare's intentions were to "glamourize" this section of Lancastrian history, and to offer a permanent "myth" of national "genius" which it is not the historian's responsibility to interrogate.

We know from the existence of the *Famous Victories of Henry V*, as well as from what appear to be references to two other plays on this subject, that Henry V was popularly celebrated by the Elizabethan stage in much the terms assumed by Hutchinson and McFarlane.[9] Shakespeare himself remarked this myth in its earliest stage of construction in *Henry VI, Part 2,* when Clifford uses it to persuade Jack Cade's followers to desert him:

> Is Cade the son of Henry the Fifth,
> That thus you do exclaim you'll go with him?
> Will he conduct you through the heart of France,
> And make the meanest of you earls and dukes?
>
> (4.8.34–37)

And Cade himself remarks its success: "Was ever feather so lightly blown to and fro as this multitude? The name of Henry the Fifth hales them to an hundred mischiefs, and makes them leave me desolate" (4.8.55–58).

It has often been assumed that *Henry V* itself participated unproblematically in the building of this national legend, an interpretation most likely to be invoked, understandably, at moments of peril. In 1914 Dover Wilson saw a performance at Stratford of "the epic drama of Agincourt" which "matched the temper of the moment, when . . . the Kaiser was said to be scoffing at [England's] 'contemptible little army' which had just crossed the Channel.''[10] He recorded this epiphany, however, in his 1947 edition of the play, which was dedicated to Field Marshal the Viscount Wavell; that is to say, it was a post-Second World War statement, designed not only to correct Hazlitt's dark view of Shakespeare's protagonist, but to make a contribution to the national spirit:

> The zenith of the play is not the victory—that is lightly passed over, and (in itself miraculous) is ascribed to God alone—but the king's speeches before the battle is joined. . . . Every line of what Henry then says breathes the English temper, but one above all—
>
> *We few, we happy few, we band of brothers.*
>
> If History never repeats itself, the human spirit often does: Henry's words before Agincourt, and Churchill's after the Battle of Britain, come from the same national mint. (P. xxxi)

As is now well known, Sir Laurence Olivier's stirring film, itself a strongly idealizing interpretation of Henry and especially of the battle of Agincourt, was produced in the context of the Normandy landings of 1944. Explicitly dedicated to the "Commandos and Airborne Troops of Great Britain . . . the spirit of whose ancestors it has been humbly attempted to recapture," the film was manifestly wartime propaganda. But the country did not have to be at war for the play and its title character to be so represented. In 1954 (the same year that McFarlane delivered his lecture on *Henry V* to the Workers' Educational Association), when England was struggling with a disastrous postwar economy, J. H. Walter established for the Arden edition of the play, and hence for generations of students, his own verdict that Henry had been "calumniated" by those who doubted his character or the justice of his war; "Only a leader of supreme genius . . . could arrest this civic entropy and raise a state to prosperity."[11]

Yet there has always existed another view, both among historians and literary critics. Among the latter, ever since Hazlitt, skeptical attention has been focused on the aggressive militarism of *Henry V:* not that there is any doubt that this is the play's central theme, but because certain readers have been uncertain as to whether Shakespeare promoted those values or whether, on the contrary, by problematizing Henry's character and the motives for the French campaign, he partially or completely undermined them, producing an ambiguous play which could point in either direction.[12]

Among historians, J. H. Wylie's often critical *Reign of Henry VI*[13] has recently been outdone in iconoclasm by Desmond Seward, whose reassessment of Henry, published in 1987, is unremittingly hostile. Henry's true legacy, Seward concludes, was the suffering he inflicted on the French people, and its consequences today:

> Henry V's truest and most lasting monument is not the beautiful chapel at Westminster, not Shakespeare's play, not the tale of Agincourt and Crispin's Day. It is that antipathy and distrust which, sadly, all too many Frenchmen feel for those who speak English as their first language. That is the king's legacy for those of us who live in the last years of the twentieth century. Other men and other wars have deepened it, but he was one of its original architects.[14]

Significantly for our purposes, Seward (like Hutchinson) aligns Shakespeare's play with idealized versions of the reign, although he wishes to displace them; but there is a trace of uncertainty in his response to *Henry V*, which he interprets as Shakespeare's hesitation:

> In Henry's own brutal words, "war without fire is like sausages without mustard." Not only emergent French nationalism but French local loyalties were outraged by his invasions and campaigns of conquest. The horror unleashed by him was unforgivable, and also unforgettable. No account tells the whole harrowing story, conveys how widespread and how savage was the misery which he inflicted on the French people. In the midst of all his hero worship Shakespeare somehow discerns the sheer callous cruelty of the king:
>
> > What is it to me, if impious war
> > Array'd in flames, like to the prince of fiends
> > Do, with his smirch'd complexion, all fell feats
> > Enlink'd to waste and desolation?
>
> But on the whole even Shakespeare succumbs to the legend. He could not know what had happened in France. (P. 216)

One is not to suppose, however, that Seward's passionate reproaches against military destruction are characteristic of late twentieth-century sensibilities; for the allure of the popular legend is once again exemplified by Kenneth Branagh's *Henry V*, a production, I shall argue, that reinstates as its theme what Dover Wilson in 1947 called "the finest of war-plays" (xxxi). My reason for dwelling on this film is that its *popularity* as a media event in the United States has a direct bearing on how and why we should continue to teach *Henry V*. While in Britain the film is reported to have played predominantly in specialized art theaters to small audiences, thousands of American filmgoers responded positively, producing a major box office success.

We could be asking our students to consider how this play, as distinct from its various interpreters, deals with the legend of Henry V, with the idea of "England," or what Dover Wilson called "the English temper"; how it relates nationalism to militarism, specifically to aggressive military campaigns abroad; and how these issues can be, have been, transported through historical time and geographical space to land up in their own territory. The very popularity of Branagh's production with American filmgoers can suggest to them the relevance of Shakespeare's play to ourselves, our political self-consciousness, and to our contested value systems. Lacking a live theatrical tradition, film gives us access to a simulacrum of the Elizabethan theater, in which issues of public importance were acted out symbolically on the public stages. A great deal can be learned about all the above issues by a careful comparison between Branagh's production and the "play itself."

This, of course, begs the textual or bibliographical question of what the "play itself" is now considered to be. Here is an opportunity not only to do some close reading, but to learn something in the process about the publication history of *Henry V*, and of how the new textual theory differs from the old with respect to the play's two surviving printed versions. In *Shakespeare and the Popular Voice*, I argued that, while it was possible to extract both the simply patriotic and the skeptical interpretation from the Folio version of the play that was printed for the first time in 1623, the simply patriotic version can be far more readily supported by the version that was printed close to the time of the play's composition, in 1600, under the title of *The Cronicle History of Henry V*. For this Quarto text, long disregarded by Shakespeareans as a "bad" quarto, may well represent, though in an imperfectly reported form, what was actually performed on the stage at the turn of the century. Unlike the so-called "Bad" Quarto of Hamlet, where shortening produced a less philosophical or talkative text, the Quarto of *Henry V* appears to have been pruned in the direction of a less skeptical staging of the Henry legend.[15]

The most striking omission is of the Choruses, which we now think of as defining this last and most sophisticated of Shakespeare's fifteenth-century chronicles; and without the choruses we lose the perception that the historical assessment of Henry's career is ongoing throughout the play, and will not be quite concluded even when the main action is over. For if the early Choric interventions resemble Hutchinson and McFarlane in their heroic descriptions of Henry and the French campaign, in the Epilogue the difference between an idealizing and a realist historiography comes to the surface, as the Chorus summarizes Henry's legacy:

> Small time; but in that small most greatly lived
> This star of England. Fortune made his sword;
> By which the world's best garden he achieved,
> And of it left his son imperial lord.
> Henry the Sixt, in infant bands crown'd King
> Of France and England, did this king succeed;
> Whose state so many had the managing,
> That they lost France, and made his England bleed[.]

I argued in *Shakespeare and the Popular Voice* that the main reason for the disappearance of the Choruses was probably the highly topical content of the fifth, with its dangerous reference to the many who were imagined flocking from the city to welcome the earl of Essex back from Ireland. In the Epilogue, the "many" who "had the managing" of the state during Henry VI's minority—that is to say, the competing barons—is an ironic echo of that popular "many," that section of society who flocked to the public theaters in the 1590s, and whose sympathy for Essex the authorities were determined to control. Also missing from the Quarto is act 1, scene 1, in which the archbishop of Canterbury and the bishop of Ely cynically discuss how to distract the king from the parliamentary program to divert ecclesiastical revenues to the support of the poor; Burgundy's moving speech on the damages suffered by the French countryside as a result of the war; and much of the material in the night scene before Agincourt, especially the king's closing soliloquy on the hardships of political leadership, which in its Folio placement, *after* Henry's debate with Williams about the justice of the war, can be read as disturbingly self-regarding. The removal of all these passages, I argued, makes for a version of the Henry V story that is unreflectively heroic and xenophobic.

Yet in making this argument I overlooked one vital counterexample. Something inconsistent with the legend of ideal leadership survived in the 1600 Quarto: the killing of the French prisoners at Agincourt. Edward Hall, whose mid-sixteenth century chronicle Shakespeare used along with Holinshed, recorded the killing of the prisoners as follows: "Certain Frenchmen on horsback . . . entred into the kynges campe beyng voide of men and fortefied with varlettes & lackeys, and there . . . robbed tentes . . . and slewe suche servantes as they could fynd in the tentes and pavilions." That is to say, the French marauding party gave the provocation. He also recorded that Henry heard "the outcry of the lackeys and boyes whiche ranne away for feare," and

> fearyng least his enemies beying dispersed and scattered abroad should gather together againe and beginne a new felde: and doubtying farther that the prisoners would ether be an aide to his enemies or very enemies to him if he should suffre them to live, contrary to his accustomed gentlenes and pitie he commaunded by the sounde of a trompet that every man upon paine of death should incontinently sley his prisoner. When this dolorus decre & pitiful proclamacion was pronounced, pitie it was to se and lothsome it was to behold how some Frenchmen wer sodainly sticked with daggers, some wer brained with polaxes, some wer slain with malles, other had theyr throtes cut and some their bellies paunched: so that in effect havyng respecte to the greate nombre, few prisoners or none were saved.[16]

Now, this has been a famous crux in the interpretation of the Henry V legend. For McFarlane, defending Henry against modern French detractors, the event was justifiable in terms of military pragmatism:

> The English were rounding up and stripping their captives when a fresh French attack was thought to be threatened. To prevent their escape while his troops dealt with the new task, Henry ordered them to put to death all but the most valuable of the prisoners. The sign of the execution of this order caused the attackers to withdraw and the English army was able to retreat with the survivors to Calais. Not an attractive episode, but it is necessary to say that it was condemned neither by contemporaries nor by the laws of war.[17]

Conversely, Desmond Seward's account of Henry's campaign as a whole was, as I have indicated, strongly condemnatory. His description of the episode deserves quoting at some length, not least because the issue of military pragmatism is here inflected (accurately) with economic interests. Seward explains the situation after the initial charge of the French infantry:

> The French were everywhere lying in heaps, sometimes higher than a man on his feet. Many were alive, prevented by their armour from rising. The English finished some off as they lay like stranded turtles, thrusting a dagger through their visors, but the majority—perhaps as many as 3,000—were pulled out and sent to the rear as prisoners for ransom.
>   Suddenly a shout went up that the third, mounted French line was

about to attack. . . . What is certain is that after the rout of the second line two brave French noblemen, the Counts of Marque and Fauquembergues, swore to kill Henry or perish and prepared to launch a final despairing charge with a mere 600 men.

The king was already uneasy enough about the prisoners at the rear. Just before the start of the battle local peasants had raided his baggage but had been driven off. It was possible they might try to raid it again. When it looked as though he might expect a serious attack from the third line and that it was possible the captured men-at-arms might break free and join their comrades, he ordered their liquidation. His men were horrified, not from compassion but at the prospect of losing such valuable ransom. Henry promised to hang anyone who refused to obey. He detailed 200 archers to slaughter the prisoners. . . . We know from a survivor, Gilbert de Lannoy, that one batch were burned to death in the hut where they were confined. Those spared were worth great sums, such as princes of the Blood like the Duke of Orleans. The king stopped the slaughter when he realized that he was not threatened by a serious attack from the French third line and was throwing money away.

This massacre of prisoners in 1415 is Henry V's one generally acknowledged peccadillo. Almost every one of his English biographers and historians tries to absolve him of guilt, referring to the lack of condemnation by contemporary English chroniclers, or to "the standards of the time." In reality, by fifteenth-century standards, to massacre captive, unarmed noblemen who, according to the universally recognized international laws of chivalry, had every reason to expect to be ransomed if they surrendered formally, was a peculiarly nasty crime—especially by someone who constantly claimed to be a "true knight." (Pp. 80–81)

It is worth noting that Seward, who refers to Hall's account of the killing of the prisoners, makes no mention of the attack on the camp by a French marauding party, unless that is represented by the raid by local peasants before the battle began.

As for Shakespearean editors, they too are divided. For Dover Wilson in 1947, there *are* ethical questions raised by the episode, but blame of Henry can be deflected onto the French: "Contemporary comment on the battle . . . shows that the treacherous assault left a deep stain upon the chivalry of France. Thus any lingering doubt about Henry's action is blotted from the minds of even the most squeamish in the audience." Altogether, he concludes:

The general impression which the incident was designed to convey, and which I do not doubt was conveyed to the original audiences, is not one of brutality at all, but of a great commander's strength, decision, and presence of mind at the crisis of the battle. No wonder honest Gower cries, "O, 'tis a gallant king!" and Fluellen goes on to speak of Alexander the Great.[18]

It is true that Hall, on whom Wilson is probably leaning, had observed that the French marauders "were long imprisoned and sore punished" by the dauphin for this breach of the law of arms; but Hall's account as a whole was less likely to banish "lingering doubt about Henry's action" than to encourage his readers' inspection and interrogation of military savagery. It is also true that Dover Wilson knew his defense of the killing of prisoners to be just that: a defense. "I have run ahead," he admits. "But the slaying of the prisoners is so famous and its misunderstanding is so generally entertained that it casts a baleful shadow over Henry's earlier actions. It is therefore well to have it out of the way . . . " (xxxvii–xxxviii).

Gary Taylor, like Dover Wilson, observes that Shakespeare's decision to include the episode at all is revealing, especially since *The Famous Victories of Henry V* omits it.[19] But he also notes the crucial textual fact that, in Shakespeare's version, the order to kill the prisoners precedes Henry's knowledge of the raid on the camp: "But hark, what new alarum is this same?" Henry asks, and answers his own question. "The French have reinforc'd their scatter'd men. / Then every soldier kill his prisoners!" (4.6.35–37). Not even Henry's famous sentence, "I was not angry till I came to France," includes a direct causal connection between one killing of the helpless and the other.

Taylor, unlike Dover Wilson, regards the killing of the prisoners as so definitive of Henry's character and the play's meaning that, as editor, he actually adds a stage direction insisting that the prisoners be killed on stage, in order to bring home the brutality of the event. Taylor does not, however, note the significance of the *Quarto's* inclusion of the episode. In the Quarto, Henry says, more briefly, "What new alarum is this? Bid every souldier kill his prisoner." Here there is not even the assumption of a French rally; so that the Quarto text offers a still darker version of the episode (figure 6). Indeed, the Quarto text makes a significant contribution of its own to the scene's interpretation; for here Pistol confirms the brutality of the order as he leaves to carry it out, shouting (ironically, in French), *"Coup' la gorge."*[20] As for the belief that the order to kill the prisoners was a legitimate response to the killing of the lackeys and boys in the camp, this derives exclusively from Shakespeare's Gower, who, exaggerating Hall's account, which stressed those who escaped, asserts, "Tis certain there's not a boy left alive; and the cowardly rascals that ran from the battle ha' done this slaughter . . . / *Whereupon* the king most worthily hath caused every soldier to cut his prisoner's throat. O 'tis a gallant king" (4.7.5–10; italics added). Students can here decide for themselves whether to agree with Dover Wilson or to find some irony in the attribution of gallantry (the term is peculiar in the circumstances) to an antichivalric decision, not least since Fluellen has just invoked (though against the French) the "law of arms." Here too the Quarto retains the substance, though not the fine details, of the irony; and it is also, for so short a version, strangely faithful to the learned intervention by Fluellen on the subject of Henry's likeness to Alexander the Great, who "in his rages and his furies and his wraths and his cholers and his moods and his displeasures and his indignations . . . kill[ed] his best friend Cleitus." We must, I think, conclude from this textual evidence that the killing of the prisoners was perceived by Shakespeare and his company to be at the very center of the Henry legend, to be, in effect, its evaluative crux, and to require both representation and interpretation in the public arena. In negotiating between the extremes of interpretation outlined above, I myself would suggest a position somewhere between McFarlane and Dover Wilson, on the one side, and Seward and Taylor on the other. The account of the event that Shakespeare provides offers both a realistic, if compressed, account of the way decisions are actually made in wartime, and also of the way they are explained later, by the Gowers and Fluellens of the administration, to bring them into line with prevailing ethical norms.

In teaching *Henry V*, then, one can use the textual evidence (in the past consigned to the specialized territory of Shakespearean bibliography) to focus the interpretive debate, to introduce students to issues of historiographical assessment that were from the start, and continue to be, imbricated in our response to the play, which in turn has played a not inconsiderable part in the historiographical enterprise. I suggest that we have the same opportunity (and the same responsibility) with respect to the two major film scripts, Olivier's and Branagh's, which resemble the 1600 Quarto in offering a condensed, production-oriented text, but differ from it absolutely on the issue of the killing of the prisoners.

In the theater or its child, the cinema, Shakespeare's plays are almost never produced in total; and much can be learned from what different directors regard as expendable. In the late eighteenth century, for example, *Coriolanus* was typically performed without the opening scene which sets the plebeians' uprising in a context of simple starvation. Such a deletion

Enter Piſtoll, the French man, and the Boy.

Piſt. Eyld cur, eyld cur.

French. O Monſire, ie vous en pree aues petie de moy.

Piſt. Moy ſhall not ſerue. I will haue fortie moys.

Boy aske him his name.

Boy. Comant ettes vous apelles?

French. Monſier Fer.

Boy. He ſaies his name is Maſter *Fer.*

Piſt. Ne Fer him, and ferit him, and ferke him:

Boy diſcus the ſame in French.

Boy. Sir I do not know, whats French

For fer, ferit and fearke.

Piſt. Bid him prepare, for I wil cut his throate.

Boy. Feate, vou preat, ill voulles coupele votre gage.

Piſt. Onye ma foy couple la gorge.

Vnleſſe thou giue to me egregious raunſome, dye.

One poynt of a foxe.

French. Qui dit ill monſiere.

Ill ditye ſi vou ny vouly pa domy luy.

Boy. La gran ranſome, ill vou tueres.

French. O lee vous en pri pettit gentelhome, parle

A cee, gran capataine, pour auez mercie

A moy, ey lee donerees pour mon ranſome

Cinquante ocios. Ie ſuyes vngentelhome de *France.*

Piſt. What ſayes he boy?

Boy. Marry ſir he ſayes, he is a Gentleman of a great

Houſe, of *France:* and for his ranſome,

He will giue you 500. crownes.

Piſt. My fury ſhall abate,

And I the Crownes will take.

And as I ſuck blood, I will ſome mercie ſhew.

Follow me cur.

Exit omnes.

Enter the King and his Nobles, Piſtoll.

King. What tire French retire?

Yer

Fig. 6. *Henry V,* 1600 Quarto

Yet all is not done, yet keepe the French the field.

   Exe. The Duke of *Yorke* commends him to your Grace.

   King. Liues he good Vnckle, twife I fawe him downe,
Twife vp againe:
From helmet to the fpurre, all bleeding ore.

   Exe. In which aray, braue fouldier doth he lye,
Larding the plaines, and by his bloody fide,
Yoake fellow to his honour dying wounds,
The noble Farle of *Suffolke* alfo lyes.
Suffolke firft dyde, and *Yorke* all hafted ore,
Comes to him where in blood he lay fleept,
And takes him by the beard, kiffes the gafhes
That bloodily did yane vpon his face,
And cryde aloud, tary deare coufin *Suffolke:*
My foule fhall thine keep company in heauen:
Tary deare foule awhile, then flie to reft:
And in this glorious and well foughten field,
We kept togither in our chiualdry.
Vpon thefe words I came and cheerd them vp,
He tooke me by the hand, faid deare my Lord,
Commend my feruice to my foueraigne.
So did he turne, and ouer *Suffolkes* necke
He threw his wounded arme, and fo efpoufed to death,
With blood he fealed. An argument
Of neuer ending loue. The pretie and fweet maner of it,
Forft thofe waters from me, which I would haue ftopt,
But I not fo much of man in me,
But all my mother came into my eyes,
And gaue me vp to teares.

   Kin. I blame you not: for hearing you,
I muft conuert to teares.

     Alarum foundes.

What new alarum is this?
Bid euery fouldier kill his prifoner.

   Pift. Couple gorge.   *Exit omnes.*

                       Enter

Enter Flewellen, and Captaine Gower.

Flew. Godes plud kil the boyes and the lugyge,
Tis the arrants peece of knauery as can be defired,
In the worell now, in your conſcience now.

Gour. Tis certaine, there is not a Boy left aliue,
And the cowerdly raſcals that ran from the battell,
Themſelues haue done this ſlaughter:
Beſide, they haue carried away and burnt,
All that was in the kings Tent:
Whervpon the king cauſed euery priſoners
Throat to be cut. O he is a worthy king.

Flew. I he was born at *Monmorth.*
Captain *Gower*, what call you the place where
Alexander the big was borne?

Gour. *Alexander* the great.

Flew. Why I pray, is nat big great?
A ſif I ſay, big or great, or magnanimous,
I hope it is all one reconing,
Saue the frafe is a litle varation.

Gour. I thinke *Alexander* the great
Was borne at *Macedon.*
His father was called *Philip* of *Macedon,*
As I take it.

Flew. I thinke it was *Macedon* indeed where *Alexander*
Was borne: looke you captaine *Gower,*
And if you looke into the mappes of the worell well,
You ſhall finde litle difference betweene
Macedon and *Monmorth.* Looke you, there is
A Riuer in *Macedon,* and there is alſo a Riuer
In *Monmorth,* the Riuers name at *Monmorth,*
Is called Wye.
But tis out of my braine, what is the name of the other:
But tis all one, tis ſo like, as my fingers is to my fingers,
And there is Samons in both.
Looke you captaine *Gower,* and you marke it,

You

You shall finde our King is come after *Alexander*,
God knowes, and you know, that *Alexander* in his
Bowles, and his alles, and his wrath, and his displeasures,
And indignations, was kill his friend *Clitus*.

    Gower. I but our King is not like him in that,
For he neuer killd any of his friends.

    Flew. Looke you, tis not well done to take the tale out
Of a mans mouth, ere it is made an end and finished:
I speake in the comparisons, as *Alexander* is kill
His friend *Clitus*: so our King being in his ripe
Wits and iudgements, is turne away, the fat knite
With the great belly doublet: I am forget his name.

    Gower. Sir *Iohn Falstaffe.*

    Flew. I, I thinke it is Sir *Iohn Falstaffe* indeed,
I can tell you, theres good men borne at *Monmorth*.

        Enter King and the Lords.

    King. I was not angry since *I* came into *France*,
Vntill this houre.
Take a trumpet Herauld,
And ride vnto the horsmen on yon hill:
If they will fight with vs bid them come downe,
Or leaue the field, they do offend our sight:
Will they do neither, we will come to them,
And make them skyr away, as fast
As stones enforst from the old Assirian slings.
Besides, weele cut the throats of those we haue,
And not one aliue shall taste our mercy.

should help to convince us of the scene's importance in creating audience sympathy for the common people of Rome. Olivier's production of *Henry V* was confessedly World War II propaganda, and its deletions were made on that principle. Unlike Shakespeare's company, who had to deal with the contemporary archbishop of Canterbury as a major agent of censorship, Olivier had no pressing reason to exclude the opening scene with Canterbury and Ely; Burgundy's lament for the devastated French countryside was perhaps too poetic to sacrifice; and he needed parts of the early Choruses to stage the representational difference between sixteenth-century theater and twentieth-century film techniques. But he could not permit his uplifting film to end with the heavily ironized vision of the epilogue, which declares that the entire military campaign has been in vain. Significantly, his final chorus concluded:

> Small time: but in that small most greatly lived
> This star of England: Fortune made his
> sword: and for his sake
> In your fair minds let this acceptance take.

In film, of course, manipulation is also possible not in terms of what is taken away, but of what is added—by developing scenes that the Shakespearean text merely alluded to. The Chorus was, after all, a heuristic device intended to dramatize this principle of limitation, this sense of what can and can not be staged. But while Olivier's film brilliantly represented this principle of mimetic restriction, by moving between the Globe's wooden O and vast cinematic expanses, it took one major liberty that actually alters the ethical structure of the play. Olivier deleted Henry's order to kill the prisoners; but he then proceeded to visualize the scene which, only according to Gower, was supposed to have motivated that order: the French killing of the boys and lackeys in the camp. Thus what is only reported by Fluellen and Gower in a few lines becomes a major episode, calling up our sympathy for the English and denying it to the French; while the slaughter of the French prisoners (whether or not reciprocal) totally vanishes from the story. Given Shakespeare's scrupulous representation of what he found in Hall, Olivier's was not a legitimate interpretation. In fact, as history, it is incoherent.

What do we make, then, of the Branagh remake of Olivier's masterpiece? Given the assumption that Shakespearean productions, especially in England, always carry some flavor of topicality, I was initially tempted to see this film as rewriting a militant nationalism for the Britain of Margaret

Thatcher. If so, the antagonist here would surely not be the pathetic Falklands, but rather, in the terms of economic militancy that the Iron Lady was famous for, a response to France's role in the Common Market and the challenge to British sovereignty signaled by the approach of 1992 and a common currency. Whether that inference is supported or denied by the rumors that the film was not popular with British audiences it is impossible to determine.

Unlike Shakespeare himself, however, Branagh provided, in the introduction to the published film script, a document that supposedly records his intentions, and it can, if read "as a text," help to explain both why the British audiences rejected his film and the American ones accepted it with enthusiasm.[21] Branagh begins his introduction by revealing how *Henry V* enters the consciousness of the British schoolboy: "Like many students I knew 'Once more unto the breach' and the St. Crispin's Day speech" (p. 9). In other words, British students are taught to memorize the set speeches, the stirring exhortations to masculine effort and violence, that Shakespeare clearly presented as military rhetoric. As for Olivier's film, Branagh described it, for obvious promotional reasons, as obsolete (actually old-fashioned at two levels):

> The powerful Elizabethan pageantry and chivalric splendour of that extraordinary movie did not accord with the impression I received as I read the play afresh. To me, the play seemed darker, harsher, and the language more bloody and muscular than I remembered. Although I was aware of bringing a particular set of postwar sensibilities to bear on my reading, I sensed that a 1980s film version of such a piece would make for a profoundly different experience. . . . Although Olivier's film had been welcomed and celebrated as part of the war effort, its seeming nationalistic and militaristic emphasis had created a great deal of suspicion and doubt about the value of *Henry V* for a late twentieth-century audience.

Branagh further observed that the "play itself" is consequently performed very rarely; that this suspicion about it is "unfair" to its true complexity; and that in his first attempt to act the part of Henry for a 1984 production by the Royal Shakespeare Company, he had "tried to realize the qualities of introspection, fear, doubt and anger" which, he believed, "the text indicated," were aspects of Henry's character: "an especially young Henry with more than a little of the Hamlet in him" (pp. 9–10).

When, however, he came to conceive of a major cinematic production, Branagh's attitude to the playtext seems to have altered. What he calls his unsurprising view of the play as tremendously "filmic" included its "exciting linear plot, short scenes, great structural variety, . . . rich mixture of low-life sleaze, foreign sophistication, romance, action, philosophy and humour." "In all seriousness," he continues in this "portrait of the actor as a great, canny, director,"

> I was convinced that I could make a truly popular film: there would be no declamatory acting and the pace and excitement of the plot would be presented with the greatest possible clarity and immediacy. It was a story that would make you laugh, make you cry, and be utterly accessible to anyone of whatever age and background. These were all ingredients that would be needed to persuade Stephen [Evans's] financial contacts to invest in the film. (P. 10)

Rather than a meditative study of the young and introspective Henry, with a touch of the tragic Hamlet in him, *Henry V* was to be marketed not only as a detailed analysis of leadership and a complex debate about war, but also as, and I quote, "a political thriller."

Branagh then proceeded to describe and justify what he himself called a "drastic" cutting and pasting of the playtext. Determined that the film should be of "commercial length," and convinced that the contemporary film audience has a maximum attention span of two hours, he decided that the cuts would have to be "even more savage" than those in the Royal Shakespeare production, which had run for three. "In any case," Branagh declared, "the cuts dictated themselves" (p. 11). Yet, apart from the leek scene between Fluellen and Pistol, we learn very little about how these excrescences took matters into their own hands; we are told only that "Elizabethan obscurities," "plot repetitions" and "excessive flights of rhetorical fancy" were "ruthlessly excised"; that Branagh decided to *include* some scenes that Olivier's film had omitted—namely, the revelation and punishment of the conspiracy by his young friends, which Branagh played with homoerotic intensity, and the savage threats to the governor of Harfleur, both of which he assumed Olivier had omitted in favor of a more idealized portrait of Henry's character.

"I hope," Branagh concluded, "we have remained true to the spirit of the play. Above all the aim of the screenplay has been to bring out what some critics have referred to as 'the play within the play': an uncompromising view of politics and a deeply questioning, ever relevant and compassionate survey of people and war" (p. 12). That is to say, there are two versions of *Henry V* as Shakespeare wrote it: the seemingly archaic, nationalistic and militaristic play that Olivier found in the text and brought to the surface; and the "deeply questioning" play that skeptical critics have pointed to as lurking in the Folio text, and that Branagh claimed to have set in celluloid. Yet which, in his practice, as distinct from his theory, is the frame, and which is the center? Just how uncompromising and questioning a view of nationalism and militarism does the Branagh production offer, especially when the economic register of film production and of "popularity" were so clearly in the forefront of the conception?

Given the assumption of rivalry with, and the desire to upstage, Olivier (and students should see *both* films), they are free to decide whether an ambitious young director casts himself as the purveyor of an ethos he wishes his audience to discard. Given the text of his screenplay and his introduction to it, they can see for themselves whether his account of his intentions was as disingenuous as I have here suggested; and they can certainly see that Branagh remained silent about one crucial production decision. For Branagh *followed* Olivier in omitting the order to kill the prisoners. He *followed* Olivier in omitting Fluellen's telling comparison of Henry with Alexander the Great. Presumably this went under the heading of "excessive flights of rhetorical fancy." But he especially followed Olivier's lead in dwelling visually on the killing of the boys in the camp (figure 7); actually, he did more than follow Olivier. He increased the weight of this interpolated scene in the story's ethical structure (figure 8). [For the text of the screenplay, see pp. 250–51.] By staging, at the end of

Fig. 7. "English Camp. Boys' Slaughter" (Courtesy of Chatto & Windus)

He gently lays the **Boy** down, kisses him gently on the head, and then stands up as the rest of the army gather round him as best they can. We cut close on his blood-stained and exhausted face, the dreadful price they have all had to pay for this so-called victory clearly etched into his whole being. His head drops as if in shame.

DISSOLVE TO:

Fig. 8. "Concluding Scene of the Battle of Agincourt" from "*Henry V*": *A Screen Adaptation* by Kenneth Branagh, 114–15 (Courtesy of Chatto & Windus)

the battle, a slow funeral procession in which one of the dead children, carried in his own arms, is the central symbol, he raised the episode to the level of a principal theme. The result is a representation of Henry V as a deeply compassionate, fatherly figure, who clearly deserves his miraculous victory, with its legendary imbalance in casualties.

As a teacher, though I try, of course, to be evenhanded, I do not conceal my own opinions. I would certainly argue that this one directorial decision conflicts with Branagh's claim to have taken an "uncompromising" view of the darker side of his subject; it overpowers the film's partial admission of doubt in the justice of the war and the righteousness (which is always on the verge of overrighteousness) of the king's behavior. Branagh's account of his relation to Olivier's film is not, therefore, to be trusted. Rather than replacing its chivalric idea of Henry V with a darker and more truthful account appropriate to a culture that has moved beyond warmongering, Branagh has in fact (and as a close comparison of the two scripts will further demonstrate) followed Olivier in the central objective—to make the battle of Agincourt seem a heroic and desirable victory.

As distinct from the reported coolness of British audiences, it was Americans who have fulfilled Branagh's ambitions to produce "popular" Shakespeare. We can only speculate as to why those viewers, most of whom left Shakespeare behind them with guilty relief when they graduated from high school, flocked to see *Henry V*. Did they experience a pleasing sensation from getting a little high culture in a popular medium? Were they taking Branagh's militarism literally as a respectable sort of Ramboism? Or did they rather, like some of the American reviewers, see it as a grim-lipped statement of the necessary costliness of war?[22] To what extent did the film succeed because of a match, or because of a clash, between its ideology and that of the United States government when engaged in promoting a militant foreign policy? Probably all of the above; but I would guess that the reviewers represent the minority position, and that the majority responded then as Branagh intended, to the allure of "a political thriller." Showing the film to students would help them to determine its intentions; to distinguish those intentions from Shakespeare's; and, most importantly, to register that it matters what version of *Henry V* we are exposed to, what account of Shakespeare in general our own generation receives.[23]

When I delivered this paper at Union College in the Fall of 1990, I made an oblique reference to its topicality in the light of U.S. policy in the Gulf. I could not have anticipated the still larger topicality that has subsequently accrued to it, as Operation Desert Shield became Operation Desert

Storm, and as we begin to assess the consequences for the Iraqi people. I could not have anticipated that Anthony Lewis would read the extraordinary disparity between American and Iraqi casualties in terms of Henry V's accounting after Agincourt, nor that since his column in the *New York Times* was published on 1 March 1991, the estimates of Iraqi soldiers killed by the Allied bombing attacks on the trenches would have risen to one hundred thousand. I could not have anticipated the extent to which the topic of legend-making or breaking, as it emerges in the historiographical record of Henry V and the interpretive history of *Henry V*, would have so clearly connected to the management of the news, to the production of patriotism at home, and to the cultural erasure of facts we prefer not to contemplate. As Lewis finally came around to remarking, after many paragraphs devoted to the pragmatic lessons to be learned from the Gulf War, Arabs "may go on asking themselves whether the world would have paid so little attention to Western deaths in such numbers." Even then, he did not suggest that Americans might ask themselves the same question. In that column, "Shakespeare" (partly, I suspect, as produced by Olivier and Branagh) operated as a talisman to screen the political commentator and his readers from intolerable sights; for as Edward Hall had put it with respect to the killing of the French prisoners, "pitie it was to se." I hope I have shown that an issue-oriented Shakespearean pedagogy, yet one that insists on a scrupulous review of the textual evidence in its complex detail, can help to prevent such a talismanic approach.

Notes

1. See Lawrence W. Levine, *Highbrow/Lowbrow: The Emergence of Cultural Hierarchy in America* (Cambridge, Mass., 1988), p. 73. This extremely useful study charts the transition of Shakespeare's plays from the American popular theater to the territory of legitimate theater, and anticipates the later move to academicism.

2. On this issue, see my *Shakespeare and the Popular Voice* (Oxford, 1989), pp. 30–31, and behind it, J. M. Nosworthy's *Shakespeare's Occasional Plays* (London, 1965), pp. 171–82.

3. See J. Hillis Miller, "Ariachne's Broken Woof," *Georgia Review* 31 (1977): 44–60.

4. See, for example, Michael Warren, "Quarto and Folio *King Lear* and the Interpretation of Albany and Edgar," in *Shakespeare: Pattern of Excelling Nature*, eds. David Bevington and Jay L. Halio (Newark, Del., 1978), 95–107; Steven Urkowitz, *Shakespeare's Revision of "King Lear"* (Princeton, 1980); "'Well-sayd old Mole': Burying Three *Hamlets* in Modern Editions," in *Shakespeare Study Today* (1986): 37–70; Gary Taylor and Michael Warren, *The Division of the Kingdoms: Shakespeare's Two Versions of King Lear* (Oxford, 1983).

5. P. W. K. Stone, *The Textual History of "King Lear"* (London, 1980), pp. 119–21, argued that the Fool's prophecy was spurious, and had been added to the text that became the Folio "for a purely theatrical purpose," probably by an actor. Conversely, Joseph Wittreich, *"Image of that Horror": History, Prophecy, and Apocalypse in "King Lear"* (San Marino, Calif., 1984), pp. 60–74, makes the Fool's prophecy one of the mainstays of his own interpretation of the play.

6. See Charles L. Kingsford, ed., *Chronicles of London* (Oxford, 1905), pp. 120–21; printed from Cotton m.s. Cleopatra C IV (1441).

7. K. B. McFarlane, "Henry V: A Personal Portrait," in *Lancastrian Kings and Lollard Knights* (Oxford, 1972), p. 133.

8. Harold Hutchinson, *Henry V: A Biography* (London, 1976), p. 131 (italics added).

9. Thomas Nashe mentions "Henrie the fifth . . . represented on the Stage, leading the French king prisoner, and forcing both him and the Dolphin to sweare fealty," (in *Works*, ed. McKerrow, 1:213); and the reference in Henslowe's diary to a new play of "harey the Vth" in the repertoire of the Admiral's Men in 1595–96, five years too soon for this to refer to Shakespeare's play. See E. K. Chambers, *The Elizabethan Stage*, 4 vols. (Oxford, 1923), 2:144–45.

10. Dover Wilson, ed., *Henry V* (Cambridge, 1947), p. viii.

11. J. H. Walter, ed., *Henry V* (London, 1954), p. xxii.

12. See, for instance, Gerald Gould, "A New Reading of *Henry V*," *English Review* (1919): 42–55; C. H. Hobday, "Imagery and Irony in *Henry V*," *Shakespeare Survey* 21 (1968): 107–13; Jonathan Dollimore and Alan Sinfield, "History and Ideology: The Instance of *Henry V*," in *Alternative Shakespeares*, ed. John Drakakis (London, 1985), pp. 206–27. See also Norman Rabkin, *Shakespeare and the Problem of Meaning* (Chicago, 1981).

13. J. H. Wylie and W. T. Waugh, *The Reign of Henry the Fifth*, 3 vols. (Cambridge, 1914–29).

14. Desmond Seward, *Henry V: The Scourge of God* (New York, 1987), p. 220.

15. Compare Gary Taylor, ed., *Henry V* (Oxford, 1984), p. 12: "Whoever was responsible for them, the effect of the differences between this text and the one printed in all modern editions is to remove almost every difficulty in the way of an unambiguously patriotic interpretation of Henry and his war—that is, every departure from the kind of play which theatrical convention and the national mood would have led audiences of 1599 to expect." Earlier, however, Taylor had argued that the main reason for these differences between Quarto and Folio was that the Quarto represented a production version cut for performance in the provinces with a smaller cast. See Stanley Wells and Gary Taylor, *Modernizing Shakespeare's Spelling with Three Studies in the Text of Henry V* (Oxford, 1979), pp. 72–113. I also differ with Taylor as to our capacity to determine "the national mood" in 1599 with such certainty as is here assumed.

16. Edward Hall, *Union of the Two Noble Houses of Lancaster and York* (London, 1548), pp. 69–70.

17. McFarlane, "Henry V," p. 129.

18. Dover Wilson, ed., *Henry V*, p. xxxvi.

19. Taylor, ed., *Henry V*, p. 32.

20. *Shakespeare's Plays in Quarto*, ed. Michael J. B. Allen and Kenneth Muir (Berkeley and Los Angeles, 1981), p. 543. Gary Taylor here transports Pistol's blood-lust from the Quarto to a text otherwise based on the Folio.

21. Kenneth Branagh, *Henry V: A Screen Adaptation* (London, 1989).

22. See, for example, Pauline Kael, "Second Takes," *New Yorker,* 17 November 1989, 105: "Branagh's interpretation of *Henry V* emphasizes the price paid for war: the bloodshed. He's trying to make it into an anti-war film, an epic noir. But he can't quite dampen the play's rush of excitement—not with Henry delivering all those rousing words to his soldiers. . . . (Shakespeare shows how the English language itself can be turned into a patriotic symbol.) In keeping with his generation's supposed disillusion with war, Branagh has minimized the play's glorification of the English fighting man." It is interesting to see how Kael, despite her recognition that "the greatest jingo play ever conceived" is also full of "doubts and complicated feelings" (p. 104), falls victim to the great military rhetoric that Branagh himself recalled learning by heart in childhood.

23. Since I gave this lecture at Union College, the following essays on Branagh's *Henry V* have appeared in print: Peter Donaldson, "Taking on Shakespeare: Kenneth Branagh's *Henry V*," *Shakespeare Quarterly* 42, no. 1 (1991): pp. 60–70; Curtis Bright, "Branagh and the Prince, or a 'royal fellowship of death,'" *Critical Quarterly* 33, no. 4 (1991), pp. 95–111; and Chris Fitter, "A Tale of Two Branaghs: *Henry V,* Ideology, and the Mekong Agincourt," in *Shakespeare Left and Right,* ed. Ivo Kamps (New York: RKP, 1991), pp. 259–75. This convergence of interests demonstrates the importance not only of using film versions of Shakeapeare in the classroom but also of subjecting them to wary critical analysis.

From *"Henry V": A Screen Adaptation*
by Kenneth Branagh

(With permission from Chatto & Windus, 1981, pp. 108–9)

English Camp. Boys' Slaughter: Day

As Gower and Fluellen arrive, the scale of the carnage is obvious. Every English boy has been killed. Fluellen and Gower walk among the pitiful pile of corpses as the rest of the English army principals arrive to be greeted by the same dreadful sight.

Fluellen kneels down beside the body of the dead Boy. Gower is beside him.

> *Fluellen:* Kill the boys and the luggage! 'Tis expressly against the law of arms: 'tis as arrant a piece of knavery mark you now as can be offered: in your conscience now, is it not?
> *Gower:* 'Tis certain there's not a boy left alive.

Fluellen breaks down in tears and, crossing himself, leans his head on the boy's outstretched arm.

The rest of the weary bloodstained army look on, stunned. Finally Henry arrives on the bank above them. Exeter stands beside him.

In despair he turns his back on the scene to deliver a great howl of rage against the French.

> *Henry V:* I was not angry since I came to France
> Until this instant.

Exeter sees Mountjoy riding toward them.

> *Exeter* (voice-over): Here comes the herald of the French, my liege.

Henry pulls the herald from his horse, forcing him to his knees. He screams at the unfortunate messenger.

> *Henry V:* How now! What means this, herald?
> Com'st thou again for ransom?
> *Mountjoy:* No, great king:
> I come to thee for charitable licence,
> That we may wander o'er this bloody field
> To book our dead, and then to bury them:
> To sort our nobles from our common men:
> For many of our princes—woe the while—
> Lie drowned and soaked in mercenary blood:
> O, give us leave, great king,
> To view the field in safety and dispose
> Of their dead bodies.

This speech has been delivered with a desperate, remote sadness.

Henry V, 4.6.1–38, 4.7.1–65

(With permission from Houghton Mifflin, *The
Riverside Shakespeare,* ed. G. Blakemore Evans, 1974.)

[ACT IV, SCENE VI]

Alarum. Enter the KING *and his* TRAIN *with prisoners;*
[EXETER *and others*]

  K. Hen. Well have we done, thrice-valiant coun-
trymen,
But all's not done—yet keep the French the field.
  Exe. The Duke of York commends him to your
Majesty.
  K. Hen. Lives he, good uncle? Thrice within this
hour
I saw him down; thrice up again, and fighting; 5
From helmet to the spur all blood he was.
  Exe. In which array (brave soldier!) doth he lie,
Larding the plain; and by his bloody side
(Yoke-fellow to his honor-owing wounds)
The noble Earl of Suffolk also lies. 10
Suffolk first died, and York, all haggled over,
Comes to him where in gore he lay insteeped,
And takes him by the beard, kisses the gashes
That bloodily did yawn upon his face.
He cries aloud, "Tarry, my cousin Suffolk! 15
My soul shall thine keep company to heaven;
Tarry, sweet soul, for mine, then fly abreast,
As in this glorious and well-foughten field
We kept together in our chivalry!"
Upon these words I came and cheer'd him up. 20
He smil'd me in the face, raught me his hand,
And with a feeble gripe, says, "Dear my lord,
Commend my service to my sovereign."
So did he turn and over Suffolk's neck
He threw his wounded arm, and kiss'd his lips, 25
And so espous'd to death, with blood he seal'd
A testament of noble-ending love.
The pretty and sweet manner of it forc'd
Those waters from me which I would have stopp'd,
But I had not so much of man in me, 30
And all my mother came into mine eyes
And gave me up to tears.
  K. Hen.   I blame you not,
For hearing this, I must perforce compound
With [mistful] eyes, or they will issue too. *Alarum.*
But hark, what new alarum is this same? 35
The French have reinforc'd their scatter'd men.
Then every soldier kill his prisoners,
Give the word through.   *Exeunt.*

[SCENE VII]

Enter FLUELLEN *and* GOWER.

  Flu. Kill the poys and the luggage! 'Tis expressly
against the law of arms. 'Tis as arrant a piece of
knavery, mark you now, as can be offert; in your
conscience, now, is it not? 4
  Gow. 'Tis certain there's not a boy left alive, and
the cowardly rascals that ran from the battle ha' done
this slaughter. Besides, they have burn'd and carried
away all that was in the King's tent; wherefore the
King, most worthily, hath caus'd every soldier to cut
his prisoner's throat. O, 'tis a gallant king! 10
  Flu. Ay, he was porn at Monmouth, Captain
Gower. What call you the town's name where
Alexander the Pig was born?
  Gow. Alexander the Great. 14
  Flu. Why, I pray you, is not "pig" great? The
pig, or the great, or the mighty, or the huge, or the
magnanimous, are all one reckonings, save the phrase
is a little variations.
  Gow. I think Alexander the Great was born in
Macedon. His father was called Philip of Macedon,
as I take it. 21

252

Flu. I think it is in Macedon where Alexander is porn. I tell you, captain, if you look in the maps of the orld, I warrant you sall find, in the comparisons between Macedon and Monmouth, that the situa- 25 tions look you, is both alike. There is a river in Macedon, and there is also moreover a river at Monmouth. It is call'd Wye at Monmouth; but it is out of my prains what is the name of the other river; but 'tis all one, 'tis alike as my fingers is to my fingers, 30 and there is salmons in both. If you mark Alexander's life well, Harry of Monmouth's life is come after it indifferent well, for there is figures in all things. Alexander, God knows, and you know, in his rages, and his furies, and his wraths, and his cholers, and 35 his moods, and his displeasures, and his indignations, and also being a little intoxicates in his prains, did, in his ales and his angers, look you, kill his best friend, Clytus. 39

Gow. Our King is not like him in that; he never kill'd any of his friends.

Flu. It is not well done, mark you now, to take the tales out of my mouth, ere it is made and finished. I speak but in the figures and comparisons of it: as Alexander kill'd his friend Clytus, being in his 45 ales and his cups, so also Harry Monmouth, being in his right wits and his good judgments, turn'd away the fat knight with the great belly doublet. He was full of jests, and gipes, and knaveries, and mocks—I have forgot his name. 50

Gow. Sir John Falstaff.

Flu. That is he. I'll tell you there is good men porn at Monmouth.

Gow. Here comes his Majesty. [*Exit*] 54

Alarum. Enter KING HENRY *and* BOURBON *with* [*other*] *prisoners;* [WARWICK, GLOUCESTER, EXETER, HERALDS, *and others*]. *Flourish.*

K. Hen. I was not angry since I came to France
Until this instant. Take a trumpet, herald,
Ride thou unto the horsemen on yond hill.
If they will fight with us, bid them come down,
Or void the field; they do offend our sight.
If they'll do neither, we will come to them, 60
And make them skirr away, as swift as stones
Enforced from the old Assyrian slings;
Besides, we'll cut the throats of those we have,
And not a man of them that we shall take
Shall taste our mercy. Go and tell them so. 65
[*Exit a Herald.*]

Palinode

ANNABEL PATTERSON

Mea culpa, twice over. This statement stands in for the transcript of the workshop I led at Union College in the Fall of 1990, and which should have appeared in this series. For more than one reason, I was unwilling to have it appear in print. I was not happy with the way I conducted the class; and since then my thoughts on the role of Shakespeare in a college education have changed—not, perhaps, irrevocably, but enough to require this substitution. In addition, what I think now has crystallized in relation to the *other* workshops directed by my colleagues in the series, whose transcripts I have been privileged to see. Their unplanned but remarkable variety, while still having a relation to each other, tells a story that gives force to this palinode, and perhaps may justify its anomalous presence in the volume.

First, then, the class I actually taught: this was to have been an example of issue-oriented Shakespearean pedagogy, relating two texts that thematize or explore violence towards women—*The Rape of Lucrece* and *The Taming of the Shrew*. In the Fall of 1990 I was still flush with what felt like the success of teaching Shakespeare, two years in a row, to the students at the Bread Loaf School of English, the summer M.A. program attached to Middlebury College, Vermont. The students in that program are mostly high school teachers, many of them from underprivileged rural teaching districts. The students of those teachers may travel several hours a day for the privilege of an education, and their own opportunities for such cultural luxuries as access to live theater may be assumed to be nonexistent. I myself was new to the teaching of Shakespeare, having been for years locked into the counterintuitive professional bind which decrees that Renaissance scholars further specialize in either dramatic or nondramatic works of that period, but not both. At Bread Loaf, where Shakespeare is central to the M.A. curriculum but often the only Renaissance author these student-teachers (and *their* students) will encounter, I discovered a way of teaching the plays of Shakespeare that was, I thought, responsive to the needs of this community. It was also, for me, intellectually challenging; and being new to the field, I gazed with the clear eyes of ignorance at texts that seemed to open up before me a very different and more engaging prospect than the one my own long-ago education in the Shakespeare canon had led me to expect.

The point was to focus on social, political, or even economic issues—such issues as, it might be supposed, were of importance to the Bread Loaf student-teachers (and their students) no matter how constrained their circumstances, or in some instances all the better by virtue of those circumstances. For instance, *Henry V* could be read, with the assistance of the Olivier film version, as a study in the interrelated problems of nationalism and militarism, topics that were certainly accessible to a generation for whom the national memory of Vietnam was already being refigured by a fairly wide selection of fictional and/or cinematographic representations. As my formal lecture indicates, and as the Kenneth Branagh film version corroborates, this was no misappropriation of the text to some misguided concept of "relevance," but rather one of the many proofs we have that in the case of Shakespeare the literary notion of transhistorical value has demonstrable content. As Reginald Foakes puts it so poignantly at the beginning of his workshop on *King Lear*, it is only through relating the plays to our own time as well as to Shakespeare's that we can release them, like Prospero at the end of his career, from bondage to time.

By a slightly different token, *A Midsummer Night's Dream* came alive for the Bread Loaf student-teachers by way of an experiment in staging the play-within-a-play of Bottom the weaver and his colleagues. Looking at the play with my ignorant eyes, it did not appear to me self-evident that the Elizabethan audience in the public theater would have identified unproblematically with the audience of aristocrats in Theseus's court before whom Bottom and his company perform, and whose mockery and condescension, as written into the playtext, is sometimes confused with Shakespeare's, and so determines how the *Pyramus and Thisbe* playlet will be staged. Since the Bread Loaf summer school is fortunate enough to have, every year, a company of professional actors on campus who will assist in dramatic readings or workshops in literature courses, we staged two different versions of the so-called "mechanicals'" play: one in which Bottom and his colleagues are merely clumsy fools, and in which the tone was therefore vulgar farce or pantomime, complete with balloon (and hence explosive) breasts for Thisbe; and another in which they retain a certain working-class dignity in the effort to please their social superiors, and in which the double entendres that Shakespeare built into their lines and the way they deliver them (the ambiguous punctuation of the prologue, for example) carry a message of mild social reproach that the artisans themselves would never have dared to articulate. I have to admit that the Bread Loaf student-teachers enjoyed the farcical version more than the enigmatic, socially discomforting one, where the problem of unequal social status they were forced to confront both conflicted with their legitimate need for carnival and cut perhaps too close to the bone. Nevertheless, I had here my first taste of the heady pedagogic brew that results from stirring together certain preconceptions about a Shakespeare play with the decision-making process that underlies any stage production; and it is interesting to see that *A Midsummer Night's Dream*, so much less venerated in the critical literature than any of the Jacobean tragedies, was John Wilders's choice for a teaching workshop, and that Patricia Parker chose the *Pyramus and Thisbe* playlet as the site for an examination of Shakespeare's subtle and even classically learned wordplay.

These experiences led directly to my writing *Shakespeare and the Popular Voice*, and hence, I suppose, to the invitation from Union College to participate in the lecture and workshop series to which this volume testifies. But time passes—more visibly, perhaps, in the academic profession than others—and the innovations of one year (which may themselves be less innovations than reinventions of old wheels carelessly discarded) may in the next seem commonplace, what everyone is doing, ho hum. By the time I arrived at Union to deliver my lecture and conduct my workshop to an auditorium full of undergraduates and some faculty, I could no longer feel in possession of a magic key that would unlock the gates behind which the sacred Shakespearean scriptures had been stashed for generations. What Professor Foakes calls "archeologizing" Shakespeare was already itself a buried layer of past behavior, already subject to critical excavation throughout the profession. And at Union College, the mixture of awe, incomprehension and boredom with which American undergraduates (I assumed) typically approach Shakespeare when deprived of an issue-oriented criticism was not in evidence, no doubt because the Union students had been so well engaged by their teachers, who had prepared them for this series of visitors with intelligent zeal; or, if there were any residual pockets of resistance to Shakespeare, the hall was too large and the time too short for me to locate them.

What I did discover, and which reflected on me, not on the Union students, was that they expected, and they had reason to expect, a much more dramatic and intense interaction between themselves and the speaker than I was prepared to provide. Having learned late in the day that the "workshop" I had agreed to teach would in fact consist of students from several literature classes, far too many for me to conduct the meeting in seminar-style, I gave, in effect, a second lecture, counting on the connection between my theme of violence towards women and the current national focus on date rape to generate discussion after I had finished. Reading the transcripts of my colleagues, who met the challenge of numbers with so much greater ingenuity and effectiveness, has only confirmed my decision not to allow my so-called "workshop" to appear in print. In particular, I was dazzled by the skill with which Helen Vendler evidently rose to the occasion, creating on the stage of the auditorium a mini-seminar of volunteer interpreters, who became jointly responsible for teasing out the meaning and significance of a Shakespeare sonnet; a pedagogic playlet, as it were. Not only was the staging inventive, the quality of the student questions and suggestions was of a higher intellectual level than most of us can dream of in a graduate seminar. Clearly Professor Vendler was able to ask the students questions that mixed cognitive depth and general humanity, and that produced between her and them, and presumably among the audience as well, an electrical current of discovery.

While Shakespeare's most tortured sonnet obviously lends itself to such penetrating analysis precisely by virtue of its emotional accessibility, one might be skeptical of what results one could get by exposing a large undergraduate class to the intricacies of textual theory or Shakespearean analytic bibliography. Even graduate students rapidly become restive against the mental discipline required to follow the highly technical and often tendentious arguments that have been adduced to explain the differences between Quarto and Folio versions; and teachers may well feel that the degree of uncertainty introduced by the revisionist textual theory of the last decade—whereby *the* text of *King Lear* or *Hamlet* has been replaced by the theory of equally *valid* versions created by theatrical practice—is simply too great for themselves or their undergraduate students to handle. Leah Marcus's workshop shows us that such fears are unfounded. By having her students look closely at the 1603 "Bad" Quarto version of "To be or not to be" beside the standard Folio version, and also by showing them that "grizzled old teaching aid," the parallel text edition of *King Lear* produced by Wilhelm Vietor in 1892, Professor Marcus generated almost as much intense speculation about meaning and intention as that passionate sonnet could do.

Helen Vendler's workshop also gives me the occasion to formulate the other half of my palinode, which has nothing to do with Union College. It concerns rather the state of literary criticism, or, since "literary criticism" is in mild disfavor as a term descriptive of what we do, the norms of discourse about literature and its boundaries. As I write in the spring of 1992, I acknowledge that we may have gone too far in changing those norms. For all the fresh air that came rushing into the field of literary studies, with the influx first of "theory," then of disputes over the "canon"; for all of the advantages that have accrued to pedagogy by our being able to set aside or problematize (provisionally) the question of literary value, which has always been one of the hardest notions to transmit to students; for all of the social advantages of allowing into college classrooms demographically trans- formed into geopolitical microcosms the possibility that literary studies in the United States should no longer be fixated on Europe; for all of the advantages of having to persuade students (and colleagues) of the contin- ued importance of Shakespeare, instead of calmly assuming it—for all of these good and energizing changes, some equally good things are in danger of being lost, of becoming forgotten or eccentric skills. Like thatching a cottage roof so as to last a decade, the skill of close reading, so brilliantly exhibited here by Helen Vendler, is in danger of disappearance, a sacrifice to the larger thrills of the rapid construction of more or less prefabricated edifices. By prefabrication, I mean the tendency to apply to literary texts a concept that the reader has inherited from one or another of the new approaches, whether it be feminist theory, deconstruction, New Historicism, or the various forms of analysis ultimately derived from Marx that seek to expose the sociopolitical underbelly of the writer and his work. As a pedagogic exercise, such applications are not to be scorned, especially when the student is advised, and honest enough, to acknowledge negative results or counterindications from the text. Prefabrication occurs, however, when the reader has already decided what the results of the experiment *ought* to be. The centrifugal structure of close reading—the patient teasing out of ever wider circles of significance from seemingly small units (a sonnet, a string of adjectives)—is reversed; instead we experience the im- position of a large conceptual structure from above. The roof is lowered from a derrick on a truck.

The other characteristic of literary studies for which I have become nostalgic is what, granting the unsatisfactory nature of the term, I am still prepared to designate "humanism." I recently examined a graduate student on the topic of *King Lear*. During that examination, my own remarks on the theme of economic inequality in that play came back to haunt me: not because I no longer regard those remarks a useful correction to the view that Shakespeare was a willing propagandist for monarchy and contemptuous of the common people of his time, but because this student had so incorporated the norms of issue-oriented criticism that she was simply unable see the play as anything but a critique of social injustice. Reginald Foakes has ably described the shifts in our modern perception of Shakespeare that have been perhaps most clearly visible in accounts of *King Lear;* but his own "workshop" focuses, with absolute appropriateness, on the scene that no shift in the critical climate can make mean anything other than it appears to mean at first sight. It is the scene of Lear's division of the kingdom, his public testing of his three daughters' affections. The Union students were evidently capable, under Professor Foakes's subtle direction, of reenacting this scene in terms of their own understanding of parent-child relationships, of the breakdowns of communication common even in families that are not dysfunctional, that are not forced to operate at the high political level of royal or presidential responsibility. The exchange between Lear and Cordelia, in particular, they were able to see as both pathetic and feisty, on both sides. My student was unable to remember that *King Lear* is, among other things, about domestic feelings, the structure of the family, about love and favoritism and parents and children who find each other too late for a fortunate ending. Issue-oriented criticism had done its work too well.

In his play about Shakespeare's retirement to Stratford, never to write again, Edward Bond transferred to the playwright now, as he imagined, embittered, Tolstoy's old cry, "What is to be done?" From time to time, as following the examination just mentioned, I find myself transferring it again, mutated, to the American academy in the 1990s: "What have we done?" But reading the transcripts of the other workshops in the Union College series has provided some considerable reassurance. This eclectic mixture of approaches is an emblem not of conflict or defeat but of a potential latitudinarianism in the profession at large, with humanist and ethical criticism side by side with a deconstructive emphasis on wordplay, for example; and the unmediated transcript has the added pedagogical advantage, for teachers, of providing the sound of students' voices—living proof of what induces learning and thinking at its best.

Notes on the Contributors

R. A. FOAKES, Professor of English at UCLA and former director of its Center for Medieval and Renaissance Studies, has written many articles on Shakespeare and is the author of *Shakespeare: The Dark Comedies to the Last Plays, Coleridge's Criticism of Shakespeare, Illustrations of the English Stage 1580–1642,* and *Hamlet Versus Lear: Cultural Politics and Shakespeare's Art.* He is the editor of several scholarly teacher's editions of Shakespeare's plays, including the recent Penguin edition of *Troilus and Cressida* and the forthcoming New Arden edition of *King Lear.*

LEAH MARCUS, Professor of English at the University of Texas at Austin, has written several dozens of articles on Renaissance literature. She is the author of *Childhood and Cultural Despair: A Theme and Variations in Seventeenth-Century Literature, The Politics of Mirth: Jonson, Herrick, Milton, Marvell, and the Defense of Old Holiday Pastimes,* and *Puzzling Shakespeare: Local Reading and Its Discontents.*

PATRICIA PARKER, Professor of English and Comparative Literature, Stanford University, has produced articles and books on deconstructive, feminist, Marxist, and rhetorical criticism. She has edited a number of books of special interest to critics, including *Centre and Labyrinth: Essays in Honor of Northrop Frye, Lyric Poetry: Beyond New Criticism, Shakespeare and the Question of Theory,* and *Literary Theory/Renaissance Texts.* She has written *Inescapable Romance: Studies in the Poetics of a Mode* and *Literary Fat Ladies: Rhetoric, Gender, Property;* has authored two forth-coming volumes, *Preposterous Shakespeare* and *Dilation/Delay/Discourse: A Study in Shakespeare and the Renaissance;* and has two more books, *Figures of Difference* and *The Metaphorical Plot,* under contract.

ANNABEL PATTERSON, Professor of English at Duke University, has published several books about Renaissance culture and literature, including *Hermogenes and the Renaissance, Censorship and Interpretation, Pastoral and Ideology, Shakespeare and the Popular Voice, Fables of Power,* and *Reading Between the Lines.* She has analyzed major figures of the Tudor-Stuart period—including Jonson, Donne, Herbert, Milton, Marvell, Sidney, Spenser, and Shakespeare—as well as of the French and Italian Renaissance. Her essays on critical theory appear both in her books and in her contributions to *New Literary History, Critical Inquiry, Shakespeare and Deconstruction,* and *Critical Terms for Literary Study.*

HELEN VENDLER is A. Kingsley Porter University Professor at Harvard University. She has written books on Yeats, Stevens, Herbert, and Keats, and is now working on a commentary on Shakespeare's Sonnets.

JOHN WILDERS, the John Hamilton Fulton Professor of the Humanities at Middlebury College and Emeritus Fellow of Worcester College, Oxford University, has taught at Princeton, Bristol, Oxford, and Middlebury. He has been director of the Oxford graduate Shakespeare programme and the Royal Shakespeare Theatre Summer School; Dean of Graduates, Worcester College, Oxford; governor of the Royal Shakespeare Theatre and member of the Executive Council; and literary consultant for the BBC television productions of the complete plays of Shakespeare. He has written *Shakespeare: The Merchant of Venice, The Lost Garden: A View of Shakespeare's English and Roman History Plays,* and *New Prefaces to Shakespeare;* he is editing *Antony and Cleopatra* with an introduction and commentary for the New Arden Shakespeare (forthcoming).

BRUCE MCIVER, an independent scholar, and RUTH STEVENSON, Professor of English, Union College, have each taught for over fifteen years and have presented and published scholarly and critical articles on Shakespeare, Overbury, Earle, Sidney, Nashe, and Marlowe.

A Short List of Recent Works
on Teaching Shakespeare

Adams, Richard. *Teaching Shakespeare: Essays on Approaches to Shakespeare in School and College.* London: Royce, 1985.

Aers, Lesley, and Nigel Wheale, eds. *Shakespeare in the Changing Curriculum.* London and New York: Routledge, 1991.

Bulman, J. C., and H. R. Coursen, eds. *Shakespeare on Television: An Anthology of Essays and Reviews.* Hanover, N.H.: University Press of New England, 1988.

Edens, Walter, Christopher Durer, Walter Eggers, Duncan Harris, and Keith Hull, eds. *Teaching Shakespeare.* Princeton: Princeton University Press, 1977.

Findlay, Heather. "Renaissance Pederasty and Pedagogy: The 'Case' of Shakespeare's Falstaff." *The Yale Journal of Criticism: Interpretation in the Humanities* 3, no. 1 (Fall 1989): 229–38.

Friedlander, Larry. "The Shakespeare Project in Multimedia." In *Hypermedia and Literary Studies,* edited by Paul Delany and George Landow. Cambridge: MIT Press, 1991.

Forker, Charles R. "Symbolic Staging in Shakespeare and Its Importance in the Classroom." *Rocky Mountain Review of Language and Literature* 38, nos. 1 & 2 (1984): 3–11.

Frey, Charles H. *Experiencing Shakespeare: Essays on Text, Classroom, and Performance.* Columbia: University of Missouri Press, 1988.

Gibaldi, Joseph, series ed. *Modern Language of America Approaches to Teaching World Literature.*

    Hunt, Maurice, ed. *Approaches to Teaching Shakespeare's The Tempest and other Late Romances.* New York: Modern Language Association of America, 1992.

    Ray, Robert H., ed. *Approaches to Teaching Shakespeare's King Lear.* New York: Modern Language Association of America, 1986.

Gilbert, Miriam. "Teaching Dramatic Literature." *Educational Theatre Journal* 25 (1973): 86–94.

Holderness, Graham, ed. *The Shakespeare Myth.* With forewords by Jonathan Dollimore and Alan Sinfield, and an afterword by Terry Eagleton. Manchester: Manchester University Press, 1988.

Homan, Sidney, ed. *Shakespeare and the Triple Play: From Study to Stage to Classroom.* Lewisburg, Pa.: Bucknell University Press. London: Associated University Presses, 1988.

Klingspon, Ron. "Teaching Shakespeare to Undergraduates: The Professor as Practitioner." *English Quarterly* 18, no. 2 (Summer 1984): 16–26.

Leach, Susan. *Shakespeare in the Classroom: What's the Matter?* Buckingham and Philadelphia: Open University Press, 1992.

Lusardi, James P. "Shakespeare's Performed Words: *Macbeth* and Improvisation in the Classroom." *CEA Critic: An Official Journal of the College English Association* 54 (1992): 1–29.

McLean, Andrew. "Teaching Shakespeare." *Shakespeare Newsletter* 29 (1979): 39.

Neely, Carol Thomas. "Feminist Criticism and Teaching Shakespeare." *ADE Bulletin* 87 (1987): 15–18.

O'Brien, Veronica. *Teaching Shakespeare.* London: Edward Arnold, 1982.

Peck, John, and Martin Coyle. *How to Study a Shakespeare Play.* Basingstoke: Macmillan, 1985.

Robinson, Randal F. *Unlocking Shakespeare's Language: Help for the Teacher and Student.* Urbana, Ill.: National Council of Teachers of English. ERIC Clearinghouse on Reading and Communication Skills, 1989.

Shakespeare Quarterly.
  Volume 25, number 2, edited by R. J. Schoeck, 1974.
  Volume 35, number 5, edited by John F. Andrews, 1984.
  Volume 41, number 2, edited by Ralph Alan Cohen, 1990.

Swander, Homer. "Teaching Shakespeare: Tradition and the Future." Vol. 3 in *William Shakespeare: His World, His Work, His Influence,* edited by John F. Andrews, 873–87. New York: Scribner's, 1985.

Watson, Robert N. "Teaching 'Shakespeare': Theory versus Practice." In *Teaching Literature: What is Needed Now,* edited by James Engell and David Perkins, 121–50. Cambridge, Mass. and London: Harvard University Press, 1988.

Wheeler, Richard P. "Psychoanalytic Criticism and Teaching Shakespeare." *ADE Bulletin* 87 (1987): 19–23.

Index

265

WITHDRAWN